Girls of the Factory

UNIVERSITY PRESS OF FLORIDA

Florida A&M University, Tallahassee
Florida Atlantic University, Boca Raton
Florida Gulf Coast University, Ft. Myers
Florida International University, Miami
Florida State University, Tallahassee
New College of Florida, Sarasota
University of Central Florida, Orlando
University of Florida, Gainesville
University of North Florida, Jacksonville
University of South Florida, Tampa
University of West Florida, Pensacola

Girls of the Factory

A Year with the Garment Workers of Morocco

M. Laetitia Cairoli

University Press of Florida

Gainesville · Tallahassee · Tampa · Boca Raton

Pensacola · Orlando · Miami · Jacksonville · Ft. Myers · Sarasota

First cloth printing, 2011
First paperback printing, 2012

Library of Congress Cataloging-in-Publication Data
Cairoli, M. Laetitia.
Girls of the factory : a year with the garment workers of Morocco / M. Laetitia Cairoli.
p. cm.
Includes bibliographical references and index.
ISBN 978-0-8130-3561-1 (cloth: alk. paper)
ISBN 978-0-8130-4441-5 (pbk.)
1. Women clothing workers—Morocco—Case studies. 2. Teenage girls—
Employment—Morocco—Case studies. 3. Teenage girls—Morocco—Social
conditions—Case studies. 4. Women—Morocco—Social conditions—Case studies.
I. Title.
HD6073.C62M833 2011
331.4'887008350964—dc22   2010031994

The University Press of Florida is the scholarly publishing agency for the State
University System of Florida, comprising Florida A&M University, Florida Atlantic
University, Florida Gulf Coast University, Florida International University, Florida
State University, New College of Florida, University of Central Florida, University
of Florida, University of North Florida, University of South Florida, and University
of West Florida.

University Press of Florida
15 Northwest 15th Street
Gainesville, FL 32611-2079
http://www.upf.com

Contents

Preface

I was standing in front of a sewing factory in Fes, looking for a girl I had met the day before. She had promised me she would return this morning and answer my questions about factory work in Fes. I was an American doing research and I needed answers. But she was not there. I ran into two other girls, girls who had also been standing at that factory gate the day before: Rhema and Fatima Zahor.

"Are you still looking around here?" Rhema asked, greeting me. "This girl," Rhema said, motioning toward her companion, "has also worked in factories for a long time. She'll tell you what you need to know. Walk with us." And so I did.

Rhema and Fatima Zahor were headed for a factory at the end of the street, where, it was rumored, cutting specialists were needed. Fatima Zahor was an expert in cutting fabric, and she walked quickly ahead of us. When we arrived at the factory gate, though, we found the factory was not hiring.

"Connections. Money. That's what you need to get a job here," Fatima Zahor said, disgusted. "You need to know someone in the factory, or you need to pay them off."

"Really? How much money would you need?" I asked.

"About 250 *dirham*, probably, to get in," Rhema said. "Unless you have connections or money, you'll never get a factory job. Those who are poor—like us—look all day long and find nothing. Not even the money for the bus ride home."

Rhema was small and thin, white-skinned, wearing blue jeans and a long shirt that hung close to her knees. She looked nothing like Fatima Zahor, who was taller and more imposing, with dark skin and curly black hair, oiled and pulled tight against her head. Rhema said she was 16. Fatima Zahor did not tell me her age, but she did not look much older. They had met just this morning at a factory gate and had decided to continue their job search together. It was now midmorning, and they had been walking since dawn, having arrived in the district at 7:00 a.m., when the factories began operations.

We passed one neat white factory surrounded by a well-tended yard where thick and sturdy red geraniums grew. "The French companies look like embassies," Rhema said. "They have heat in the winter and air-conditioning in the summer, like this one. You need to make a formal application to even get inside there. Nobody stands at the door there." Indeed, there was no clutch of girls at the gate as there were at other factories.

"How do you know whether a factory is a good place to work?" I asked.

Fatima Zahor answered immediately. "Three things tell you if a factory is good: the factory follows the law, has good pay, and has respect. These are the three things that matter."

"Respect is important," added Rhema. "They should respect the girls who work there. What matters is that they don't yell at us; they don't constantly berate us. Like at Confection—where I worked last year—they would constantly yell at us. They'd call us prostitutes, treat us like dogs. This is what we don't want."

We continued to walk. The morning had dawned cold, but as the sun reached higher into the sky we could feel its warmth. We moved from factory to factory knocking on gates, talking to the small clusters of girls waiting in front of each, speaking with factory guardians. Sometimes we were encouraged to wait, told there might be work. Other times we left almost without stopping: the group at the door was too large, or the chances of latecomers finding a space would be impossible. Sometimes, after we had waited, a factory guardian would appear at the gates, telling the job seekers to go home. No workers would be needed today.

As we moved, I asked questions, first trying to understand Fatima Zahor's history. As a girl of 12, she had been sent to Tangiers to live with her mother's brother. There, in the house of her uncle, she had "worked a little"—probably as a child servant, although she would not admit to having been sent there as a maid. When she grew older, she found work in a Tangiers sewing factory and eventually returned to her family, to work in the sewing factories of Fes. From her estimates, she had been working in factories for at least five years.

"I know how to do the fabric cutting, which is a good skill to have—it is difficult and important. For cutting you must have a sharp mind and you must be able to write. And I know other things—packaging, final control." She pointed to a blouse she was wearing. "You see this blouse? I made the whole thing by myself. And I have sewn other things—entire outfits."

"Why are you out of work now?" I asked.

"At the last job they just got rid of me—they just threw me out. I had been there awhile, I was earning a lot of money, so they just threw me out and let in someone new."

"Was that the last job you held?"

"No. Then I got a job at another factory. I was there for four months, and then I had an accident. I fell out of a taxi as the cab was moving. The door of the cab was no good. I was in the hospital for fifteen days. I thought I would die, but I didn't. But after that, the factory where I was working did not want me back."

"Why not? Was it their taxi?" I asked.

"No, the accident had nothing to do with them. But I think they were afraid that I was going to blame them. But I wouldn't have, because the accident had nothing to do with them. Now my family is trying to get a lawyer, to get some money for the accident. But that probably won't happen. We really don't have laws like that in Morocco. Do you have those laws in America?"

I did not know what to say. I didn't answer her question and it was quiet for a while. And then I asked her if that was the last job she had had, before now, before this current job quest.

"Well, after that I worked at a plastic bag factory, right here, in Sidi Brahim. But I only worked there for one week. They trained me to use a machine—I would push a pedal to seal the bottom parts of plastic bags closed. But the factory was full of dirt, and there was a bad smell, and I just could not bear it. That kind of factory is for a person who has no skills at anything."

We kept walking. Time was passing and there seemed to be no hope of a job for these girls. The sun kept rising higher in the sky, blinding us as it climbed. The girls walked slowly, moving their hands to their foreheads to shade their eyes when we turned a corner to face into the sun. We were silent again, and then we came upon the factory from which Fatima Zahor had been unceremoniously released, for reasons of seniority. I crossed the street with Fatima Zahor, since she wished to avoid seeing anyone she might recognize at her former place of employment. But Rhema approached that factory gate, hopeful. Before long, Rhema ran back across the street to tell us she had found an old acquaintance in the cluster of workers standing at that factory gate, and this girl had told her to wait—there might be a job.

"Go ahead—go on without me," Rhema told us. Then looking at Fatima Zahor, she said decisively, "The important thing is that we meet again here tomorrow morning, so that we can search together." The two made a date to meet in front of one particular factory and invited me to join them. Rhema dashed eagerly back across the street, and Fatima Zahor and I continued on out of the district and toward the center of town. It was almost noon now, and there was no use searching any longer.

•

It was January 1995. The hard morning air had grown soft and the sun was burning like an African sun in a never-ending blue sky. I was living in the ancient Moroccan city of Fes, doing ethnographic research on the lives of the young girls and women working in the city's garment industry. I would stay there for a year, learning what I could about the workers and their lives. I spoke with the workers and their families in their own language, a dialect of Arabic spoken in Morocco. It was not my first time in that country: I had lived there as a Peace Corps volunteer, in a small town close to Marrakech, and I had later returned to do research in the capital city, Rabat. This time I traveled to Morocco with my husband, who had a position at the University of Fes as a professor of English. We rented an apartment in the Ville Nouvelle, at the center of Fes, and I spent my time with the factory workers, in the streets, in the factories, and in their homes.

Rhema and Fatima Zahor, like all the other individuals in what follows, are real people, although these are not their real names. I have, in the tradition of ethnographers, used pseudonyms to afford them privacy. I have also obscured the names of the factories where I met them and the exact location of the homes we frequented. Fifteen years have elapsed between the period of research and the publication of this narrative, and during this period I have published several articles, theorizing the data I collected and arriving at conclusions about the implications of garment factory work for girls and women in Fes.

In my previous publications I presented my observations and the statistics I collected in a dispassionate voice, in conformance with the traditional standards of academic writing. In my field notes, however, there remained the whisperings of the girls and the stories they told me. These whisperings haunted me, for I knew that what I had written thus far was an inadequate testimony to the complexity of the workers' lives and the challenges they faced. These women were not just statistics. I had known them intimately, and the stories they told me mattered. With this book I give voice to their experience and provide readers with a more personal understanding of their lives; it is meant to augment my earlier work and make it more complete.

Today, the Moroccan government continues its quest to open the country's borders to foreign trade and to promote industrialization; Moroccan girls continue to labor in sewing factories there. Certainly, conditions in these factories and in Morocco generally are not precisely the same as they were at the time of my research. But my account offers insight into the lives of Moroccan women at a particular moment in that country's march toward globalization. It chronicles the lives of the women I knew, their struggles as I witnessed them, their stories as I heard them. As such, this narrative explores the process of globalization itself and speaks to the experience of young women the world over who have toiled in factories and struggled to accommodate the intrusion of new forms of labor into their lives. In what follows I pass along the words of the workers I knew.

The book begins with an introduction which sets the research in its academic context. A reader who is not concerned with the scholarly precedents of this sort of writing might skip the introduction and begin with the first chapter. The remainder of the book describes in rough chronological order the year I spent in Fes. It begins with my attempts to meet and interview workers in the streets of the factory district, progresses to my experience working inside one Fes factory, and then moves into the household of one young woman as she endures a very typical cycle of employment, unemployment, and job hunting. The book concludes with a brief discussion about conditions in the Moroccan garment industry since 1995.

A Note on Transliteration

Darija is the spoken vernacular Arabic of Morocco and is not commonly written. This dialect of Arabic varies regionally in form and usage throughout Morocco. It is characterized by the use of loan words from Berber, French, and Spanish and varies widely between men and women, particularly in informal usage. Here I have relied on the general guidelines provided by the *International Journal of Middle East Studies* for Arabic transliteration, particularly for words commonly used in Modern Standard Arabic. The majority of Arabic words in the text are directly derived from Darija, and for these words I have relied upon Harrell 1966 in transliteration, with the following proviso: I have taken the liberty of eliminating the diacritical marks and in some cases have added vowels to render as closely as possible, in phonetic English, the sounds of the Darija word. I have anglicized the words in this way in order to make them immediately accessible to the English-speaking reader. I believe speakers of Moroccan Arabic, relying on English phonetic conventions, will recognize the Darija term being rendered.

Introduction

I was motivated to write this book by the discrepancy between doing ethnographic fieldwork and writing about it. Anthropology demands objectivity; theorizing and data collection eclipse any need for sensory descriptions. And yet it is a visceral experience to do ethnography. The acrid stench of the leather tanning factory I passed each day on my way to the sewing factory, the cacophony of roosters and Moped engines that woke me at dawn, the thick roundedness of the young workers' hands against the seams they inspected, the intense listening to stories that are sometimes amusing and at other times tedious, or poignant, or depressing. All these things were lost in "writing up" the research. This book is my attempt to recapture them and share this vivid realty.

This book has several goals: to detail the nature of the ethnographic encounter, to convey a sense of how life is lived in Morocco, and to describe how one group of females—Moroccan girls and women—experience the impact of globalization in public spaces, inside the workplace, and in their homes.

I do not theorize or interpret the data collected, nor do I arrive at a definitive conclusion. The text recounts my encounters with the women and the stories they told me. I have minimized my use of academic jargon to make the research accessible to students and other readers. Anthropologists, sociologists, and economists in other locales have elegantly theorized data on females working in factories in newly industrializing regions. I describe some of their research in this introduction, and throughout the text I compare and contrast my findings with theirs. This book, however, is not an attempt to replicate any of this work. It is different from what has already been published. First, it describes the industrial experience of Moroccan girls, who are Arab and Muslim. (Little has been written about girls in factories in the Middle East.)[1] And second, this book uses the narrative form.

Anthropology, Ethnography, and Writing

In recent decades, ethnographers have experimented with multiple literary forms in response to questions about how best to represent other realities. The use of personal narrative as a genre to convey the results of fieldwork has a long history in anthropological writing and has received increasing attention in recent years.[2] With personal narrative, a sequence of events is related through the perspective of the narrator, and the narrator's point of view is never obscured. There is no claim, then, to objectivity. The narrative form puts the actions, voices, and experiences of individuals at the center. Thus these individuals appear as undeniably human, and their behaviors appear as a recognizable expression of the human condition. Through the narrative form, the anthropologist allows what were once called "informants" to become fully human actors; the lived experience of the people who are being studied becomes the focus of the ethnographic project.[3]

The use of the narrative style allows me to give a detailed and intimate account of my encounters. I have placed myself at the center of the text. It is always clear that I am speaking and being spoken to. This makes it evident that the truths produced by the ethnographic encounter are the results of constant negotiations—discussions between myself and the workers and the owners, factory families, and other inhabitants of Fes. Because the reader can observe the interactions, he/she avoids the impression that ethnographic understandings are bits of cultural facts extracted from willing informants, and sees instead how ethnographic knowledge is often produced through a particular kind of interaction between ethnographer and "informant." The reader witnesses how ethnographic knowledge is gleaned and can, perhaps, evaluate the information that is generated.

The use of the narrative style makes the realities of ethnographic research apparent. Ethnography by its nature is time-consuming and imprecise; information gathered is often contradictory and uncertain; in the course of the research, the ethnographer is never sure of what an observation or encounter means and whether it will be significant to the research conclusions. Most of all, this research is very personal, and it is affecting.

For the most part, I have avoided voicing my personal reactions to what I see and hear. I do not want my reactions to distract the reader from the words and experiences of the workers themselves, for this is what I seek to transmit as directly as possible. There are transitory moments in the text where I do allow myself to give voice to emotion; I leave these in place to remind the reader that a sentient observer is viewing and recording the actions of others and as a comment on the personal intensity of the fieldwork experience. I use the present tense frequently, throughout the narrative. This is a stylistic choice not meant to impose timelessness on the experience of Moroccan females and/or industrialization in Fes, but rather to draw the reader into the experience of fieldwork and the lives of the people.

During my research, I was engaged daily with working people. While conducting formal interviews I wrote openly as people spoke. When speaking informally, I took notes unobtrusively, often jotting down words or phrases in a small notebook, and as quickly as possible recording them more completely. I never used a tape recorder. I believe I have rendered the conversations here faithfully. I use direct quotations throughout the narrative to give a sense of intimacy and immediacy to the text.

The people of Fes, like most speakers of Arabic, repeat phrases thanking and praising God in their speech—phrases like "God willing" and "thank God." This linguistic habit is particularly strong among those in the lower classes who have less schooling. I have eliminated most of this repetition because in translation these reiterations make the speakers sound quaint and foreign. I have used a limited number of Arabic words in the text; some words were used frequently, and others had a specific meaning that would be difficult to translate.

I record here many evocative tales told to me, usually, by workers. I present them not simply because they are interesting and entertaining, but because they are the kinds of stories I heard repeatedly. The stories represent the nature of my engagement with the people I was researching. These stories also tell something about the people themselves—they tell of how Moroccans speak of their own lives. I hope to show the reader how it feels to do ethnography—in this instance, how Moroccans speak and behave and how they interacted with me.

The book records the fieldwork experience in rough chronological order. It begins with my initiation into the field and my search for factories and workers, and it ends with my departure from the field. The book is divided into three parts, which correspond roughly to the way the girls themselves divide up their world: street, factory, and home. Moroccans imagine a strict division between the public and private worlds. The street—the public realm—is juxtaposed with the home—the private world of family and friends. The factory is both: it represents something that is foreign and outside the home, but the girls who work in factories use their relationships to one another and to the factory owners to transform the factory into a private space, a kind of home. This juxtaposition between home and factory is also an issue brought to the fore by theorists of second wave industrialization. They have asked questions about whether work in the factory would alter the nature of family relationships or whether the patterns of relationships at home would be replicated in the factory. These kinds of questions have also influenced the format of my narrative.

Gender and Factories

By the early 1980s, researchers had begun to describe and document a new global process. International capital had begun to invest in poor and less developed countries, not in plantations and mines as under colonialism but in industry. The countries of the periphery had become the sites of a new industrial production. All over the globe, factories were built to produce or assemble electronics, textiles, and clothing. Much of this industry was based in subcontracting, with the wealthier nations supplying the materials and equipment needed for production and the poorer countries offering up the labor. In this "new international division of labor," it was women who, more often than not, became the workers.[4]

The feminization of the labor force in sites of new industrialization is not new. Historians have described how women, and particularly young unmarried women, were recruited as accommodating and easily disciplined workers at the time of the first industrial revolution.[5] The recent incorporation of females into the industrial labor force of newly industrialized countries, however, has been a trend intensified by the imposition of structural adjustment policies on these countries. Debtor nations (strapped by debt payment schedules they could not meet) have been compelled by their creditors to introduce economic restructuring programs designed to open their economies to foreign trade and investment and to decrease government spending. The programs cut and often eliminated popular benefits, such as food and rent subsidies; they restricted access to the secure, well-paid government jobs that had kept many afloat; and they tightened economic conditions in a way most painful for those already at the bottom. For households suffering from restructuring, women's paid labor became a way to counter the costs of economic restructuring. At the same time, international capital found a cheap and flexible female workforce.[6]

The literature analyzing this feminization of the labor force has taken for granted that around the globe gender ideologies that subordinate women to men, and the feminine to the masculine, helped to devalue women as workers and make their labor cheap. Women working in the new factories (which came to be known as the "global factory") have been widely considered supplementary workers and have been given positions and wages inferior to men. Elson and Pearson outlined much of the earliest debate by recognizing three effects of factory work on local gender systems. Factory work, they argued, could "intensify" local forms of gender subordination, it could "decompose" them, or it could "recompose" them, creating new forms of subordination. Following on these questions about whether incorporation into the new industries damaged or improved female status, later researchers focused on the relationship between the international industry and local patriarchies. They began to look more closely at how the labor process has varied culturally in specific locations and how cultural specificities affect workers and their actions. Within the enormous diversity (and persistent similarities) in the forms and expressions of gender hierarchies in industry around the globe, a set of issues has emerged.[7]

Who are the workers? In some cases, it is the working girl's status as a daughter, often a "dutiful daughter," that makes her amenable to factory work.[8] In other locations, wives and mothers get access to the factory. For all these women, employment in the factories allows them to develop their own skills at various levels. Some workers gain valuable proficiencies while others gain little, and this affects their ability to create careers that last beyond any particular job.[9] Different styles of labor control on the shop floor—work regimes—use varying methods for controlling the workers. Sometimes these involve highlighting the sexuality of female workers, as male managers often do in the Mexican Maquila industry, which helps to trivialize their labor contributions.[10]

Nearly everywhere, the entry of females into the factories is followed by new kinds of modern consumption. The workers begin to purchase lipstick, face cream, and sunglasses with their wages—or with whatever portion of their earnings they are left to control. They begin to participate in leisure activities previously unknown to those of their class, particularly to women. The working women's choice of new and foreign forms of "modernity" causes suspicion and tension in local communities. At best, their new and "inappropriate" behaviors are seen as selfish. At worst, the workers are believed to be disease carriers. Malaysian workers, for example, are suspected of carrying HIV/AIDS, females in Sri Lanka are victims of rape and violent crime, and women working in Mexico become the victims of lethal violence.[11]

The morality of working women is often called into question, perhaps because in fact they often do adopt a new sense of personal autonomy as a result of their wage labor, a sense of personal independence considered unseemly for women (or even for men) in traditional, kin-based communities. This autonomy can result in greater personal influence in courtship and marriage decisions, altering local traditions in China, Malaysia, Thailand, Sri Lanka, India, Mexico, and—as I will illustrate—in Morocco. It also opens up new public spaces for women who enter the public domain and interact with men in unprecedented ways.

To what extent do women accommodate themselves and their own understanding of gender to the new factory regimes, and to what extent do they resist gendered power at home and on the shop floor? As Marybeth Mills points out in her review, women may not struggle against harsh work regimes on the shop floor if there are no alternative work options available to them, or if available alternatives are seen as far less desirable, household labor, or sex work. In many locations, though, women do resist, and researchers have documented multiple forms of resistance on the shop floor—from nightmares and menstrual problems to more culturally specific forms of revolt, such as spirit possession and hysteria. Women have protested through outright labor actions, such as strikes, but very often the complicity of governments with the power of international capital makes it almost impossible for women to directly and successfully protest in such a way.[12]

How do Moroccan females experience work in the garment factory? How do their experiences on the shop floor translate to the home? Does the women's participation in these new forms of wage labor—with the money and autonomy they may bring—give them novel ways to contest their subordination at home? Around the globe, working girls and women make new claims to spatial mobility, hide their wages from husbands and parents, and buy for themselves new kinds of commodities. In Morocco, as I detail here, working girls stroll the streets after work, streets their own mothers cannot negotiate, free of the watchful eyes of brothers and fathers. They manage to forge romantic relationships and purchase highly desired consumer goods. But their actions are always conflicted and ambiguous; they continue to accept the gendered ideals of their own societies even as they resist them.

Thus with this narrative I look in the streets, in the factory, and at home to see how the factory girls of Fes, their families, and their community live the experience of the global factory.

Garment Factories in Morocco

Beginning in the 1980s, the feminization that typically accompanies economic liberalization became evident in Morocco. Having begun its own economic restructuring program, the Moroccan government opened the country to foreign trade and actively promoted the growth of private enterprise—of export manufacturing specifically. In search of cheap foreign suppliers, European garment manufacturers looked to newly open and nearby Morocco for labor. Sewing factories sprang up in Casablanca, Rabat, and Fes. These factories hired females.[13]

The city of Fes emerged as a leading Moroccan garment-producing center by the mid-1990s. The Fes garment industry was based largely on subcontracting with European firms: The foreign firms supplied the necessary materials—patterns, cloth, zippers, thread—to the Moroccan entrepreneurs, who then hired the workers to sew and package up finished garments for export to Europe. Fes's wealthy elite (known locally as the "Fassi" families) provided much of the start-up money to open the small, private sewing factories to meet European demand. These factories were low-tech, family-owned businesses typically operating with an average of 50 workers. They, together with a few much larger, foreign-owned (and in some cases well-established Moroccan) firms, hired a third of all the city's factory workers, nearly all of them female.

Over time, the Fes garment market became increasingly narrow and focused on French suppliers. Local Moroccan enterprises competed intensely with each other for contracts. The factories were supplying neither the sewing patterns nor the fabrics, so the essential difference between one firm and the next was the cheapness of the labor. European subcontractors jumped from manufacturer to manufacturer, seeking out the best deal. Fes factories opened and shut as contracts were won and lost, delayed and cancelled. Although Moroccan labor law legislates the registration of factory workers to ensure they receive benefits—minimum wage, paid overtime, sick leave—the small Fes shops never registered workers. They relied on a flexible labor force of skilled and semiskilled workers who could fill orders after they were received.[14]

In this context, employment in a sewing factory was insecure and everchanging. Workers experienced sudden, unexplained layoffs followed by mysterious rehiring as factory owners made, lost, or reworked contracts with their foreign clients. Factory work was a kind of temporary yet long-term affair. While a worker might be in the labor force for years, she would never be at a single factory for an uninterrupted period. She could never count on having her job next year, next month, or perhaps even next week.

The factories operated with little government interference. Work hours were erratic, and overtime pay was not standardized. When a contract demanded immediate shipping of goods, factories compelled workers to sew throughout the night—what workers called "sleeping at the factory." Workers received no sick leave or vacation pay, and they could be fired without warning. Although the minimum monthly wage in 1995 was recorded as 1,200 *dirham*, workers I encountered throughout Fes reported earning anywhere from 300 to 800 *dirham* a month.[15] (Workers at foreign-owned factories acknowledged that they were receiving minimum wage.) Factory workers frequently reported that they had been fired for "growing old." After having spent several years at one factory, workers were often dismissed. These firings were never explained, but the assumption was that such highly skilled and savvy workers would begin to demand the benefits legally due them.

The garment factories worked on a Taylorist system,[16] and conditions were difficult. The workday was at least nine hours, often longer, and workers were rigorously monitored. The more rigid factory administrators might prohibit them from leaving their assigned places, or even speaking during work hours. In many factories the doors were locked once the workday started, and workers were not permitted to leave the building, at risk of being fired. Workers were often kept at the job long after quitting time and told they would not be permitted to leave until the day's quotas were met.

During my own research period (1994–95), I encountered a handful of workers who had been employed in the sewing industry since the early 1980s. These longtime workers were aware of a significant decline in their working conditions over the previous decade. Historically, since the colonial period, Fes had been the site of four government-run textile factories that provided secure, highly coveted jobs mostly to men—but to a few women as well. Moroccan labor unions had been a powerful force in these early textile factories, protecting the rights of the workers and ensuring government-approved benefits. Union activism was a legacy of these factories, and the garment workers among the first ranks of the garment girls (before the effects of the economic reforms became acute) remembered the unions' impact and the protections they once received. It was these relatively few older, experienced workers who articulated a decline in the conditions of their labor.

In addition, many Fes garment workers believed that labor conditions had seriously deteriorated after the workers' strike of December 14, 1990. This strike erupted into rioting, looting, and civil unrest that lasted several days. Fes locals widely asserted that since the strike, one-third of all Fes's factories had remained shut down.[17] The availability of garment factory jobs was then significantly reduced. With fewer positions available to an ever-growing number of poor young women, owners could easily deny workers their legal rights to equitable wages and fair working conditions. Older workers consistently reported that they had participated in organized labor unions and labor activism before the strike; such activism was no longer apparent among garment factory workers in Fes in 1995.

Given the conditions of factory labor, why would Moroccan females strive to supply these factories with their labor? The restructuring of the 1980s looked like real economic development: Morocco's gross national product increased during this period. Refrigerators, telephones, televisions, VCRs—once considered luxury items for the rich—appeared in urban apartments everywhere. Ovens for baking bread, which are very expensive to operate, became popular in private homes. Boutiques selling the latest French fashions proliferated near fancy ice cream shops in the city centers, where the streets became clogged with cars that even teachers could afford. Hawkers selling contraband—shoes, sunglasses, radios—brought in through the Spanish enclaves of Ceuta and Mellilia trawled the city sidewalks, particularly in the country's north. Enclaves of spacious green tile–roofed villas in various states of construction began to pop up on city outskirts. Some of these even had swimming pools.

But these apparent improvements were illusory. During the 1980s, disparities sharpened between rich and poor in Morocco more than in any other Magrebi society. Of course, some Moroccans grew rich, but their numbers were relatively few. The overwhelming majority of Moroccans experienced the economic boom as further impoverishment.[18] Under its new economic policies, the Moroccan government cut food subsidies that had made bread and sugar affordable to the poor. Hiring in the public sector—for civil service jobs, which were the most secure and protected—was frozen. Rents became astronomically high. By the mid-1990s some 30 percent of the urban poor were unemployed. Even those who did find work often found that their incomes would never cover the costs of rent and food needed to support a wife and children.[19] The poor and middle classes struggled to cover the cost of living while they watched the wealthy minority—those able to participate at the highest levels in the new export industries—shop for high fashion clothing in the new boutiques and eat pastries in shiny mirrored cafés.

The Garment Girls of Fes

In Fes, as in Morocco generally, not all females were considered eligible for garment factory work. The workers I encountered were young, between the ages of 13 and 25, unmarried, living at home with their parents and siblings. Married women rarely worked in the sewing factories, especially if they had children. The few I encountered were either newly married and as yet child-less or else destitute because their husbands were unable to work.[20]

Fes garment workers were daughters in relatively poor households. In a quarter of the factory workers' homes, the fathers were gone. Workers would claim that a brother or uncle had "taken charge," but despite this nod to patri-archal ideals, households were actually headed by widowed (or perhaps aban-doned) mothers of large broods. The factory households suffered from high rates of male unemployment. The fathers and brothers in these households who did indeed hold jobs were employed in low-wage positions as construc-tion workers, salesmen (vegetable sellers, perhaps), or taxi drivers.

The factory families were only one generation removed from the country-side. In most factory households, the girls' parents had grown up in the coun-tryside surrounding Fes, or in other rural regions, and had come into the city as part of the vast and ongoing rural to urban migration that had begun in colonial times. Thus the garment workers had been born and had grown up in the lower-class neighborhoods of Fes. They were not migrants from the countryside who had come to Fes simply to work, as are many of the garment workers described in the literature on the global factory (particularly in Asia). The Moroccan factory girls lived at home and made the daily commute to work, sometimes transported from their homes or neighborhoods by factory-sponsored buses. This is in contrast to other globalizing countries where young females often left their homes in the countryside to live in large factory dor-mitories for years. In that context, the labor of those girls in factories involves issues of rural to urban migration and the proletarianization of the peasant family. These issues do not pertain to Morocco, where most factory families had settled in Fes before the emergence of the garment industry there.[21]

Many of the workers had entered the school system, but on average they had achieved at best a fifth grade education. Financial needs at home demanded that all children in the workers' large families contribute to the family's upkeep. As food bills, rent, and school costs for younger siblings mounted, a collection of meager wages would ensure household survival. Almost every worker con-tributed some or all of her salary to her family. As mentioned above, workers earned anywhere from 300 to 800 *dirham* per month, significantly less than the national minimum wage, and a factory salary fell severely short of meeting the needs of any single family. Nonetheless, these salaries were considered significant in lower-class households where men had difficulty finding work.[22]

Under other circumstances, in earlier periods, it might have been expected that girls in the workers' age category would marry. Traditionally girls in Morocco marry shortly after the onset of puberty, and workers' mothers reported on their own early marriages. But in Morocco it is assumed that the husband will act as breadwinner; the girls' hopes of marriage were evaporating as steady employment became increasingly elusive for their male peers. Factory labor was not highly esteemed, especially for females, but girls of this class had few other options. Earlier generations of Moroccan women had entered the professions as teachers, nurses, and office workers; Moroccan women were visibly present in universities and hospitals, as professors and doctors. But these professional women were usually of a higher class than the factory girls, who, with their dismal educational histories, had little hope of attaining such status. For a girl of this class, wage-earning options were narrow. She might serve as a maid in a wealthy home—perhaps even the home of a relative. She might weave in a carpet factory or sort and pack vegetables in a food-processing plant, both forms of factory labor perceived as even more menial than garment manufacture. She might do seasonal agricultural labor in the fields surrounding Fes, or work at home as a seamstress, doing piecework for local tailors, and earning what amounts to pennies per piece. Garment factory work was a comparatively good option compared with any of those.

The girls work in four factory districts, created with the support of the Moroccan government, that surround the ancient city of Fes. Moroccans see Fes as a bulwark of Moroccan and Muslim tradition. Its central mosque is an international pilgrimage site. Residents live and work in a cultural ethos typical of what has been described as Arab and Muslim: The working girls of Fes bless their bread before breaking it. They visit the shrines of saints, where they ask the departed holy ones for help and intervention. They struggle with *jnun*, mischievous spiritual beings that exist on a plane somewhere between humans and the angels and that can create havoc. The girls also hold tightly to traditional Arab and Muslim understandings of family, gender, and sexuality.[23]

In Morocco, the family is the center of an individual's life and the source of personal identity, as is generally true throughout the Arab world. No one should be alone: everyone must marry. "Marriage," one worker told me, "is like death. It is necessary." As a wife, a woman's place is in the home, caring for children and keeping the house. As she grows up, a daughter is encouraged to stay close, so that she may be trained in the skills necessary for homemaking and lend her support to her family. Although a wife might earn a wage and contribute to the household income, ideally she is not obligated to do so. It is the man's duty to support her and their children. (Children are desperately desired by men and women alike.) Moroccans widely believe these roles to be assigned by God and that to faithfully enact them is at the heart of being a good Muslim.

The Moroccan family is a patriarchal family in which males have authority over females, husbands over wives, fathers over daughters, brothers over sisters. Females must behave in a way that demonstrates their subservience and their acceptance of this very "natural" order. This social order makes sense to Moroccans because they accept that females are less rational, less disciplined, and more dependent than men. Females are believed to be vulnerable and to need male protection. Thus male authority is more than simple dominance: fathers, brothers, and husbands are expected to support and protect their daughters, sisters, and wives.

At the time of the study, this understanding of gender, marriage, and family was part of the Moroccan Code of Personal Status, which then governed family relations. This set of statutes, based on traditional Islamic law, placed women under male tutelage throughout life and institutionalized a division of gender roles with the man as the head of family.[24] Legal consent for marriage was to be expressed not by the bride but by her father or male guardian. (Although Moroccan girls insisted that a righteous father would ask his daughter's permission before giving her hand in marriage, compulsion was possible.) Divorce at will was the prerogative of men, while women were severely constrained in their ability to divorce. Polygyny remained legal, with a man having the right to marry as many as four wives. (Although taking four wives was indeed rare, the possibility of a husband taking a second wife hovered as a threat to first wives.)

Ideas about family honor are a crucial component of the Moroccan system of family and gender. The honor of a family is displayed through its members' piety, generosity, and hospitality. But family honor hinges most critically upon the proper comportment of the daughters. Virginity before marriage and fidelity throughout marriage are cultural absolutes in Morocco and the burden of these values falls most heavily on females. A girl's public display of modesty (with the virginity it implies) is possibly her single most important characteristic and a measure of the honor of her father and brothers. Like many in the Muslim world, Moroccans perceive human sexuality as a powerful force demanding constant vigilance. Females, with their passions and vulnerabilities, are felt to be at particular risk for stepping outside the accepted boundaries and thus putting family honor at risk. But there are cultural systems in place to help control women and prevent the danger of lost virginity.

Moroccans believe it is best to separate unrelated males from females and strive, whenever possible, to do so. In their roles as mothers and wives, women are associated symbolically with the home, and generally it is believed that this is the best (and safest) place for girls and women to be. The home is seen as a private space—for women and family—in contrast to space that is public—for men. Thus the difference between male and female is expressed in spatial terms as a division between public and private space, a division between work and home. Honor is bestowed upon those families who display an ability to keep their women under control—in their proper place—thereby preserving the sanctity of the gender boundaries.

It is impossible to argue, though, that women in Morocco are secluded. Females are visible on the streets and in the nation's schools and offices. But female seclusion retains significance both as an ideal and as a practice, particularly among the lower-class people of Fes. In Fes, girls and women of childbearing age are restricted in their movement outside the home. Fathers, husbands, and brothers often control their comings and goings and demand an accounting of where they have been. Girls and boys might sit near each other in a classroom, but they ought not to spend time together in the streets after class. Girls and women are discouraged from sitting in cafés or movie theaters or strolling through the streets without purpose. Most lower-class Fes families guard and limit the mobility of their daughters in the effort to ensure the girls' morality and the family's honorability.

Girls and women signal their conformity to the ideals of female modesty through the use of appropriate dress. Outside the house, lower-class girls of Fes wear long polyester robes, the *djellaba*, and those who have reached puberty often cover their heads with a loosely tied scarf. Married women frequently wear a head scarf to assert their status as wives. By the mid-1990s, the use of a more complete form of covering, the *hijab*, a style of dress associated with fundamentalist movements throughout the Muslim world, had taken hold among high school and university girls in Morocco. Most factory workers, however, had not adopted the *hijab*. Many seemed uninterested in the academic religious arguments made by those who had adopted fundamentalist clothing;

others claimed that the factory owners would not permit this form of dress, lest the European clients find it unacceptable.

No one—including the girls themselves—ever called the factory girls "workers" or "employees" or any word that might translate as "factory hands." Although there is a form of apprenticeship in the factories (a period of training that often goes unpaid), no one referred to these trainees as "apprentices." They were "girls." In Arabic, a *bint* (girl) is a female who has not yet married. By cultural definition, a "girl" is not simply a child or immature female. A "girl" is a virgin, a daughter. A female loses her status as a "girl" and is transformed into a "woman" through marriage. Being a "girl" then has less to do with biological age and more to do with social—marital and sexual—status. The fact that Moroccans, and the workers themselves, always spoke of factory "girls" says something about the importance of the workers' family position to their identity.

Garment factory workers are often demeaned by Fes inhabitants for their participation in factory labor. Girls who engage in factory labor are assumed to be related to males who are unable to appropriately support and protect them. Their glaring presence on the streets suggests a lack of family honor and the real or potential loss of personal virtue, proof of the inadequacy of families to control and monitor their daughters. And yet, usually pushed by economic necessity, the workers continue to labor in Fes garment factories. Their notions about what gender means, many of them fundamentally associated with Islam, affect the way in which they understand their work, how they behave on the factory floor, and how the work ultimately affects life at home. Their understanding of Islam and gender, however, does not prevent them from entering the factory, working for a wage, or wishing for an improved professional future.[25]

Research Methods

The book is based on research I conducted in the city of Fes from August 1994 through August 1995. By the time I arrived in Fes that August, I had lived in Morocco for more than two years previously, and I was already able to communicate in the dialectical Arabic that Moroccans use in everyday conversation. As an anthropologist, my research method was based on intensive ethnography. I began the research by attempting to find the factories (their location was not always publicly documented or marked on a map). Ultimately I obtained a list of local enterprises from the Fes Chamber of Commerce and began to contact factory owners. I also began to make contacts with workers, often by searching for and speaking with them in the streets of the factory districts where they looked for work.

Over the course of the year, I was able to interview the owners of twelve factories in Fes, many of whom allowed me to tour their factory sites. On the whole, owners were reluctant to speak with me. They were well aware that they did not comply with Moroccan labor law; the Moroccan government turned a blind eye to their operations, and the owners were suspicious of having an "American researcher" investigating their enterprises. Nonetheless, two owners permitted me to carry out random surveys of their employees. I asked a set of formal interview questions aimed at uncovering basic statistics on the workers: for example, the size and income level of their households, their age and educational attainment, and the number of years they had worked. In many ways the survey data confirmed details about the workers that were widely known in Fes. I also began to collect longer survey questionnaires from workers whom I had befriended in the course of my factory visits, and who were willing to meet me outside the factory for further discussion. These initial surveys and interviews helped me shape ideas about the meaning of factory work.

In January 1995, I secured a job in one of the factories and worked in its packing department over a period of three months. Ultimately, I was asked to leave the factory when the manager began to suspect my motives. This factory officially employed some 150 workers (although on a given day, fewer workers were there) and had been in operation for six years by the time I arrived. This factory was typical of the other garment factories I had visited in Fes. It was one of the larger operations in the city. With my position as packaging worker, I was able to observe and converse with workers throughout the day and after work as well. I carried out both informal and formal interviews. This is the factory experience I describe in detail in the narrative that follows.

As I spent time with workers in the streets and in the factories, they became my friends and companions. In my free time, I visited with them and their families in their homes and came to know something of how life was lived there. This household visiting and the development of what would become close friendships continued throughout the research year. This I describe in part III.

PART I

In the Streets

CHAPTER 1

Finding the Workers

My husband and I arrived in Rabat. He would be teaching at the university, and I was to begin my research into the lives of factory workers. Everything was terribly familiar, for I had lived in Morocco before. I recognized the singular smell of dry heat and the feel of the constant dusty wind that rips across the flatness. Cars and motorbikes were everywhere. The fumes of strong unfiltered exhaust and the powerful shrieking of vehicles permeated the atmosphere. Everything was as I remembered it and yet, somehow, it was shocking to be back.

We were greeted at the Rabat airport by a representative of the American embassy who drove us to the quiet and green section of the city where the foreigners lived. He then deposited us at a hotel close to the embassy offices. Weary, we slept in the warm, barely ventilated room for several hours. Then we returned to his office, where we were given the paperwork confirming our purpose in the country. I gathered together my documents, which certified that the Moroccan government approved of my research on the garment industry and that I was licensed to conduct research.

Leaving the embassy office, I felt the heat beat hard on my head. The coastal cities are the coolest in Morocco, but still the August sun burned bright and white. We walked back to the hotel to make preparations for our departure. We were not planning to remain long in the capital; tomorrow we would travel to Fes. I had a fleeting feeling of exhaustion.

The next day we arrived in Fes and settled into an apartment in the center of the modern city, the Ville Nouvelle, the newer section of Fes that was built up by the French colonists. In the heyday of the French, this section was defined by lovely white villas, enclosed by walls that hid lush gardens. Its organized grid of streets stands in direct contrast with the old section of the city, the *medina,* with its maze of cross-cutting streets and alleys. Today, however, the Ville Nouvelle is no longer a haven for wealthy foreigners. Rather, it is made up of tall apartment blocks that house the teachers and civil servants of the city—those who have managed to secure jobs that allow them to live outside the walls of the old section but do not allow them to build villas far beyond the city limits.

For days, I walked back and forth between the Ville Nouvelle and the *medina*. I walked the crooked *medina* streets, looking at the men selling plastic shoes, watches, studded blue jeans, chic lace tops for women, stylish polyester shirts for men, and bright *djellaba* (a traditional long, loose-fitting outer robe with full sleeves). I passed women selling bread from carts and tailors working on their machines in shop windows. I passed back and forth through the old French market in the Ville Nouvelle, down a long city block where men sat on the ground, their wares on top of blankets, selling contraband clothing snuck in from Spain. But I could see no factories. I knew that they existed because the government statistics claimed that Fes was an industrial center in Morocco, the third largest after the coastal cities of Casablanca and Rabat. Industry was planted there purposefully by the Moroccan government in a push toward industrialization that gained momentum in the 1970s. I bought a map of the city sold at a tourist kiosk but could find no section marked as industrial. Where were the factories? "Sidi Brahim." This is what everyone in Fes said when I asked them this question.

Sidi Brahim is, in fact, the largest and oldest industrial district in Fes. It was built in the 1970s by the Moroccan government, eager to launch the country into a new industrial era. And so I got in a taxi and asked the driver to take me to Sidi Brahim. We headed out through the Ville Nouvelle and past the university district, where the busy streets are lined with cafés and small trees. We drove across a bridge over a dried river bed. Suddenly the road widened and the trees and cafés disappeared. Big yellow concrete buildings appeared in the horizon. There were no trees at all, just dirt blowing up into little dust devils on the side of the road. The first factory we came to was a huge white building with red trim and a large Coca-Cola sign at the top. This was Sidi Brahim.

The driver stopped and let me out of the cab. I wandered aimlessly down the wide avenue, down side streets. It was five o'clock.

The factories of Sidi Brahim are large flat structures, unevenly built. Like the buildings everywhere in Morocco, parts of them seem to be unfinished cement block. Some have clean, modern facades, but most look like unfinished warehouses, made of cement worn gray from the dust and sun. For the most part the factories are unnamed. There are no signs announcing that these are factories, that the factories are owned by a particular person, and that they are producing particular kinds of goods. I see no indication that these factories actually house workers. The factories are silent.

The buildings seem not to have any windows, only narrow horizontal openings on what looks to be the second floor. There is no light shining out. Buses are lined up in front of some of the factories, but no one is around. The broad dusty streets are empty, uninhabited, noiseless. To the east, the edge of Sidi Brahim is visible, and I see that nothing lies beyond it but the immense flat plains that circle Fes and end in the enormous treeless mountains on the horizon. There is dirt swirling and sand is in the air. It starts to get dark, and I head back toward the university district, searching for a taxi to take me home.

•

The tourist map I had purchased did not mark Sidi Brahim or the urban sprawl that I knew surrounded the center of the city. This map limited Fes to the Ville Nouvelle and the *medina*, places appropriate for the tourist to visit. It made the city look far smaller than it is. I rented a car to take me beyond the limits of walking. For two days I drove through the sprawling city. On all sides of the old center, Fes is surrounded by neighborhoods of cement block buildings that stretch endlessly. Signs mark out the other industrial districts that lie at the borders of this sprawl: Ben Souda, Doukkarat, Sidi Brahim. These districts house the factories that produce canned fruits and vegetables, leather, and clothing. I had found the factories. Now I needed to find the workers.

The Chamber of Commerce, at the center of the Ville Nouvelle, supplied me with a list of factory addresses. The Chamber of Commerce was interested in making the advantages of Fes's industry known to foreigners who might wish to invest. I found brochures there advertising the beauty of Fes industry to global industrialists. I was told that I should go to the government department that oversees industry. There was an office here in Fes, and the government agents would be happy to supply me with information. And so I went to the government office.

There I met a young, bearded man named Malik. I told him that I was researching the garment industry in Fes and he assured me he would help. "Return here tomorrow morning," Malik said. "Once a month, I drive through the factory districts, inspecting the buildings, monitoring any changes, checking on garbage removal. It's part of my drive. I can take you along with me. You are welcome." So the next morning I arrived in the office.

"First," Malik said, "I must of course introduce you to my boss. He is the head of this province, the director of industry for the whole area." I was led into the office of the director. I sat in one chair, Malik sat in another chair, facing me, and the director sat at his desk. We made a triangle. Another man then entered the room. He, they said, was another director.

And so, once we had formally greeted one another, the director asked me, "What is it you want to study?"

"Sidi Brahim," I said at first, knowing that Malik's tour was taking him there.

"But what specifically? What is your focus?"

"Well, my study is about the women who work in the factories."

The director became visibly angry. "Well, we cannot help you with a study like this." He looked at Malik accusingly, and Malik looked at me, shocked, as if I had betrayed him. I faltered. I realized that when I had first spoken to Malik, I had said simply that my study was on the garment industry in Morocco. I had said nothing about workers. This mattered. I tried to explain that my study was on the garment industry, but that I was particularly interested in the workers themselves. The director stayed angry. I feared that perhaps I had put Malik's job in some jeopardy. Perhaps he would not have offered to help if he had known everything. But Malik spoke up in my defense.

"You can see," he said to the director, "her study has two separate aspects, one aspect being the industry itself, the other aspect being the workers." I repeated, heartily, what Malik had said. I did not know why he was trying to protect me.

The director then turned to Malik. "You can take her on your tour, but she is not allowed in any factories. Don't take her inside—not any of the factories. Just show her around, show her where they are. That is all." And then he turned to me. "This office can give you a certain number of facts. We can supply you with the statistics about the industry, tell you the number of the workers, give you technical information. But we will not talk to you about the workers. For that, you need to go to the Ministry of Labor. Now, like I said, Malik will not bring you into any factories."

Malik and I left the office. I felt sick, frightened that perhaps Malik would suffer repercussions. But he seemed unfazed. We got in his car and Malik tried to explain his boss's reaction. "This director was upset, you know, because he just began at this job. He is new. He only started two months ago. He has come from Meknes and he knows nothing of the owners in Fes. He knows nothing about Fes's industry. He is afraid that if I bring you into the factories, the owners will wonder why he is allowing you in. You will want to ask the workers about how much they earn, and the owners will wonder why you are asking such questions. This director needs the confidence of the owners, you know. And he does not have it yet."

I listened and wondered why Malik cared to bother about my research. But then he went on. "Do you know there were big riots here in Fes in 1990? There was a three-day strike. The police and army came in. There were big problems in the streets. The incident got a lot of press overseas, but it was exaggerated. The workers were fighting for human rights, and the unemployed were fighting for jobs. But as far as this director is concerned, he doesn't need bad press."

And again, Malik told me he would help. "You are a sister to me," said Malik. But I thought that perhaps I would stay out of government offices.

•

I found a tutor to help me with my Arabic. The tutor was a middle-aged man named Abdul-Haq. At one time Abdul-Haq had been a primary school teacher, and now he taught Arabic to foreigners visiting Fes. Beyond this, I knew nothing of Abdul-Haq. Although he was willing to teach me Arabic, he never asked me anything about myself. He never told me anything about himself. Over the months I came to believe that Abdul-Haq was certain I was a spy.

There is a certain amount of fear of the police and of government security action among Moroccans, particularly those old enough to have lived through the reign of King Hassan II. These fears were not without reason: this king's government had demonstrated little tolerance for dissent, and there was widespread evidence of government abuse during his reign. Abdul-Haq often whispered when he spoke of anything that might even mildly question the political status quo. Moroccans were careful, but Abdul-Haq was particularly so. My sense was that although he was willing to tutor me, he was careful not to put himself in any danger by revealing too much. He also devoted much time to warning me about potential perils I might pose to myself or to others.

During what were supposed to be our Arabic language classes, Abdul-Haq delivered long, detailed lectures on Moroccan society. He knew that I was investigating the lives of factory workers, and so he tailored his lectures to this topic for me. Sometimes he strayed. He never called on me to respond to his statements, and so I sat, writing down, word for word, the words of Abdul-Haq. Abdul-Haq understood that I was not a native speaker, and so he carefully chose his vocabulary, expertly conveying complex and detailed ideas in the simplest of terms. He spoke slowly and enunciated everything.

In part this was because he understood me to be a language learner; but, as I came to realize, Abdul-Haq spoke like that because he was a storyteller. Once he started speaking, he could speak for a long time, without searching for an idea. He spoke, it seemed to me, in paragraphs, as if he were reading aloud. His face became animated, and his eyebrows moved furiously as he spoke.

As the months wore on, and I listened, I realized the things Abdul-Haq told me about Moroccan society were widely held as true. What Abdul-Haq said, other people believed. Other people said those things, too. And so Abdul-Haq helped me understand what was happening around me.

After my tour with Malik, I asked Abdul-Haq about the strike of 1990. What had happened? And Abdul-Haq began to speak:

In 1990, the Fes strikes occurred, and conditions have changed dramatically because of these strikes. The strikes lasted for three days. Soldiers came into Fes from everywhere, from all over the country, even from the Sahara. They had machine guns and just shot—because some soldiers just shoot without thinking. Some of the soldiers, though, were on the side of the people in the strikes—about 50 percent of the soldiers were on the people's side and against the government. It was the Arab soldiers who were with the people, the Berbers against.

The strikes were the people acting against the government; they were not against foreigners. No foreigners were hurt at this time. (Abdul-Haq said this, I think, to reassure me.)

Only one foreigner was hurt in Casablanca; he was killed. But the foreigners in Fes were mostly left alone. Even when the rioters entered the Hotel Merinedes, they did not touch the foreigners there. As a matter of fact, the strikers were happy to see the foreign journalists, and boys cleared a path for these journalists in the streets. They encouraged the journalists to take pictures of the riots, so the foreign countries would know what was going on here.

These were not just strikes. They were huge riots. There were fires burning all over Fes, at every edge of the city, north, south, west, east, one could see huge fires burning. Little boys, and big boys, but lots of little boys were throwing gasoline on cars and just burning the cars. All the cars in Fes were burnt; parking lots were turned into huge fires. Little children were slashing into stores and hotels, carrying everything out. Even old women were entering hotels and looting them, taking what they wanted and then returning for more. The cabinets and beds had legs, I'm telling you. Looking down from above, from my window, looking down at the action on the streets, it was as if the cabinets and the beds had legs. In fact, though, they were being carried by little children.

The Moroccan press had been predicting the strikes for months. For months before the strikes began, the newspapers had been saying that the workers would strike for a higher wage. The newspapers even reported that the strike would begin on December 14. But the government said nothing. The government did nothing. The government paid no attention to the newspapers; it gave this report no importance. If the king had even said one word on December 13, the evening before the strikes, if the king had said just one word about the striking, if he had at least recognized the threat, perhaps the actions on December 14 would never have happened. But the king and the government said nothing. They did nothing.

And so then, on the morning of December 14, I woke up and took the bus to work. (At this point he bent at the waist and leaned forward, with one finger to his lips to signal the hush in the streets, and said, "Scoot," meaning "Silence.") People were in the streets, but there was silence in the streets. And boys started throwing rocks at the bus I was riding in, and the bus had to stop, and the people had to get out of the bus and walk. All was quiet. And then later that day, the rioting, the looting, the fires began. And the strike was on.

Work stopped in the factories. And because of the unrest, thirty factories closed here in Fes. These factories are still closed.

•

At the Chamber of Commerce, I had been given a list of the garment factories operating in Fes, complete with addresses and phone numbers. I called owners and asked to interview them, to see their factories. I spoke with many owners and toured many factories. In some of these factories I was able to conduct worker surveys, always under the watchful eye of a floor manager. Still, I had only a glimpse into the workers' lives.

Early in the morning, workers clustered at the factory doors, hoping they would be called in to work. In the evenings, workers emptied out of the factories; some walked home through the city streets. And so I began wandering through the factory districts, finding workers to speak to me. But I worried constantly: Would factory owners see me and object to my presence in the factory district? Would they assume I was attempting to organize workers? Would they complain to government officials and have me removed? But even worse, I feared for the workers. What if they were seen speaking with me—a foreigner? Would they be assumed to be aligning themselves with political action? Could they be blamed for this? Could they be fired? The Moroccan system of justice, I knew, might not offer protections to factory girls—people at the bottom of the social and political hierarchy. I did not want to hurt them.[1] But I needed to speak with them. Abdul-Haq had said to me:

> *Some people will not understand the idea of your research. They will not comprehend what you are doing. These people will understand you better if you just explain that your husband is a teacher here and so you are here with him.*
>
> *But some people will understand your research and will believe that you are here to help them, and they will speak with you. You must be patient, and you must not fear. You must wait, with patience. Be patient, do not fear. Fear is a sickness. When people trust you, they will begin to speak to you and tell you about themselves. You must wait patiently and not fear.*

Nearly all of the garment workers in Fes are unmarried females between the ages of 15 and 25. These girls, I found, were eager to speak with a curious foreigner who wanted to hear them talk about their work. Many were remarkably trusting, sharing with me their secrets and confidences even after a very short acquaintance. These initial disclosures, I would quickly learn, were often only partial truths that would, over time, become more and more complete.

One evening I went to the center of the Ville Nouvelle, where I had visited a small factory the day before. It was, as far as I could tell, the only factory located in this section of the city, and the owner had given me a tour of the factory and allowed me to stay for a while to watch the girls work. Now dusk was approaching. I stood across the street from the factory and watched the workers exit. Waves of girls stepped onto the sidewalk in groups of two or three. I crossed the street and sat on a bench, and the stream of workers thinned out as they moved further from the factory. I followed one small group into a small city park and got close enough to interrupt them.

"Excuse me, please, excuse me. I would like to speak with you," I said. They stopped. One girl with a bright face and shiny lipstick smiled and said she remembered me from the day before. "I am doing research," I told them. "Would you speak with me about your work?"

"You mean you want to learn to sew?" one of them asked. I tried to explain to them why I wanted to speak with them. I was not sure whether they understood. But they were obliging and tolerant, and they invited me to walk along with them. We moved together slowly, heading through the park and down the main avenue of Fes. "We feel for you," they said. "We like the way your Arabic sounds." "You are beautiful." "You are welcome among us." "You will stay in our hearts." All these things they said to make me feel like I was accepted among them.

When everyone understood why I had been in their factory yesterday, and when I had made my interests clear, we began to discuss whether or not I should return to their factory. "Yes, you must come back. You will be welcome there," some of the youngest among them assured me.

"No," said Hajja, an older girl in the group. "You cannot come back. They will not let you talk to us there. And if you do talk to us there, we will not tell you the truth." And she described how once someone, whom she presumed was a government official, came to the factory and conducted a survey. "I did not tell them the truth. They asked me questions, there, in the factory, and I did not answer truthfully. Why would I, with my manager looking on?"

Hajja spoke with authority. She said that she was 30, but to me she looked a lot older. She wore a scarf tied under her chin in the French peasant style and a *djellaba*. She was married, she said, and her husband was in France. She had lived in France until just recently and had only just returned to Morocco because, she said, she was unable to become pregnant and had returned to seek medical help. I knew this made no sense, but I did not question her explanation. Hajja understood my purpose, and she tried to explain it to the other girls. "She is writing a book about Morocco. People write books about Morocco, about life in Morocco, about culture and habits." Hajja had lived elsewhere. She understood this.

As we stood in the middle of the sidewalk on the main thoroughfare of town, clustered in a group, a fancy-looking woman and a man approached us. "Excuse me, sisters," she said. "Please, can I speak?" The girls nodded yes, and she motioned forward the man who was with her. He opened a briefcase displaying children's language learning cassettes and some perfume and began his sales pitch. The girls listened patiently and then told the pair, "We have no money now. We would very much like to buy these things, but we cannot. But really, you should go to the offices here in town, even go to our factory. Our owner will let you in, and perhaps you can try to make a sale there." The woman asked them which factory it was, and they told her it was the garment factory in the town center. "Oh, really," the woman said, excited. "I used to work in a garment factory as a manager. Do you think you could get me a job?" And the girls said immediately, "Oh, yes, sister, you should come to the factory during the day. Ask there." Then the couple walked away. When they were past hearing, the girls said, "We don't need any more managers. Managers are our problem." And then the group dispersed, but a girl named Fatima stayed with me, and we talked as we walked toward my home.

Fatima was somewhat older than the other girls. She was tall and skinny, dark-skinned, with buck teeth and a thin sallow face. Her cheeks were sunken, so she looked underfed. She wore a plain and tattered *djellaba*, unlike the younger girls, who were dressed in jeans and fancy western style clothing. "I live with my parents," Fatima began. "They are very old. My father is 83, and my mother is around 62—or something like that. They had children late in life, and they only had us—me and my brother." Fatima's brother was 18. He had gone to school, left school, and was now jobless. And so she was the only one in the family who worked. "My parents are too old to work, and my brother cannot find a job. So I must support them. I feed them, and I pay the rent." Fatima said that men had come for her asking for marriage. "But I cannot marry. If I do, who will support the family? I have to stay with them. I have to take care of them. My parents often say, 'Listen, Fatima, you must think of your own future. You must marry.' But I tell them, 'How can I marry? How will you eat if I marry?' Yes, of course, I'd like to think of my own future. But what can I do?"

I asked Fatima about her brother. "He cannot find work. I have to give him money. I even give him money to buy cigarettes because he asks me. He asks for money. He needs money. And I'm afraid. If I don't give him money for what he needs, what might he do? Perhaps he would get involved with something bad, something criminal. And so I give him what he needs."

We were quiet for a few moments. My mind wandered. When Fatima spoke, her lips pursed as if to cover her front teeth, which stuck out slightly and were slightly gray at the roots. These lips, I thought, are hiding something, perhaps hiding teeth that are missing, which would explain why her cheeks are so sunken. And as these thoughts crossed my mind, the disparaging words of people in Fes, people who had no daughters working in factories, kept echoing in my head: "Factory girls work to buy lipstick," everyone told me. Abdul-Haq had only recently seconded this opinion, with his usual asperity:

Girls in the factories work for the mul dheb (gold salesman). In the past, women thought a lot about wool. Women bought wool. Now they think about gold and want to buy gold.

Women in the Middle East have long valued gold as an investment, a source of personal wealth that might steel them against future calamity. But Fatima wore no lipstick nor did her wrists jingle with bangles of gold. She did not seem to be working to collect gold—or any other wealth. She seemed to be working, quite selflessly, to support her family.

And then Fatima told me about her old job, at the state-owned factory, where she had worked for many years with Hajja. The factory closed, she said, when the workers went on strike. "I am certain," she warned me, "that the owners of our factory do not want you back. Don't visit us there. Things are not being done according to the law. We have no benefits, and we do not receive the minimum wage. They will not want you to see how things are being done." Once again I heard the echo of Abdul-Haq's words. I could see him counting off on his fingers, starting with his pinky, pushing each finger down to form a fist as he elaborated:

And now, since the strikes, we have even more girls working in factories in Fes. More and more factories are employing girls. Why?

1. A girl does not strike. Girls do not organize strikes.

2. A girl is willing to work more than the hours allotted by labor law. She will work more than an eight-hour day.

3. A girl does not have a skill; she does not have a specialty. Girls are untrained. So a boss can say to a girl, "Sew today, and then clean up the factory tomorrow." And if he has wheat at home to clean and work on, he can tell the girl to clean his wheat, clean his house, and then sleep with him, if he wants.

We arrived at the door of my apartment, and Fatima continued on to her home. She said that she would bring the workers to my home, now that she knew where I lived. They would come back and speak with me on Saturday— Saturday at 1:00 p.m. if they were finished with work. If they were not finished by 1:00, that would mean they would finish at 6:00, and so they would come then.

•

On Saturday I waited at home for the workers at 1:00, and then I waited again at 6:00. They arrived at my home at 7:00. They had not expected to work all day, but they were kept at their machines until six. Now they could not stay, as they needed to get home. "Come to the park near the factory on Wednesday, in the evening. We will meet you then. We will answer your questions then."

On Wednesday evening, I sat on a bench in the park. I sat facing the direction of the factory, which is one block down from the park. I started waiting for the workers at 5:00, not knowing when they might be released. I stood up every once in a while and walked toward the factory, thinking that perhaps I would just go to the door and ask the factory guardian when the workday would be finished. But I knew it would be best if I did not make myself known. And so I just kept sitting on the bench.

The night falls differently in Fes. It falls quickly. Very suddenly the light takes on a magical quality, and then everything grows dark so that you are sitting underneath a velvet sky that is not black but a sort of deep purple gray. Tall palms line the walkways of the park. The trunks are bald, but at the top they flower out with dark green leaves. When the sky changes the massive tree trunks reflect the remaining light of day off their white surfaces. And from the top of these long faintly glowing trunks come thousands of tiny little chirping sounds.

As the color of the sky changes, the birds come out, delicate black swallows moving in huge flocks. They sweep across the sky, separate groups of them streaming in separate directions, heading toward each other across the sky. And then, just before they might collide, they disperse. And without warning a flock swooping across the sky will alight upon a single palm ,and the birds will disappear into the canopy. The chirping of swallows in the tree the flock chooses grows so loud that the noise is almost deafening, blocking out the street noises. You cannot see the birds once they have lit upon a single tree because the palms in which they must be sitting are so high up. You know they are there only because you have watched them swoop down upon the tree top and you hear their sounds. When the sky becomes completely dark, the birds disappear, and only the shape of the palms in the dark remains.

I sat on a bench in the park waiting, but the doors to the factory never opened, and no one came out. It grew dark, and fewer and fewer people passed through the park. Young men passing me on the bench kept stopping and asking me, in practiced English, "What time is it?" I waited some more and thought again about going to the factory door. Then I went home.

•

I was, at this point, dependent on chance encounters. I kept wandering factory streets early mornings and late afternoons. In the evenings, clusters of workers exiting the factories warmly welcomed my approach, and often one or more of them would promise to meet with me at a later, agreed-upon time. I would wait for these girls at the appointed hour at the end of a workday, standing alone at a bus stop or near a factory gate, watching Mopeds speed by on the dimly lit avenues of an industrial district, conspicuous in my solitude. But the workers never appeared.

I became discouraged. How could my research succeed if workers would not speak with me? Why did these girls not keep their appointments? Abdul-Haq had a ready answer to my question:

> *The word miwaad can refer to a business appointment or to a social sort of engagement. In Morocco, it is considered a bad thing to "tie yourself down with appointments." This is not a good thing to do. In Morocco, you might see a friend in the street and say to him, 'We must meet in a café tomorrow.' The friend will automatically reply, 'O.K.' The friend does this unthinkingly, automatically. But both people know that it is not a sure thing. Both know that everything is in God's hands and that something else might come up tomorrow. And if one friend shows up and the other does not, they both know that something happened that just kept the other from showing.*
>
> *So there is really no way to make appointments in Morocco. People do not keep appointments. Everyone assumes that all is in God's hands, and if you do not show up for an appointment, it is simply because you could not, because something came up. Americans have to rip up their appointment books when they come to Morocco.*

I knew that Abdul-Haq, with his instinctive discernment of Moroccan culture, was correct. But I knew, too, that there was more to these missed appointments. It was certainly possible that these workers never really intended to speak with me at all. Moroccans are far too courteous to refuse to accommodate someone and would prefer to agree to any sort of invitation, no matter their intentions. But in many cases, it was very likely that the workers could not keep their appointments because they had no control over their departure from the factories; they never knew when they would be released from their machines. After hours of toil inside the factory, they needed to begin what might be a tiresome commute home. Their families expected them. They had little control over their own time.

More and more I began to avoid making appointments, and I spent my time roaming the factory districts in the early mornings, where I would always find unemployed workers seeking work. One morning I ran into a young girl standing outside of a factory in Sidi Brahim. Immediately we recognized each other—I had met Zahor in the factory in the Ville Nouvelle. She had been standing at the end of an ironing board, distracted, hanging skirts on hangers as they were handed to her, and we had spoken briefly that day. Now, with the instant intimacy so prevalent among some of the girls, she said: "Come with me, back to the Ville Nouvelle. I need to go back to my old factory to meet up with my friend. And then you can come with us. We are looking for work." So we left the crowd of workers standing in front of the factory in Sidi Brahim and started back toward the city center. When we arrived at her "old" factory, Zahor crouched behind a van parked nearby and called into the group of workers clustered at the door. "Khadija, Khadija," she shouted for her friend. Finally a girl turned her head and walked toward the van.

"Why are you hiding, Zahor?" I asked.

"I fought with the manager in charge of the ironing here," she said. "That is why I left this factory. I don't want her to hear that I am back here." And with this, we three headed back toward Sidi Brahim, to find a factory hiring workers.

"I am getting married next summer," said Zahor.

"Who will you marry?"

"A boy who lives near me. He has asked for me."

Khadija, then, launched into a series of stories about marriage—dramatic stories, in which no one was happy. She told of a girl in her neighborhood who was engaged. The groom did not appear at the wedding party. He simply did not show up. The girl's mother was devastated. She was close to death. Then she told several stories about Moroccan men she knew who had married Christian girls. And then she told of her father's sister's son, who recently married a girl of 14. This girl did not want to marry. She cried for a long time after the wedding. Khadija said that she herself had no plans to marry soon. Boys came to ask for her, but her father refused them because the family had to wait for her elder sister to marry first. She could not marry before her elder sister, but nobody had come to ask for this sister. Marriages, impending marriages, failed marriages, foiled attempts at marriage—these were the topics that occupied us as we found our way to Sidi Brahim. These subjects were, as I was coming to realize, a standard topic of conversation among the factory girls. The pursuit of marriage, as these girls portrayed it, was a serious business, fraught with formidable consequences.

We arrived at the gates of a factory in Sidi Brahim. There were ten girls standing there already. It was about 10:30 a.m., and the others at the door said they had been there since 8:00. We waited with the group, sitting on a cement wall. Every once in a while a man would stick his head out the factory door, and the girls would get up and gather around him. "Wait," he kept telling them. "Don't leave. Wait here. There is work here. We'll call you soon." And the girls would return to the wall and sit, waiting. At 11:30, Zahor and Khadija grew weary. They decided to leave. "There is nothing here," they said.

Zahor and Khadija gave up hope of finding work. As we wandered, fewer workers were gathered at factory doors, and we no longer bothered to stop and ask those we saw about prospects. But Zahor and Khadija were happy to remain in the streets, chatting with me and passers-by. We strolled on in the sun, which had become strong and hard on our faces. No longer job hunting, we walked back into the center of town, into the *medina*, having traveled miles since the early morning. The girls were telling me of the problems with marriage and the evils of Moroccan men. A young man passing us overheard the conversation. Impulsively, and unexpectedly, he joined us. "Look," he said, "do not tell this foreigner that Moroccan men are bad. That is not true. We are not all bad. Take a good look at me: I'm not bad." And then he pulled out his wallet and began to show us photographs of himself, identification cards. "Try me—look at who I am," he said. "I am a good person, a good man." The girls were cordial, apologizing for what they had been saying, discussing openly with him the trials of love and marriage in Morocco today. They were young, unattached girls, moving unrestricted in the streets, free from constraints, socializing with a foreign woman and an unknown Moroccan man. As job hunters in an unpredictable job market, these young women were free from their family's watchful eyes, enjoying an autonomy that would have been unimaginable had they not been forced to look for work.

•

Zahor and Khadija were both teenagers, about 15 years old. Neither had been sent to school for more than a year. Instead, as children, they had worked in carpet factories.[2] Many of the garment girls had worked in carpet factories, and employment in the garment industry was considered far superior. Zahor had spent the past five months as a garment worker in the Ville Nouvelle, but for Khadija this would be her first job in a garment factory, were she to find one.

Leaving the young man behind, the girls offered to show me the carpet factory where they had once been employed. We continued through the *medina*, into the popular quarters sprawling around Fes. As we walked further, the pavement disappeared and large mud puddles filled the center of the dirt roads. Garbage littered the sides of the streets. The girls led me toward a cement block building indistinguishable from the others surrounding it. They pushed open the big blue metal doors.

We walked down a steep stairwell into a warm dark room smelling of sweat. At first I saw only looms, large wooden frames of looms that stretched from floor to ceiling. And life was everywhere—small, squirming bodies seemed to be everywhere, crawling and moving in between the looms, through the threads that stretched to the ceiling from the floor. And when my eyes adjusted to the dark from the hard sunlight outside, I could see that the looms were lined up in rows, about five deep, and there were several rooms full of looms. In front of each loom were narrow wooden benches where the weavers sat. The weavers were girls, some of them tiny little girls. They sat on the benches. Some stood to weave. Some were so little that, even standing, they were shorter than others sitting to weave. And they moved so fast the movements of their hands seemed to make their small thin bodies shake, so that their whole bodies moved as they wove. It seemed as if the room was moving, as if the bodies were squirming between the threads. They were not. But the whole space vibrated.

When the weaving girls noticed me, they stopped. They left their looms and ran to me, surrounding me, some of them touching my hair. They were laughing and shouting, and when they heard me speak in Arabic, there were loud whispers. "She speaks Arabic, a little Arabic." They surrounded me and led me from room to room, through the looms, showing me the threads and the unfinished carpets. They called to me, "Come here, come here. See me weave. Look at my carpet!" There was an older woman who stayed at her loom, and when I approached she encouraged me. "Stay here. Stay near me. Learn how to weave. Learn." And one big girl, a fat girl with a round face made rounder by her frizzy, curly hair, followed me through the rooms, saying, "Bring me a Christian to marry!" which made everyone laugh.

But the tiniest girls did not join in the crowd around me. They stayed in their places; they did not move. One tiny one seemed entranced. Her head was bent, leaning on one shoulder, and her body seemed convulsed with movement. It seemed that she could not stop weaving. It was as if the weaving controlled her. She did not stop to look at the Christian or the commotion around her. And then another little one, with a dirty face and a runny nose, her hair hanging loose around her head, stopped weaving suddenly to look at me. She was so small that she actually climbed onto the metal bar that was the central part of the loom. Her weight was nothing. I smiled at her, but she looked as if the smile frightened her, as if she might cry. So I looked away.

It was at that time, when the French left the country, that the carpet factories began. There was little industry in the past—most of it was centered on the traditional crafts that were mostly the province of men. But with independence and the departure of the French, the carpet factories began. A huge carpet factory opened up in Fes El Djedid, "Bab Mekina," which was at one time an arms factory. They turned it into a carpet factory. . . .

Now the carpet factories are everywhere. Why? Because the carpet factories do not pay taxes. The carpet factories are in rooms that look, from the door, like houses. You cannot tell it is a carpet factory until you enter, and so the carpet factory owners do not have to pay their taxes. They just pay off the inspector who comes one or two times a year. They are able to just pay him off, and then when he is on the street, counting out the number of businesses on the street, he will count the small food shops and everything else, but he will ignore the existence of the carpet factories. Thus the carpet factories are everywhere, and they are a cheap way to make money.

There is a Moroccan proverb that says: "Girls of the carpets have neither a handicraft nor a childhood." The carpet factories are considered the worst business in Morocco. If a father puts his daughter into a carpet factory, it means this is a parent who has absolutely no choice at all. This is because everyone knows that when a girl first enters the carpet factory, she gets no pay at all. And children enter at young ages, as young as 4. Everyone knows that a girl who enters the factory gets hit a lot. A carpet factory girl gets beaten a lot, and she is not allowed to cry when she is beaten.

So everyone knows that a little girl in a carpet factory has no childhood at all. It is the last resort for a parent. A mother must hit the girl at first, to tell her to go to the factory. She must hit her at first, to get her out of the house to go to the factory, because at the beginning the girl cries and cries. But then when she grows up, the mother must hit her again, because she does not come home—she has become reckless, a girl of the streets, a girl who strolls the streets with men.

The little girls in the carpet factories learn bad things from the big girls. They learn filthy songs. And the older girls send the little girls to the local shops with messages for the shop owners, messages such as, "I will meet you at six o'clock when I leave." So the little girls learn these things, and in the end when they grow older their mother hits them for not coming home after work.

Now the other very, very bad type of work for girls is the work of mtaalma or an apprentice maid. A mtaalma is a young girl, a little girl, who is

*from the countryside and is brought to the city to work in someone's house.
. . . These girls are terribly mistreated.*

Khadija had worked in this factory for ten years. She told me she would be proud to show me another one, right there, in the same neighborhood, and so Zahor and I went with her. After the tour, Zahor courteously asked me if I wished to continue with her to her home, despite the fact that she feared trouble. Her mother, she said, would be angry that she had been gone all day, and yet she had not found work. For the girls' parents, the liberty that the girls have while looking for work is problematic. Garment work is unpredictable, so the parents have to be accommodating, but there is always the fear of undisciplined behavior. I declined the invitation, not wanting to aggravate the situation.

Khadija escorted me out of the neighborhood, back into the *medina*. "Zahor's family," she said, "is no good. It is good you did not go there, because they would not want to have you. Her family does not like Christians. But my family, we like Christians a lot. We are all very blonde, like me," and Khadija pointed to her hair, which, although dark brown, was lighter than most Moroccans' hair. "My mother likes tourists very much. When my parents first married, they lived in the Ville Nouvelle, near a tourist hotel. My mother stared at the tourists every day, throughout all her pregnancies. And so we all look like you Christians—we are all blonde, like you."

I nodded, as if I now understood the origins of Khadija's "blonde" hair. My own hair is dark brown, nowhere near blonde. But I was "blonde" in Morocco. I knew that Moroccans believed that women could control their children's features by staring at particular persons or objects while pregnant. For instance, a mother who looked long and hard at light-haired people during her pregnancy could bear a child with the much coveted blonde hair. And so Khadija had been blessed with a lighter shade of hair.[3]

With this, Khadija and I parted.

•

I spent long mornings and afternoons with workers. Some came to visit me in my home, and others took tea with me in fancy cafés. They shared their tales of intrigue and woe and offered immediate familiarity and friendship. They enthusiastically answered my interview questions. We always parted with plans to meet again, but most often they vanished into the city and the factory districts. I was wearied by the appearance and disappearance of their intimacy. And yet I continued to seek out workers on the streets and to call factory owners.

One factory visit led to another. Many owners agreed to speak with me, perhaps owing to the congeniality of Moroccans, but most attempted to make our meetings short, and not all actually allowed me to tour the factory floor. Moroccan labor laws assure workers of the best wages and work conditions, but very few of the Fes factories operated according to the law. Owners were well aware of their own noncompliance, which went unnoticed by government officials interested not in workers' rights but in promoting industry and the export trade. Despite their impulse to offer hospitality, these owners did not want a foreigner reporting on factory conditions or, even worse, speaking with the workers themselves. There were a few industrialists, though, who seemed unfazed by my research.

One owner who had studied in Florida and who fondly remembered his student days in America gave me the phone number of his cousin, who also owned a garment factory. The industry tended to run in families. "Call him, he is open-minded," he urged me. "Tell him I spoke with you. He will give you a tour of his factory, too." And so I called and was invited to visit Couture, a newly opened factory on the margins of Ben Souda.

Couture was a small factory employing, so far, only twenty workers. It was clean, and the cement face of the building looked fresh and new. Inside, the cement floors and walls were still almost white, not yet having taken on the battleship gray of the older factories. At the center of the workshop floor were two lines of sewing machines, ten in each line, at which sat twenty girls, heads bent forward, sewing clothing.

The owner of Couture was a tall, lean man with white skin and thick black hair. His skin was doughlike, and when he moved his mouth to speak, a large dimple formed in one of his cheeks. He assumed I was a friend of his cousin, so he spoke with me openly, without reserve. First, he told me that his factory was not intended to house so few workers. He had opened this factory only a year earlier, and he would increase the workforce as soon as he could gain more clients from Europe. "All of this stuff we are sewing now will be sent out to France and Belgium. As soon as we have worked out our problems and as soon as we find new clients from Europe to work with, we'll expand. We hope to have at least 100, maybe 200, girls working here in the near future."

As we finished our tour, we passed the factory restrooms. The owner pointed to the wall, lined with four separate doors, each of which opened to a small room, containing just one toilet. "The communal toilets are a big problem in factories, you know." I nodded, not really wanting to know what he would say next. "Girls go into the bathrooms and spend time in there. They talk. They spend ten minutes, a quarter of an hour, just standing in the bathrooms. They live in there. They live in the bathrooms. So we have created these individual toilets so the girls will not stay in there. Now there is no talking in the bathroom. They go in, they come out quickly."

I nodded. I said nothing.

Usually my factory visits and tours were rushed by owners fearful of my questions, unwilling to speak freely with me. But not now. I had time. This owner was willing to talk. I asked him, "What about men? Why don't men work here?"

"Let me say first. When men and women do the same thing, the same task, there is no question that the man's performance is better. This is a given. Men can do anything better than women. Men sew better than women. But men are not working in the factories anyway because I do not hire them."

"But why not?"

"It is not because the men choose not to work here. It is because I—we—all the owners do not hire men. At the beginning, I did hire men. I hired three or four men here, but then I fired them."

"Why?"

"Men cause severe problems when they work. They are constantly making demands. They refuse to work overtime. When they are told to work overtime, they say, 'No, I did my work today. Things are not finished because he—that is, the other guy—did not work hard enough.' So even though men here would be willing to work in this industry, they are no longer hired here. I myself prefer the lower productivity of women workers to the problems that men cause."

"The girls accept things as they are, I guess."

I thought I was agreeing with him, but he got angry. "There is nothing for them to accept. We pay them the minimum wage."

And so the conversation ended. I asked the owner if I might survey his workers. I showed him my survey form, which asked workers their names, their length of tenure at the factory, and questions about their families—how many children there were, and whether or not their parents were alive and working. The owner agreed. "Ten o'clock tomorrow morning," he said. "You can ask these girls these questions."

And so I returned the next morning and was led onto the shop floor. One by one the workers were escorted by the factory manager, from their machines, to stand next to me and, with the manager watching, answer my questions, which they did, politely. And then the owner offered me a ride home; he was eager to get me away from his factory. He had helped me, and he had cooperated with his cousin. He was done. This is what I sensed.

We drove through the November rain from the factory to my house. Cold and wet permeated the town. I listened to the windshield wipers on the tiny European car. I hadn't heard that sound in a while. "The rain is good," I said. Everyone had been saying this, everywhere, in every interaction I had had since the rain had started some days earlier, but the owner and I had not yet discussed the weather. And so, politely, we chatted about the prospects for a successful harvest next year, now that the drought had broken.

We got to my house, and I opened the car door. The owner turned to me, smiling oddly, and said, "You are with the CIA, aren't you?"

"No, I am not."

"Just tell me the truth. I know you are with the CIA."

Poor people never asked me this, as if the thought that any one would bother to spy on them just did not occur to them. Rich people generally assumed I was an American spy. I knew I would never convince him. But I tried.

"Don't you think the CIA would have at least given me a car?"

"Maybe not."

"Do you really think the CIA cares about the factory girls?" He didn't answer. I thanked him for letting me do my survey. And then I closed the car door.

•

The next morning, the sky was leaden and the ground was wet. It seemed like the rain would continue. There would not be many girls walking the factory districts. I called the owner of Couture to ask if, perhaps, I could return to his factory and interview the workers in greater depth. Now the owner was angry. I felt sorry for him—he could not get rid of me.

"These girls will not want to speak with you anymore," he said.

"But perhaps, if you let me come back for one day, I could speak with them at lunch."

"They need to eat their lunch; they'll have no time for you."

"Well, maybe I could invite them to my house, after work, on their day off."

"How would you meet them? You don't have a car."

"I'll meet them on the bus route somewhere, in town."

"These girls all live in Ben Souda. They don't ride the buses."

"I'll pay them."

"These girls work. They have no free time for you. They wouldn't want to come on their day off to talk with you."

But I wouldn't stop. The owner of Couture couldn't get me off the phone. And so finally he agreed. "Okay, I'll ask these girls. I'll ask if anyone wants to meet with you, to speak with you again. I'll call you back." And then he hung up.

A few minutes later, he called me back. "Tomorrow, on Sunday morning, at 10:30, two girls will meet you in front of the French Center, in the Ville Nouvelle," he said angrily. "But I want to know what you will be asking them. Send me a copy of your questionnaire."

"Of course." I thanked him profusely, and then we were rid of each other.

The next morning, I met the workers who were sent to speak with me. They were nervous. They had been unable to find a bus, so they had taken a taxi, which cost them a lot of money. They arrived at the French Center, uneasy, uncertain, dressed in western style clothes and uncomfortable-looking black plastic pumps, worn without socks. I immediately regretted that I had forced the Couture owner to help me. I felt sorry for these workers, who clearly had not chosen to speak with me.

After we exchanged greetings, I asked them if they knew why they were meeting with me. They did not. "Well, how is it that you came then? Didn't the owner explain? Didn't he ask for volunteers?"

"Well, no," said the one who had introduced herself as Nadia. "The manager just came up to our sewing line and said, 'Who goes to the Ville Nouvelle often?' And we thought he was just joking with us, because we never come here. So we said, 'We do.' And then he said, 'Who will do me a favor tomorrow? Who will do an errand for me in the *ville*?' And joking again, we said, 'No problem.' So he said, 'Okay, you'll go to the *ville* for me tomorrow.' We still thought this was a joke, but then he said, 'Seriously, you're going to the *ville* for me tomorrow.' We told him we couldn't go. We couldn't afford the taxi ride. We told him he'd have to pay for the taxi. But he said, 'No, you have to go, and I'm not paying for the taxi. You have to meet that American who is doing research.' That is all we were told."

Guilt washed over me. This was my fault. I told them I would pay them for the taxi ride, and I would pay them for their time today. I explained my research to them and assured them they did not have to speak to me—they could go home now. But they said they would stay and talk. And then, trying to make conversation as we walked, I asked them if they had worked all day yesterday.

"Oh, yes, we did. That son of Satan made us work all day." The anger seemed to come spitting out of Nadia. "That owner is bad, that manager is bad, evil. The manager forced us to continue working, despite our hunger. We worked until a quarter of three. He would not let us leave our seats. He knows we have no time to eat in the morning. We leave the house with nothing. We just drink a glass of tea. And he would not let us stop for lunch. Our heads were spinning with hunger."

And so we continued to talk and walk. I invited the girls to my home, where we ate and drank and they talked, or Nadia talked. About her work, about her family. When it was time for them to leave, Nadia invited me to her home. Her sister, she told me, had once worked for Germans as a maid. Her family loved Europeans; I would be welcome among them. And so we set a date for me to return, the following Sunday, for a visit which would turn into many visits and a friendship that would provide me with insight into the home life of a Moroccan factory worker.

PART II

Inside the Factory

CHAPTER 2

Gaining Entrée

The factory where I spent the next few months working and learning about the lives of the factory girls is a large gray cement building sitting on a paved road in one of Fes's industrial districts. It sits near a leather tanning plant and across the street from an olive packing factory. On some days the whole factory block reeks of tanning chemicals. My factory is large enough to house 1,000 workers (the owner once proudly told me this), but in fact, since it opened seven years ago, it has operated with fewer than 150 workers. Factory work is intermittent: whenever there are garments from European manufacturers that need to be sewn, the factory opens and the girls are hired to work. When I arrived there as a worker, it had only recently been reopened, after having been closed for about a year.

Like all garment factories in Fes, and most in Morocco, the factory produces clothing made to order on the specifications of its French and German clients. These clients send all the fabric and supplies needed to produce the clothing, and the Moroccan girls sew, tag, and load the order into trucks that will carry the clothing north to Tangiers and then out of the country to Europe. Transit through Tangiers was always said to be a problem, as customs regulations and paperwork slowed the movement of goods through this port city. When work slowed down or came to a halt, the owner, and the workers as well, usually said there were problems in Tangiers.

The number of girls working in the factory on any given day fluctuates, based on the size of the order and the immediacy of the order's due date. Although there is often a shortage of work for the workers, there is never a shortage of workers, a fact made obvious by the clutch of girls who stand at the factory door throughout the morning, hoping to be called inside to operate a sewing machine, clip threads from finished pieces, or pack boxes. Several weeks before I became involved at the factory, the owner had received a rush order from France. After he hired all the girls who happened to be standing at the factory door that morning, he got into the factory van and drove through the streets of Fes's other factory districts, offering work to the girls who stood at the doors of other factories and bringing them back to staff his factory, if only temporarily.

It was agreed that I could work in the factory as part of a deal with this owner. He would allow me to conduct my research inside his factory if I would help him improve his English: he felt he needed to expand his business vocabulary as he hoped that, one day, he might secure his orders from the United States. Actually, this young man, who I refer to as the owner, was not really the owner. He was the owner's son. He had left his university studies after the third year, never completing his degree, because he believed that a university degree would be useless to him. He was young and open-minded—to a degree. In the end, I could not help him with his English at all, as he never found time to study and seemed to have little interest in the language. Eventually, I think, he came to distrust me and my motives. Over time, he began to behave like other factory owners in Fes had behaved toward me: suspicious of my intentions, believing perhaps that I wished to undermine his business. But his hospitality never failed him, and he never directly told me to leave his factory, although he certainly could have.

The owner, as both the workers and I continued to refer to him, was rarely seen on the factory floor and had little to do with the everyday workings of the factory. A Frenchwoman named Sylvie was the general manager. On my first day of work in the factory, the owner introduced me to Sylvie, telling her she was to find me a suitable position on the work floor. Immediately I could tell that she was hostile to the idea of my being in the factory. Sylvie did not like me. When the owner introduced us and explained my research agenda, she looked at me very quickly and then turned around, so she could not see me. On my first day of work in the factory, she spoke to me only from this position— her back to me—tilting her head back slightly to be sure that I heard what she said, unwilling to say it to my face. Middle-aged and with years of experience as a garment factory floor manager in North Africa (she had previously worked in Tunisia), Sylvie saw no point in the owner allowing me into the factory. From the start, she was convinced that I was only there to spy. Sometimes she seemed to think I was spying on her specifically.

On my first day of work, I was escorted onto the factory floor by the younger sister of the owner, Amal. Like her brother, Amal was a university dropout.

She had left university only recently, having completed one year. In lieu of study, Amal was put to work in the factory office, where she sat out long days, preparing tea, waiting for the phone to ring. Like her brother, Amal had been eager to leave the university, thinking it was not worth the bother. But now she regretted her move. Work in the factory office was boring and uneventful. She was eager to greet the foreigner.

The main factory floor was a cavernous cement space in the middle of which were twelve rows of sewing machines with a worker seated at each machine. The rows were spaced such that every two rows were pushed close together to form six double rows. Each of these double rows of machines and workers were called a "sewing line." Standing at the sides of these lines were the youngest workers in the factory, usually about 13 years old, whose job it was to clip and pull out extra threads as the garments passed from worker to worker, down the line. These were the "finishing workers." Walking up and down the lines were the line managers. They would collect sorted bundles of fabric from Sylvie and then direct the process of sewing these pieces together. Bit by bit, the pieces were passed down the lines, and the line managers checked them along the way. They were also responsible for keeping records of how many bundles of fabric their lines had completed and exactly what their lines had produced. Line managers were responsible for ensuring that the garments were put together flawlessly.

Almost everyone here was female, except for several male line managers, and Si Wardi, the chief of all the line managers and in charge of the entire factory floor. Si Wardi looked to be at least 50 years old, with a deeply lined face. He wore a small wool cap and had a cigarette hanging from his mouth at all times. He walked slowly with a slightly stooped back and seemed to do and say nothing all day long. He kept himself to the edge of the workshop floor, always adjusting the electric lights overhead, and he spent a lot of his time sitting in the lunchroom. Si Wardi, it seemed to me, had no real role in the factory. I had the sense that he did not wish to be on the factory floor among all those females.

I asked about the importance of his position. Amal told me the chief on the factory floor was always a man. "A man is needed," she assured me. "A man can make the girls afraid. A woman is far too soft. She cannot make them fear." That was what Si Wardi was for.[1]

On this day, my first day, Sylvie was preparing to set in motion the sewing of a new order for 22,000 nylon jackets. Having given me the opening tour, Amal took me to Sylvie, who told me to follow her. Sylvie was a small woman, short, with fair skin and light blue eyes. She did not smile, and she always moved brusquely as if she had no time. Today, she said, was a particularly serious day because no mistakes can be made in the setup of a new order. Mistakes could result in the loss of time and materials. Fabric, for example, would be destroyed if it were cut incorrectly.

Sylvie walked back and forth through the main factory floor. Contrary to what Amal had said about a man being needed, Sylvie was clearly frightening the workers. She walked around the workshop, stopping at each line, leaning over workers and yelling in Arabic *"shwiya"* (a little) or *"bezzaf"* (a lot). I followed her as she approached machine operators. She would approach a worker, lean over to check the girl's work and then scream, using one Arabic word or the other. The girl would look at her silently, poker-faced, and continue to work. As I followed Sylvie around, waiting to be assigned a position, she explained that she needed to yell in this way. "The workers talk too much, and their chatter slows down the work." As far as I could see, no one on the work floor was talking. In Morocco, though, everyone says women talk too much. Females, people always say, are full of empty chatter.

Sylvie eventually returned to her office, satisfied that the work process had begun. I was still following, and so I settled myself in a corner of her office, which was strewn with fabric swatches and supplies. Within minutes a worker came in, holding up a finger she had cut on a machine needle. Sylvie screamed at her, again using her favorite words, this time with a questioning tone: *"Shwiya? Bezzaf?"* She kept repeating these words, louder and louder, as she applied an antibiotic and a Band-aid to the wound. "It is the antibiotic that is making your finger sting, you know. It's not the wound that hurts that much," she said to the girl in French. The girl just sat still, her head down, holding her bleeding finger, not responding. As soon as she left, another girl came in, and Sylvie went through the same procedure, this time explaining to me, "These girls do not work. They just talk and pay no attention to what they are doing, and that is why they hurt their fingers." This girl did not look up either.

I strongly suspected that the workers did not understand Sylvie, because it was likely that they did not speak French. Sylvie, I could see, did not speak Arabic, except for the two words she continually repeated, very loudly. It appeared to me that the workers were frightened, or perhaps they were just bewildered, because they had no idea of what exactly Sylvie was saying. Sylvie herself did not seem aware of this communication glitch.

As I was puzzling this out, the manager of the packing department entered Sylvie's office. Her name was Hannen, and she looked different from the other workers. She wore a stylish skirt and sweater under her work smock. Her thick, hennaed hair was twisted into a glamorous French knot on the back of her head. Hannen was responsible for ensuring that all finished items were properly folded, tagged, and packed into cartons to be loaded into trucks. She had come to collect the tags that would be attached to the completed garments. She asked Sylvie for the instructions she needed for tagging and packaging this run of jackets. Sylvie pulled from her desk a large piece of paper covered with words and illustrations and directed Hannen to read the instructions. The girl's hands were shaking as she took the paper from Sylvie. She began to read silently, her lips moving, her index finger following the printed words on the page. She then handed the paper back to Sylvie and left the office, heading downstairs, to instruct the other packaging girls on the procedure. She soon returned to the office to show Sylvie how she had applied a tag to a jacket. The tag was in the wrong place. Hannen had tagged the side of the jacket, as the illustration seemed to indicate, but she had not followed the print instructions. She had not read the printed text, which was in French. Sylvie berated her loudly for her mistake. Hannen just stood still, looking fearful. It seemed to me that, despite her fashionable hairdo, Hannen could not follow Sylvie's loud French rantings, and based on her tagging method, she could not read French print. Sylvie seemed unaware of this fact.

Sylvie's patience, or what there was of it, was clearly running thin. "These people," she said to me, "do not do what they are told." And mistaking my look for sympathy, Sylvie went on to tell me of her problems. "Let me tell you," she said, "for example, that Abderrahim, whatever I say to him, he answers, '*D'accord, d'accord*' (Okay, okay) and then he goes and does the opposite of what I have told him." Abderrahim, I knew, was one of very few men on the workshop floor. He was one of the two male line directors, a skinny young man, always wearing a woolen cap and a pair of slacks that looked like they had been purchased in the secondhand clothing market. Sylvie continued, "Yesterday, I told him exactly how to sew a jacket, and of course he answered, '*D'accord*,' and he did it all wrong, nonetheless. These people are like children. These people, you know, have small heads. But they are even worse in Tunisia."[2]

I was certain that Abderrahim, in his wool cap and secondhand suit trousers, had not remained in school long enough to learn French. I did not dare to speak. It seemed glaringly apparent to me that no one in this factory except Sylvie spoke French. I could have argued with her, but I knew I needed her on my side. Eventually Sylvie told me it was time to go. I had done nothing but follow her around the factory floor, watching her every interaction with the factory staff. It had been a long day.

"Tomorrow," she assured me, "I will give you a job to do."

"Thank you. Good-bye, Madame," I said, calling her Madame only because I was not quite sure how I should address her.

"Oh, no, you cannot call me that," she said. "Everyone calls me Sylvie. You must call me Sylvie. We are all a family here in this factory." She said this harshly, without a smile.[3]

As I walked from Sylvie's office, the workers were leaving their seats, heading to the locker area where they stored their personal items. It was after 6:30. I could see from the wide rectangular windows high on the factory walls that it was dark outside. I walked to the lockers and watched the workers transform themselves for the trip outside the factory. Inside the factory, the girls dressed in the same kinds of clothing they wear inside their homes: polyester house dresses and worn nightgowns covered with heavy acrylic sweaters, and slippers or plastic sandals. A minority wore scarves on their heads, but those whose heads were bare wore their hair tied back. Workers make little effort to appear attractive inside the factory: they feel, within the factory walls, as if they are among sisters and family and have little need while working to style themselves. Standing at their lockers, they put on brightly colored *djellaba*. The *djellaba* covers the form of the body and expresses modesty in the streets, and most workers use it to move to and from the factory. But as they prepared to leave the factory, many stood applying makeup and lipstick, brushing and restyling their hair using big plastic barrettes and decorated elastics. Some put on plastic pumps. Eventually they moved downstairs, to the factory door, where they formed a long line in front of the exit.

Before leaving the factory, each worker must pass through the "search," a curtained room where they are frisked and their hand bags are searched by the factory secretaries. As Sylvie had explained to me earlier, "They will steal anything. They might steal the sleeve of a jacket today, another sleeve tomorrow, until they have the entire jacket to sew together at home and then sell in the *medina*. This is a war." I put myself through the search room, curious to see what was happening there. The workers snickered and giggled in line. "The Christian," they laughed, "is being searched."

Walking home through the darkness of the factory district, scattered with figures moving out of the factories, a worker hurried to walk along with me. She was a young girl with a long braid down her back, tied at the end with a giant bow. She was eager to meet the foreigner she had seen today on the factory floor. "Do you like this work?" I asked immediately, eager to start my questioning.

"Only because of the girls. I like it for the company of the girls. When you stay home, you get very bored." She told me that she had stayed at home over the past year, while the factory was shut, following three years of steady work. "During that time my mother allowed me to leave the house only once a week. This is because, in Morocco, girls are not in charge of themselves. When you are working, you can come home late and they cannot say anything at all because you will say that you were working. How can they know?"

She was engaged and planning to marry soon. "I need to marry now. It is best. If a girl is still unmarried at the age of 30, no one will take her. No man will like her. Maybe only a very old, old man." She said that when she married, she would stay at home. She would not return to the factory.

"But won't you find that boring, if you find it boring to stay home now?" I asked.

"Oh, no, when I am married, the situation will change completely. Especially when I have children. Every Moroccan man wants children. With children, it will be possible for me to stay at home."

With this, we parted ways. These were some of the same thoughts and opinions I had heard from workers standing at factory gates and strolling the streets. And I would have this conversation, or variations of it, over and over again in the days ahead.

•

The next morning I was given a position on line number six. I would be responsible for checking the seams of jackets as they moved down the sewing line. The day begins at 7:30, although many machine operators were already seated and sewing before the 7:20 warning whistle sounded. I took my place at a table placed to the side of the double lines of machine operators where I worked with Fatima, the line manager. We bent over garments for hours, inspecting them and folding them into piles according to size and color. We pulled at threads to make sure they were tight, and checked linings to be certain they were sewn perfectly into the nylon jackets. The skill here lies in concentration: being able to repeat a task incessantly for ten or more hours without losing focus. It is cold and damp in the factory and my legs ached from standing on the cold concrete floor. The workers lightened the tedium with occasional fits of giggling. They passed little scraps of gum or pieces of sweets down the line to their friends as schoolgirls might pass notes around the classroom.

At 10 a.m., a whistle blows, signaling a ten-minute break. Workers drop what they are doing, race to their lockers to collect the breakfast they brought with them, and then dash into the lunchroom to eat it.

The whistle blows again at 12:30 for the half-hour lunch break, and this scene repeats itself. The lunchtime race across the factory floor, to the lockers and up the steps to the lunchroom is more urgent than the breakfast race. Each worker needs to be certain she can get to one of only two propane gas heaters, where she can heat up the leftovers she has brought for lunch.

The girls from line six work the lunchroom routine together, a routine they repeat every day. A few girls seem to designate themselves as food warmers. They collect lunches from the others and race to get in line in front of the propane burners, where workers wait to heat their dishes over the open flame. Everyone has brought with them portions of the *tagene* (stew) that they have saved from the family's lunch the day before, carried to the factory in small glass jars. The girls warm the stew just enough to melt the fats, in flat metal dishes brought from home. And then they hurry back to our spot at the long lunch tables and place the flat metal dishes in the center. Everyone samples each other's meal. As some workers warm meals, others rush to fill jugs with water and place them on the tables, while others clear the tables, which are still strewn with refuse from the breakfast break. Workers huddle with friends, squeezed closely together on the narrow lunch benches over shared dishes. They pull out large pieces of bread, which they break up and dip into the stews. They pass large clay cups of water hand to hand and bits of hot pepper from table to table. There is little time to eat once the food is heated, so they finish quickly and wash the plates in a large long sink that lines one wall of the lunch room. When lunch is over, the tables are left strewn with chunks of dry brown bread, plastic jugs of water, clay drinking cups, and orange peels.

Today, when the lunch whistle sounded, Fatima had grabbed my arm and told me to stay with her: "I'll take care of you," she had said, and led me to a lunch table. While we had been working, I had explained to Fatima that I was doing research on the garment factory. She had asked me no questions, just looked at me seriously, lifting her eyes for a moment up from a jacket seam and nodding knowingly, as if this was of no surprise to her. And now, introducing me to the others who regularly sat together, she explained my presence: "She is doing research."

Immediately a tall brown girl came over to us. In her hands was a necklace of small plastic bead pearls. "Do you like this?" she asked, thrusting the necklace before me. "It is from Nador. I am selling it. I have more things like this."

"It's beautiful. Maybe I'll buy one another day."[4]

"Well, what kind of research are you doing?" She changed the subject immediately, not pushing for a sale.

"Workers' lives," Fatima answered for me. "She is studying the life of factory workers."

I had not phrased things in exactly this way when I had told Fatima what I was doing in this factory, but she seemed to understand intuitively. "Fatima," I asked, "how do you know about such research?" Together, Fatima and the girl selling bead pearls launched into a description of a television show they had once seen, about a Christian who went to Egypt and took an apartment in a popular quarter. This Christian, they said, wrote down the exact words of what people said. This, they presumed, was what I would be doing. They knew about people doing research, they assured me.

At this table sat Fatima and many of the workers on her line, some of her friends from the factory, and some workers who had just joined the table, eager to hear the foreigner speak. "*Mrehba bik aandna*" (Welcome to our place). Again and again they said it, as if to be certain that I understood. "Are you Sylvie's daughter?" they asked. "You look just like her. You must be her daughter."

Like Sylvie, I was pale and small with light eyes. "No, I am not." I wanted to be clear on this point, but the workers, I sensed, were not convinced. The resemblance for them was too strong: two small, pale female foreigners in the same factory. For lunch I had wrapped a long loaf of white French bread spread with processed cheese in a napkin, and when they saw this, they laughed and insisted that I eat from their plates. They pulled choice pieces of meat from the stews with their fingers and handed them to me. "What you have is not enough. The food you have brought is what we feed little babies. Babies love that kind of cheese, because it is soft, you know. Only children eat that kind of bread and cheese."

Throughout the half-hour lunch period, a girl named Arbea, whom I had met some months earlier through another factory worker acquaintance of mine, remained at my side. She had recognized me immediately and was eager to help me adjust to this new environment. She appointed herself as my manager, telling me whose stew to eat from and holding onto a small bag of crackers I had brought with me. When I went to eat one, she pulled the bag away. "No, not yet. Don't eat these now. Save them for later." She warned, "You will be hungry again in the afternoon."

And so, with me at the lunch table, the girls began to discuss the differences

between themselves and "the Christians." This difference was largely about sexual morality. I was weary of this conversation, having heard Moroccan females
contrast themselves with the entire western world on this point many times
before. The tall brown girl named Salima Bendoun asserted, "The problem
in Morocco is that if there is no blood on the sheet your father will slice your
throat. And if the man finds out before the wedding that you are not a virgin,
he will not take you." After she made her claim, Salima said in a tone that was
loud, flat, and matter of fact: "I would like to go to America, where these things
don't even exist. I'm lost. I'm broken. I'm not a virgin." Although I was tired of
this conversation, I had never heard a girl assert so publicly a fact so shameful
in Morocco.

"Be quiet. Speak softly," said a young woman in a white scarf sitting next to
Salima. She pushed her on the arm as if to remind her of where she was.

But Salima refused to withdraw her claims. "My condition is a fact," she
insisted. "I would be better off in America."

"These are our traditions," Fatima said defensively, as if she did not want to
hear such an overt social critique aired in front of the foreigner. And for a few
moments there was silence at the table.

Then, as if to lighten the air, someone else announced that there existed
another serious problem for Moroccan girls, which also made them unlike the
Christians. "When you are 30," the girl stated, "it is over. People will say, 'She
is a *sherfa*' (an old woman). It is impossible to get married after 30, unless of
course you marry a very old man." This, they could all agree, was a fact.

Moroccans, to be sure, are concerned with issues of virginity, marriage, and
sexual morality. But typically, among women in Moroccan homes, I did not find
these topics to be a matter of inordinate interest. Daughters would be reluctant
to discuss such topics at home, for it would be disrespectful to their parents.
In the factory, however, I would be witness to the girls' incessant conversation
about these issues. I sensed that workers were drawn to discussing these issues
with me. As an American, I was automatically identified as a Christian, and
it was assumed that my attitudes would be in sharp contrast to their own. My
presence may have given them the opportunity to confirm their own identity—
as Moroccan and as Muslim—with me as a foil. Sexual morality has long been
considered an issue that distinguishes Muslim from Christian and East from
West in some Muslim discourses. But many, if not most, of these conversations,
I believe, would have gone on without me. This kind of talk reiterates for the
workers the idea that, although they work in a factory, they are not factory
workers. The talk helps them to remind themselves of who they wish to be:

respectable Muslim girls, well behaved daughters, expecting and awaiting marriage. The Moroccan factory girls sought no identity as "workers"—such an identity was worthless to them. Given the low wages, indignity, and insecurity of factory work, their unwillingness to define themselves as workers is logical. Instead they strove to frame themselves as the dignified people they wanted to be: Moroccan girls, daughters, potential wives.[5]

Lunch ended, and we returned to our places and worked until 6:30. "An afternoon break," Amal explained when I asked her, "would ruin productivity." At 6:30 we were permitted to leave our posts. Workers surrounded me, asking, "Are you tired, are you tired?" The factory is cold, and my legs and back ached from standing on the damp concrete. When I answered yes, they worked to assure me. "You will get used to it. We were tired at first, but we got used to it. Be patient. Be patient and endure. You will get accustomed to this kind of work." These words, too, I would hear repeated over the coming weeks.[6]

•

The next morning it seemed to have grown even colder. The concrete walls and narrow windows of the factory seemed to concentrate the dampness, making it penetrate the bones. The workers said that the morning cold made their hands less nimble, and on frigid mornings like this, they said they found it harder to work the machines. By the end of the day, Fatima was complaining of the pain in her legs. She had spent much of the day moving back and forth across the workshop floor, managing production problems. She had given her workers the fabric to produce size 6 linings when they should have been producing size 5 linings. Her mistake generated a general work slowdown as the other lines—unable to work without the correct size linings—came to a halt. Fatima became involved in a series of heated disputes with Absellem, the manager of another line whose production had been interrupted by her mistake. Absellem kept walking over to Fatima's line, deriding her and shouting in his frustration. She responded, "Don't yell at me." She never deferred to him, always defending her actions. When Absellem threatened to report the problems to Sylvie, Fatima told him to go ahead. "I am not afraid of Sylvie or of anyone," she retorted. "I am afraid only of God."

At the end of the day, our line had to remain in place while the other workers left the factory. We had produced only 1,000 linings, while the other lines had produced 1,300 pieces each. And so we worked several hours into the night.

As a line manager, Fatima holds one of the most skilled positions in the factory. She knows the production process, coordinates production with the other line managers, and manages the twenty-five sewing operators in her own line. The position requires a strong and assertive personality. Fatima is skilled not only in the production processes but also in handling individual operators and other line chiefs. At the age of 24, Fatima has worked in sewing factories for seven years. She is articulate and powerful. She understands her job. And as she says, Fatima fears only God.

I had watched Fatima fight with Absellem freely throughout the day. But at the lunch table earlier, Fatima had fiercely defended the rights of husbands. The workers had asked me if I would go to a spa with them—a special hot spring, on the outskirts of Fes, that was considered a wonderful picnic area. "Will your husband allow you to come?" they had asked, maybe just testing me. And quickly I answered, "Yes, I have my freedom," using a phrase that they use all the time, meaning that I could make my own decisions about my movements here and there. Quickly, Salima Bendoun exclaimed, "Oh, it is that freedom that I want!" And Saudi, as a way of instructing me on Moroccan habits, said that she could not go anywhere unless her husband allowed her to go. If he said no, then she could not leave the house. And Fatima, just like the day before, said, "This is our tradition," as if to defend herself against me and Salima Bendoun. And I wondered, when Fatima did marry, if she would fight with her husband like she fought with Absellem.

Finally we met our quota, and the line six workers walked wearily out into the dark. The factory bus had left some time ago, so the workers headed for the public bus station in the town center, about a mile and a half from the factory. There, they would catch a public bus to take them home.

I walked with a worker from line six, Zaynab, and her younger sister, Fadela, who was a factory maid. As we moved slowly through the industrial district, a young girl caught up to us, looking for company on her walk home. I recognized her immediately. I had met her and interviewed her some time ago, in a different factory, in a different factory district. I had marked her in my notes as the "orphan" because at the time, she told me that she was living with her maternal uncle and his three children and that she had no parents. Her aunt, her uncle's wife, she had told me, did not like her and did not want her to live with them.

"How are you? How are you doing with your uncle?" I asked her immediately.

"I'm not with them anymore. I'm living alone."

"Why are you alone? Where is your mother?" Zaynab cut in, surprised to hear this girl was on her own.

"Oh, sister," she said, "my life story is long. You don't want me to tell it to you."

"Yes, tell me, where is your mother?"

"My mother was a maid, living with the people she worked for. My father died just before I was born, and so I was fostered out as an infant. I grew up in another family's house, as a *mtaalma*" (a word that means apprentice literally, but that is also used to refer to a girl who lives with a family and serves as their maid). "As I got older, they began to beat me more and more. I grew tired of them, and so I went to live with my mother's brother. He is my only relative. His wife, however, soon grew tired of me. So now I am living alone."

I had heard most of this story before. Zaynab and Fadela said nothing. Then the girl said good-bye, turning onto a side street toward her rented room. When she left, I told Zaynab that I had never heard of a girl living alone in Morocco. "Yes, it happens," said Zaynab, "but never when they are so young. She is too young. She has to watch out for herself." None of us commented any more on this story. Neither Zaynab nor Fadela spoke for a while.

.

The next morning, Sylvie and her husband, whom I had met briefly the day before and who also seemed to be part of the managerial staff—although he rarely spoke—passed me in their car driving to the factory. They stopped to pick me up as I was walking along the road. Amal was in the back seat. I got in the car, unable to refuse the ride but fearing the workers would now be unwilling to speak with me: perhaps they would associate me with the factory administration. But at lunch, my fears were not realized. Again today, the workers of line six had saved me a seat and were waiting for me to join them for the lunch break.

On the way to work, Sylvie told me about the factory's terrible productivity level. The conversation started when I asked Sylvie about the requirements for this shipment. "Twenty thousand jackets have been ordered," she told me, "but the shipment date is uncertain. Yesterday, one shipment was completed, and we managed to get about 3,000 pieces into the truck by four in the afternoon. But these shipment dates are critical—the buyer has the right to refuse a shipment that is more than twenty-four hours late. We are talking about a lot of money."

"The shipments are death," said Sylvie's husband.

"Oh," I said, wanting to express interest but not knowing what to say here. I felt that, perhaps, Sylvie's husband was attempting to excuse his wife's behavior.

I had come to the conclusion that she was explosive in nature, mean, and perhaps racist as well. He, I sensed, was aware of how his wife might appear. Sylvie continued to illustrate her difficulties to me. She repeated one of her favorite phrases, "These people are children," and then she explained:

"Factories in France, you know, produce the same amount of materials in a single day with one half of the staff. These people just do not know how to work."

"But how could this be so? We don't take any afternoon break here." This was, in fact, the first time I had witnessed factory work, but it seemed to me that humans could not work any faster.

Sylvie could not really explain. But then she and her husband began to calculate the costs of labor and the costs of living in France versus Morocco. "Everything here is just so much cheaper that it makes it all worthwhile," she concluded. The claim that French factory workers could sew twice as fast as Moroccans seemed, to me, extravagant. But I didn't argue.

•

The next day, many of the workers walked slowly into the lunchroom, letting the others rush in ahead of them, and seated themselves in the back of the room, removed from the crowd. Ramadan, the month of fasting, was to begin in less than a week. Females must not fast while they are menstruating, so these girls were fasting in a last-minute effort to make up days still owed from last year's Ramadan.

"There is no grace in fasting during the second half of the month before Ramadan, you know," Saudi admonished the workers. Even though she reminded these girls that their fast was less worthy because it was being committed so soon before Ramadan, she also congratulated the fasting girls. "It is good, though, to fast," she kept telling them.

Saudi was the most openly pious of the girls at the table. She said that her name signified that her people came from Saudi Arabia a long time ago. Thus, she claimed, they were direct descendants of the Prophet, particularly holy. She was proud of this fact.

Saudi wore a white scarf that covered her head completely, although she said that she was not wearing the Islamic veil, but was simply preparing herself for Ramadan. "Before I was married," she told me, "I never covered my head." And as proof of this fact, she pulled from her purse a picture of herself and her husband before their marriage. "I was fat then, and now I am too thin." She had grown thin, she told me, from being ill after a recent miscarriage. Saudi had a baby daughter who was very smart, and she wanted another baby as soon as possible.

Saudi's taking the picture from her purse set off a chain reaction. Suddenly it seemed that everyone needed to show pictures of themselves. Young Moroccan women like to visit professional studios to have their pictures taken. Many pose alone, in their best clothing, traditional or modern; they take glamorous pictures of their heavily made-up faces. If they cannot afford the professional photographer, they hold on to photographs of themselves taken at parties or on other occasions. I saw a picture of one girl milking cows in the countryside at a relative's farm. Zaynab pulled out a folded photograph of herself with a French child she used to care for. Fatima showed me a close-up professional picture of her face, asking, "I am ugly, right?" to which I responded, "No, you are beautiful." The photographs seem to validate the girl's sense of self-worth. They prove that she is, in fact, beautiful. And this matters.

·

At lunch, some days later, Kenza showed me her address book. She considered herself married and wore a faux diamond ring on her left ring finger, although when I questioned her on her wedding, it turned out that she was actually only engaged.[7] They would sign the marriage contract in the summer, when the family held the wedding. "Our family," she told me, "signs the contract at the ceremony and never before—to avoid problems." Today she pulled out a small black book filled with addresses written in both French and Arabic, to show me the address of her mother's sister's daughter who lives in Florida, a place which was in the same country I had come from. And she then had me read aloud all the addresses of people she knew who live abroad. Although she carried her address book with her, Kenza, it turned out, could not read. As I read the entries aloud to her, she explained how she was related to the people recorded in her address book. Included in the book were two addresses, one in Switzerland and the other in Sweden, the addresses not of relatives but of places she has sent letters to work overseas. "I am crazy," she told me, "about the idea of working overseas. I would go anywhere. I don't even care where. I am not afraid." But, alas, the letters, written for her by friends and relatives, went unanswered. "I have no luck," she said.

She had also once tried to get to France to stay with her sister's daughter who lived there with her husband. Her family believed that in France she could get a needed operation on her foot, an operation the family could not afford in Morocco. She completed the paperwork for her passport and visa and had all her papers in order when she found she needed one final piece of documentation, which, for reasons unknown, she could not obtain. And therefore, her quest for a visa had been unsuccessful. Her foot would simply stay as it was, without the operation. But the point of her story was not, it seemed, about her medical condition. In fact, her foot condition did not cause her problems with walking or working. The point of the story was that her efforts to go abroad had been foiled. "You see," she repeated, "I have no luck."

Soon other workers began to talk about their plans to find work outside of Morocco. One girl pulled out a worn, crumpled advertisement for employment on a ship in Panama. She asked me for my opinion on this sort of work, but since the ad was written in Arabic, and I could read only the word *Panama*, I could not advise her. Another girl said that she had heard there were many factories in Spain that were hiring women. She planned, one day soon, to go there.[8]

·

The next day when we finished eating, the lunch group began to put on makeup. Someone placed a small case containing a lipstick, an eye liner, mascara, and hand cream on the table. The workers shared the cosmetics like they had shared their stews and bread at lunch, each girl using the lipstick and passing it on to the next. They encouraged me to put on the makeup, too. "Girls in America wear lots of makeup," someone said. "We see it all the time in films."

"In Morocco, you know," someone else said, "girls should not wear makeup at all. It is actually shameful for a girl to wear makeup. But a married woman should—to please her husband." I knew that unmarried girls were disdained for wearing makeup. Girls, it was said in Morocco, should not know too much, and a girl with her face adorned would be displaying a lack of appropriate modesty. But I was married, they knew. There should be no reason that I would hesitate to wear makeup. And so they continued to urge me to participate.

"My husband doesn't like me to wear makeup. That is why I don't," I said.

"This is good," said Kenza, her shiny black eyes newly outlined in liner. "That is smart. It is good to do what your husband wants."

As soon as I said this, and as soon as I had heard Kenza's response, I regretted my words. What I said was not true: I do wear makeup, whether or not my husband cares for it. But, at this moment, I did not want to share everyone else's lipstick. I understood that their invitation was a way of welcoming me into the group; it was an expression of their endless hospitality. And from experience, I knew that they would not easily give up: it was their duty to welcome me in this way. How could I refuse? In the moment, though, I knew that this lie, invoking my husband, would be the most efficient—and least offensive—way of refusing their kindness. And it had worked. But I had betrayed myself.

Upon hearing this, a tall and commanding looking girl who sat alone every day at the end of our lunch table, eating silently from her own plate placed carefully on a cloth napkin, stood up in the middle of her own solitary makeup session. She had outlined her lips with a dark red pencil, and she had not filled in the outline with lipstick, so she looked like a clown. Her height and bearing intimidated my group as they huddled over the shared mirror. She announced in a deep voice, "I wear makeup for neither a man nor a girl. I wear it for myself." We stopped. Her statement silenced us all for a moment. And then Kenza began to giggle and told her to finish painting her lips.

This girl's bold proclamation made me recognize, rather suddenly, exactly what was happening here. This makeup session, I thought, is a subversive act. As young, unmarried Moroccan females, these girls should hide their eyes and their charms. Makeup, as they themselves report, is to be used by married women to attract their husbands. "Moroccan men" the owner had once mentioned to me, "do not like a girl who knows too much." Makeup might suggest too much knowledge. And yet here they sit, putting on lots of makeup, putting on too much makeup, so that when they are finished, they look cheap and silly, with red lips and pink cheeks.

But it is not for men that they are applying this makeup at the lunch table. There are not enough men in the factory for so many girls to make up for. Indeed, there are only four men who work on the factory floor, not including a 12-year-old boy who is the mechanic's apprentice. This makeup session could not be for the benefit of those four men. Instead, in putting on this makeup, these girls are expressing a newfound sense of self. They are taking advantage of a new kind of freedom, an independence that might be denied them if they stayed at home under the watchful eyes of parents and brothers. These girls are on their own here, in the factory lunchroom; indeed, in the lunchroom, they are free, if only temporarily, from Sylvie.

This latitude that they were experiencing came also from their ability to purchase this makeup for themselves. People in Fes always derided factory girls, claiming that they did not give their money to their families. They worked only to purchase face cream and lipstick for themselves. As I would soon see, most of these girls worked, indeed, to support their impoverished families, in an economic context where their fathers and brothers could find little work. But most could keep some money, amounts so small that they could be used only to purchase the occasional lipstick or maybe a pair of stylish shoes. And so these girls did use their money to make their own choices about what to buy and what to wear, and they could display these choices inside the protected walls of the factory. Perhaps they were subverting the authority of their fathers and brothers, who would not allow them to wear makeup. Perhaps this was a new kind of power. Or maybe it was simply the novelty of spending money on silly things that nobody really needs, like lipstick.[9]

The factory lunchroom provided a free and safe space where the girls could experiment with their identity or their sense of self. Among their peers, workers could speak freely of things it would be unseemly to discuss in the presence of kin and elders: their interest in marriage and their future husbands; their discomfort with the constraints of Moroccan social mores; their personal transgressions; their desire to leave Morocco. Such topics were not likely to be discussed at home. Moroccans do not traditionally recognize the teenage years as a distinct phase of life. Yet there was something in these lunchroom discussions that was very reminiscent of adolescence as I knew it.

As we cleared the lunch dishes, Salima Bendoun began to joke loudly and lewdly about men and sex, looking for my reaction. I smiled weakly, embarrassed, not knowing how to respond to her, and Saudi cut in and told me to pay her no attention.

"Those things are all she speaks about," Saudi said. Salima Bendoun, everyone seemed to know, was shameless in her talk.

•

The next day was a Saturday. Saturday was usually a half-day, but today no one knew what time work would finish, as we had just begun production of the new shipment. By lunch the rumor had spread that we would finish by 3:00. The workers were excited by the prospect of leaving the factory while there was still daylight, after a week of tense eleven-hour days.

Zaynab dashed past me after lunch and whispered, "Don't leave without me. I will walk home with you."

We met at the front gate as she and Fadela were coming through the search. I blinked as my eyes adjusted to the Moroccan afternoon sun, glaring even in February. "It's beautiful out," I said. "It's not dark yet."

"Yes, it's beautiful. It's beautiful to be outside in the afternoon."

Zaynab and her sister liked me. Mostly, Zaynab liked me. I noticed her the first day of work, when every time I looked up she seemed to be looking at me, smiling. On the second day she slipped past my post and placed a piece of gum on my table, whispering, "Shewing gum." We had already walked to the bus stop together, and today as we were walking down the stairs out of the factory, Zaynab said, "I like people like you. I like foreigners." And Fadela started to explain.

Zaynab had worked for a year for a French family in Rabat as a maid. They owned a factory, and she could have worked in the factory, but she preferred to work in their house. They did not speak Arabic, and she did not speak French, so they never really communicated much. Her job in the house was mostly to care for their child, a blond-haired baby boy. She loved him and she loved them. They planned to take her with them when they returned to France and helped her get her visa. But in the end, they told her they could not afford to pay her a salary in France, so they would not take her. She said she would go anyway, without pay. She only wanted to stay with them. But they refused the idea. When she first left them, she cried a lot.

Now, whenever she sees a foreigner, she remembers them and wants to cry. As proof of this fact, she said that she likes Sylvie, even though she is difficult, because Sylvie is French, and this reminds her of them.[10]

She does not like living with her own family. Her father and brothers are very difficult; they are "hard, very strict." Life with the foreigners was better, and although she was only with them for one year, she knows she loves the life of foreigners. Now she cannot bear the thought of marrying a Moroccan. She wants to marry a foreigner.

Zaynab is delicate, petite, with fine facial features and an almost waiflike appearance. Her sister Fadela is powerful with a thick body seemingly made for heavy work and a forceful round face. They do not look related. Zaynab is the elder sister, at age 21, and Fadela is 20.

Both girls had begun working only two months earlier, and Zaynab got her position on the line because she already knew how to work the machine. The French people she lived with taught her to sew at their factory. Fadela had no skills and was given the position of factory maid. When I asked them why they were working, Fadela looked at me quizzically, her eyes suggesting the answer was obvious and the question unnecessary. (Everyone works for money.) But this was a question I always asked workers, wishing to know exactly what the conditions were that spurred them into the factory. "Why have you—just now, just this year—begun to work in the factory?" I clarified my question.

"Because our father is sick," they told me. "He is very old and cannot work anymore even though our mother is still young." Their father worked for many years in a sugar factory north of Fes, but had recently stopped working. I asked if they had other siblings, and they told me they had three older brothers, all living in the household. One was married to the daughter of their father's sister, and she, too, lived with them. The brothers, they complained, refused to give the family any money—especially the two who were still single. They complained bitterly of one brother who wasted his money in the streets. "He goes to cafés and to restaurants, he buys clothes, and he goes out with girls."

And then Zaynab illustrated the problems this brother caused with a story. "Listen to this. Fadela had a gold necklace, and our brother—the second eldest one—took this necklace. He told her he was going to add to it, that he was going to buy more links for it to make it longer. But he sold the necklace and spent the money. He spent all the money taking girls out and buying meals in restaurants—eating out, eating in the street." Zaynab recounted the story in a soft voice, without much outrage displayed, and Fadela only nodded and said, "It's true," when I expressed dismay and disbelief. Their voices belied no anger, as if it was just a story, among other stories, to be told, as if they were used to the idea of people taking things from them.

"That is terrible," I said at the end of the story. "It's shameful."

"It is very shameful," they agreed. "But that's how boys are. Aren't they like that in America?"

"Sometimes," I said. "I don't know." I was trying to sort out the story in my head. It was not so much that the brother did this; some brothers are not nice, I knew. It was more that they seemed so resigned to it.

And then there was silence, until Fadela volunteered more information. "Zaynab was very sick for a while. That is why she always wears a scarf." Zaynab always wore a brightly colored scarf wrapped loosely under her chin. The scarf always looked as if it were slipping off her head; the top of her head was exposed while the scarf covered mostly her neck and the back of her head. Few of the girls in the factories cover their heads. I had counted only three of the entire workforce wearing the scarf of the *Ikhwan*—the Muslim movement—a distinctive style of tying the scarf so that all hair is kept from sight. A few of the older women in the factory wore head scarves in the French peasant style, heavy scarves tied under their chins that warm the head against the cold. Zaynab's scarf was worn like neither. It left most of her head bare, and thus seemed neither to make a statement about modesty nor to serve against the cold.

Now Fadela was explaining Zaynab's illness and her strangely worn scarf. "Zaynab was very sick for a long time."

"With what?" I asked.

"With fever."

"Were you in the hospital?" I asked Zaynab.

"Yes, I was in the hospital for two months," she said. "I thought I was going to die. And then my hair started falling out." This happened after Zaynab left the French people's house. Her hair was now falling out. And so she wore the scarf to hide her head.

"But it does not look like it is falling out," I said looking at the top of her head. So she pulled her scarf down. The hair on her head was very thin, tied back in a ponytail that was just a scraggly bundle of a few hairs pulled together with an elastic band.

"I cried and cried for my hair," Zaynab said. "I used to have hair that everyone envied. All the girls wanted hair like mine."

"It will grow back," I said. "It will grow back."

"But it will never be like it was before," Fadela reminded us. Moroccans can be brutally honest with each other. In a difficult world there are no false hopes.

"What kind of sickness did you have?" I asked her. "Do the doctors know what was wrong with you?"

"It was tension, they said. We spent a lot of money on drugs, but none of the drugs did any good."

"She still takes drugs," said Fadela, and she pulled a packet of pills out of her purse to show me. She waited for me to read the label, written in French, as if I—a foreigner—would have some insight. They were vitamins. "They are very expensive," Fadela said, "and they don't help her much."

I don't know what might be wrong with Zaynab. I could not understand this illness.[11] The girls left me in front of my house, and they continued to the bus station. "Don't forget us," they called to me. I told them I would not be leaving the factory yet and that I could not forget them anyway.

CHAPTER 3

The Girls in the Packing Department

On Monday morning Sylvie sent me to work in the packing area. Here the finished products are inspected, tagged with tickets from foreign department stores, packaged according to the clients' specifications, and loaded onto the trucks that will carry the garments to Europe. The packing workers are considered unskilled workers, as skill is defined as either the ability to operate a machine or to read and write and thereby be capable of taking inventory. The packing workers fetch finished garments from the workshop floor, carry out final inspections on them, tag them, fold them, and assemble them in cartons. Thus, while the workers on the sewing lines are completely constrained and leave their seats only twice a day, there is more opportunity for movement in the packing department. Between eight and ten girls work together, spending the entire day working around a large table.

As I would come to see, the girls in the packing area are among the least educated in the factory. Many of the machine operators had had some formal schooling, and many had attended a sewing school before finding work in the factory.[1] The girls in the packing department had had little formal schooling; none had gone to a sewing school. The packing department is down a short flight of steps from the main factory floor, and so the workers are safe from Sylvie's constant presence. Sylvie, however, frequently leans over the railing on the floor above and glares down at the workers, and she makes sporadic visits, yelling at the workers in French, even though none of them speak anything but Moroccan Arabic. Things can easily go wrong in the packing department: items are often tagged incorrectly, miscounted, or boxed inadequately.

There are two managers in the packing area. Hannen is responsible for taking inventory as the goods are packed and loaded onto the trucks. Fatiha Alami is responsible for ensuring that the finished product is in perfect condition. In the packing department, the tasks are divided among the girls so that particular girls regularly tag goods, others always inspect seams and threads, others always fold, and others always gather jackets from the workshop.

When I approached the table on my first day as a packing worker, the girls were in quiet commotion. One had carried the plastic box of packaging tools down from Sylvie's office, where they are stored overnight, only to find that the tiny metal point from the tag gun was missing. In whispers they were blaming each other, each girl defending herself, swearing she had not taken the tiny needle. The girl who had carried the box down swore the point had been there on Saturday afternoon, when she had returned the box to the office, and all began feverishly looking for the point. The point is an inexpensive and replaceable item. But each of these workers was terrified that they might be accused of stealing it. Eventually the workers decided that they must admit that it had disappeared and request a replacement in order to carry on with the day's work. One worker bravely went upstairs to the office and returned with a new gun point. The fear subsided as it became evident that no one would suffer any repercussions. Now work could begin.

My job was to assemble tags which were to be attached to the jackets being produced. I was given a small table, I found a chair to sit on, and I began to assemble tags for the workers to collect. Latifa, one of the workers, came to my table to help me quickly make a supply to start with. "Sit down," I said. "Here is a chair."

"We are not allowed to sit. They won't let us." Embarrassed, I stood up.

"Oh, no," said Latifa. "You should keep sitting."

Latifa was young looking with a round face, clear complexion, and big black eyes. She wore the veil of the *Ikhwan* and the modest dress that accompanies it. "You speak Arabic," she said. "God's blessings on you. Will you work with us long?"

"I will work for about three months, I think. But I am really working just to do research here in the factory—to research the workers."

Latifa invoked more blessings on me. "We won't get enough of you in three months. Stay with us longer." Latifa's graciousness was typical of Moroccan women, and I knew her response was just an ordinary form of politesse. But still I was touched by her kindness.

"Where do you live?" I asked her.

"I am far from this factory—out where the fields begin." Latifa told me that she walks to work because the factory transportation does not travel that far. She leaves her house in the morning darkness and returns in the dark of night.

"Why do you work in this factory?" I immediately asked Latifa what I asked all workers.

"My father cannot work. He has gone mad. He is crazy," Latifa said with no hesitation.

"What do you mean?"

"He is crazy. He used to go out with many girls, and now he has gone crazy." This was something Latifa would repeat to me as I got to know her, with utter candor and simplicity. Latifa went on to explain that her mother used to work in a pharmaceutical factory, but since the daughters have grown, they are working and she is at home, taking care of the house. Latifa has only sisters.

"There were two boys, but the boys died. Two of the girls are married, and three are still at home. All three of us left at home work in garment factories—each one in a different factory." Latifa was eager to tell me about herself.

"It is not enough money here. They only pay me 12,000" [600 *dirham* per month].[2] Latifa volunteered this after she had finished telling me her life story, a tragic tale involving the death of children and a father who has gone mad, which she recounted as a series of everyday events.

"I know, it is not enough," I said. "People always say that you girls don't really need to earn money, because you are only girls." This I knew was another fact people in Fes commonly stated about factory workers.[3]

"If we didn't need money," she said, "why would we work like this? But what are we to do?" she said with a resigned smile. And then she finished assembling a supply of tags and went to tag jackets.

Later I asked her about her veil. "Tell me, Latifa," I said, "are you wearing the Muslim veil?"

"Yes, it is the veil," she said proudly. "I have done this myself. I have chosen this veil on my own." She was indicating that she made the decision to don the Muslim head dress without familial pressure.

"And your sisters—are they veiled, too?"

"No, I am the only one in the family. I have done this by myself," she repeated.

"God bless you for this," I said, and she smiled and blessed me back. Latifa finished her set of tags and walked back to the main table where she could begin tagging. I sat and wondered why I had asked God to bless her.

I had come to question the social and political arguments associated with the Muslim veil, but I was impressed by Latifa's decision to veil, perhaps because she was so proud of it. The Muslim veil was a frequent sight on Moroccan university campuses, where educated young women read Muslim texts and participate in academic discussions about their meanings. But it was a rare sight in the factory. The interests of the factory workers were distinctly different from those of university girls. On average, workers had completed no more than the fifth grade. Even if their reading skills would allow it, workers had little time for the analysis and discussion of the religious texts that guided so much of the Islamic movement among the educated youth. The workers are teenagers. It is difficult for girls at this age to accept the veil because a veiled girl cannot easily display her beauty or her fashionable clothing. And once the veil is chosen, it cannot lightly be removed. Workers had told me that owners do not widely accept the veil because it is believed that the European contractors do not wish their garments to be sewn in factories staffed by veiled women. The few owners I was able to question denied having any opinion on the veil (a wise public stance, of course). Whatever the European opinion on veiled Moroccan factory girls might have been, I knew the Moroccan government was threatened by conservative Islam, and factory owners would have been unlikely to welcome this kind of activism into their factories.[4]

The factory girls understood that veiled women were respected and that the veil would protect a girl from harassment in the streets. The other girls in packing thought of Latifa as authentically religious, "the only true Muslim among us." They would often claim that they prayed that God would help them to don the veil, although they had not yet arrived at this level of piety. Latifa had taken this step, a fact which gave her a sense of dignity in a world where she had few other sources of personal pride. Also, I could not help thinking, this veil helped Latifa walk safely, through the dark of the early morning and late evening, on her long trips to and from the factory.

Later Latifa asked me if I went home at night and wrote everything down. These workers, I thought again, know how to do research.

"Yes, I write down what I see."

"Well, when you start asking questions, don't forget to ask me. I'll tell you things." And she held one hand up to slap me five, smiling. "I'm your friend," she said.

•

On Monday morning I nodded to Saudi as she stood outside Sylvie's office. Most mornings there stood a few girls outside the office, huddled in pairs, talking, nervous, like children standing outside the principal's office, waiting

to be chastised. These are the workers who did not appear for work the previous day or days, who must now show medical proof of the reason for their
absence. They understand that they may be loudly reprimanded by Sylvie.
They may also be fired. Saudi's face was set hard in the same distant, stony
stance that all the workers held when faced with Sylvie. When Saudi stepped
into the office, Sylvie began to berate her, complaining loudly in French that
Saudi was always absent and that she always had the same set of problems:
Saudi's young daughter was frequently ill. Like most of the others, Saudi did
not understand Sylvie's words, but she held her face still and unmoved, as
one of the line managers interpreted Sylvie's words. Quietly, in Arabic, the
interpreter told Saudi that she would have to go home and that she would
not be allowed to return until she secured a medical certificate explaining her
absence. Saudi was handed a small slip of blue paper, a pass that she would
show to the factory guard so that she would be permitted to exit the factory.
She walked, her face showing no emotion, out of the office. We would never
find out what had happened with Saudi, or her daughter, as Saudi never returned.[5]

Sickness is a severe liability in the factory. It causes absence and loss of
pay because there is no sick leave. But it causes additional hardships: no girl
can return to the factory without a doctor's note, and so even minor sickness forces the workers to spend the extra time and cost needed to get to the
government health clinic for documentation of their illness. Many workers
live far from the nearest clinic, and getting there means added expense and
possibly an additional day off, with more pay lost.

I had been in Sylvie's office, observing what was happening to the absentees.
I was there only because the packing girls had elected me to go into Sylvie's office each morning to gather the department tools kept there. In fact, they had
begged me to take over this aspect of the job, so they could avoid Sylvie. And
in this way, while I worked with them, I could relieve them of one of the more
dreadful aspects of their day. They assumed that Sylvie would never dare yell
at me, a Christian and a foreigner. As it would turn out, this assumption was
not entirely true.

I went down the steps into the packing department and began to assemble
my tags. I was working hard to keep a careful count of what I was doing. On
my first day in packing, I had inadvertently lost count of my tags and almost
caused a crisis in the department. Every day Hannen is handed a chart with
each batch of tags she receives, written in French, which she can barely deci-
pher. She must keep count of the tickets and jackets that move through the

department. My carelessness could easily have caused a disaster, which would certainly have ended with Sylvie yelling.

Latifa came immediately to my table to help me. "Oh, Titia, I could hardly wait for Sunday to pass. I wanted to see you again. I swear, the day could not pass fast enough for me. You are in my heart—I need a picture of you. Don't worry, I'll also give you a picture of me." I smiled. Moroccan girls often speak like this, openly expressing their joy in a friendship, extending hospitality to those who they perceive might need it. I knew Latifa's words were formulaic. Still, each time I heard words put together in this way, I was impressed by the girls' graciousness.

Latifa gave me her version of the history of the packing department. Four of the girls in this department, herself, Hannen, Hayat, and Mina, were "old," meaning they had worked at this factory previously. Over the past year the factory had been shut down. But during the three years previous to that, she and these other three worked together, often doing the tagging. In those first three years, Latifa said, the factory business was booming and orders were being shipped out constantly. They were often so busy that they would sleep right there, in the packing area, among the garments, sometimes not going home for three days in a row. Ultimately, the other workers went on strike and the factory shut down. It had remained closed over the past year. Latifa and the veteran packing workers did not participate in the strike. When the factory reopened this year, none of the workers who had participated in the strike were allowed to reenter. When they are found at the door, looking for work, the administration says, "You did not like working here. Why are you back?" and they are sent away.

Latifa's description of the factory closing did not coincide with what the owner had told me. He never mentioned the strike but said that the factory closed simply because he could negotiate no more orders from his client. It is possible that both worker and owner were reporting partial truths: wildcat strikes occur frequently in the garment industry, and workers are known to strike when they hear that their factory will close. The owner had told me that he had negotiated a new contract for the garments we were sewing now, but that this work would last them no more than ten months. After that time, he said, he would likely be forced to shut down again. Latifa and the other workers had little expectations about the work. They did not know from day to day how long the workday would last, how long any particular order would take to complete, or whether or not the factory would stay open in the future. They worked when they could.

"Why don't you get trained to work the sewing machines?" I asked Latifa. I wondered why she, such a loyal employee for so many years, had not moved up the hierarchy.

"They won't let us. They won't train the packing girls to sew."

"Why not?"

Latifa just shrugged. "What are we to do, sister? We are just working for our parents here. What can we do?" And with that, Latifa again told me about her father.

"Is he with you, living in your house?"

"Yes, and he screams a lot. When you come over, you can see how he is. You'll see him when you come to my house. In Ramadan. Your husband will let you come over, won't he?"

"Oh, yes, of course," I answered automatically. But, over the time we knew each other, Latifa never pursued her invitation and I never visited her at home, nor did I meet the father she so often spoke of.

•

At lunch I returned to my seat among the workers from line six and the conversation quickly turned to Saudi. A new worker had already replaced her on the sewing machine. Salima Bendoun reported that Saudi had been absent because her young daughter was possessed by *jnun*—devilish, troublesome spirits that exist in the netherworld, between humans and angels. The child's small body frequently went into convulsions, and this spirit possession kept Saudi at home, caring for the girl

The conversation turned to *jnun* and to the saints' shrines where healing and relief from the threats of spirits can be found. The shrines of saints dot the countryside and urban neighborhoods of Morocco. Women particularly like to visit these tombs where extraordinary people are buried and where prayers can be offered and spiritual solace is sought. Kenza reported that her mother is possessed by a spirit that speaks in the tongue of the Berbers, the Soussi Berbers specifically. "When my mother becomes possessed by this spirit," she said, "she begins to blabber quickly in the Soussi tongue, even though she does not even know the language. She never learned this language." Fatima reported that her paternal grandmother quite frequently gets struck by spirits who speak English. She then turned to me and began to mutter in a low voice a strange kind of garbled language.

"This is what she said. Do you hear it? It is English. Do you know what she is saying?" But I could not understand the strange sounds that Fatima was making.

·

The next day I was sitting at my table, handling the tags, when Hayat approached me. She placed a book in my hand. It was a bound book with a black fabric cover, full of blank white pages, so small that it fit in my palm. "This is for you to write things down in. My brother made it." I thanked her. I thought I might cry.

"This is so beautiful," I said.

"I'll bring you another even more beautiful one. My brother makes even better ones than this," she responded. Hayat is quieter and more serious than the others, always standing back. She wears glasses with lenses so thick her eyes look like black specks inside them. Her nose is slightly beaked, and her face is spotted with red sores, as if she has an illness, although she is not sick. For the past several days she had been wearing a long flannel nightgown, her bare feet in broken plastic sandals. She looks different standing next to the other girls around the table. They, too, look poor, but no one's clothing looks as desperate as Hayat's.

As the day wore on, Hayat kept urging me to move away from my small table and join the other workers at the shared packing table. "Come here. You must come and watch us work. You mustn't stand there alone, working. You must see how we work the tag gun so you can learn it, too." I moved over to their table, and Hayat demonstrated exactly how to load the gun with a tag, aim the point directly at the proper place, and then press the button to attach the tag by plastic thread to the jacket. "You press the button twice, not just once," she repeated as she showed me precisely how to tag the clothing. "It is important to learn," she said earnestly. Hayat was proud of her skill.

We stood at the packing table, all of us checking jackets, when Najia, who worked upstairs in inventory, leaned over the railing from above on the factory floor and said something I did not understand. Several of the girls became angry and started to argue with Najia. Hayat and Latifa were near tears.

"They are going to subtract the cost of the tag pistols and the scissors from this paycheck. We are going to get nothing for our work this month," said Hayat, "and tomorrow is Ramadan. We need money. We need to buy wheat and oil."

"How much money do you think you will get then?" I asked.

"We would have received about 250 *dirham* for the ten days we've worked so far. But now, with the price of the equipment extracted from the pay, we probably won't get any more than 100 *dirham*."[6] Hayat looked at me, checking for my reaction. "You see? Do you see what they do to us here?"

"I can see."

The workers continued to discuss this devastating piece of news, some with outrage, like Hayat. But even as they spoke of their anger, they recognized there was little they could do to change the situation. And so the conversation petered out, with comments such as "What can we do?" and "We will bear it, we can endure this." They would be able to withstand their troubles, they said. God was watching them, and God saw them suffer. Some of the packing workers just shrugged their shoulders as if they did not care. Perhaps they had not expected much anyway.

Hayat explained to me that the price of the packing equipment is always subtracted from their paychecks after the first month of the job. "This," she said, "is a kind of insurance for the owners against stealing." The girls understood this as an initial investment on their part, which would be refunded to them when they left the factory, if they were trustworthy and, indeed, had stolen nothing. But factories often shut down suddenly and with no warning. Girls are fired frequently. This investment, I thought, and Hayat must have known, would never be repaid. Hayat did not seem to want to acknowledge this. Right now, for her, the expense of Ramadan was the problem.

Even for the poor, Ramadan celebrations require cash: dates, figs, orange juice, milk, honey, and sweets are needed to properly end the day of fasting. Hayat called Najia to come back to the top of the stairs and pleaded with her. "Please, Najia, please don't take it from us all at once. Take it away slowly, a little each month. Don't take it all now. It's Ramadan." Najia had completed high school and held an enviable "clean" position in the factory. She kept track of inventory and thus was close to the administration. Although Hayat knew Najia did not make these decisions, she was much closer to the factory administration than anyone downstairs in the packing department, and Hayat believed Najia might act as intermediary.

Najia looked down at us from the top of the stairwell. She was dressed in a fashionable *djellaba* and matching Muslim headdress—she wore the *hijab*. Not a speck of hair showed from under her scarf, and her face looked fresh and unblemished as she smiled down at us and laughed. In a broken voice, Hayat called up the steps to her, "Najia, why are you laughing? Don't laugh at us."

"Why shouldn't I laugh?" Najia answered lightheartedly. "Tomorrow Ramadan begins!" For Hayat, Najia's show of unconcern was just one more insult. Hayat, leaning against the table, her hands empty of the tagging gun, in the nightgown and broken sandals she had been wearing for days, just said softly, to no one in particular, "It's the rent. I need to pay the rent."

Najia disappeared. Hayat turned her energies back to teaching me the skills I needed in packing. I was unable to clip excess threads off the jackets as swiftly and surely as the others, and Hayat was determined she would teach me the trick of it. One by one she held down nylon jackets, pulling taut the extra threads for me to snip. Each time I snipped a thread correctly she nodded, her eyes marking her approval. When I had mastered the clipping of threads at good speed, she suggested that I ask Sylvie to allow me to train with the workshop mechanics once I had learned all the skills needed in the packing department. "If you followed the mechanics around the workshop for a while," she argued, "you would learn how to repair the sewing machines. You should learn everything about this factory—everything." Almost entirely unschooled, Hayat had a reverence for knowledge.

At 4:15 we were told we could leave. The workday had been shortened so that workers could begin Ramadan preparations and visit the public baths, to cleanse themselves before beginning tomorrow's fast. Workers were summoned in small groups to join two long lines leading into Sylvie's office. There they would receive their pay in cash. I put the equipment away and went to look for Zaynab, so we could walk home together. Her line had fallen behind in production and they were still sewing. They had not been permitted to stop for lunch, and few had left the line for the breakfast break. Zaynab's head was bent over her machine, where she had been sewing seams since 7:30. I said good-bye to the packing girls as they stood in line. I walked home alone.

•

The next day was the first day of Ramadan, and we all arrived at work at 8:00. The work schedule was changed to accommodate the fast, and now we would work from 8:00 to 3:00 with a fifteen-minute break at noon. The new hours were written yesterday on the blackboard outside Sylvie's office, with a warning that any girl who had unfinished work would not be permitted to leave until the work was finished.

I arrived at the work table and the girls were talking in ferocious whispers. They were trading numbers across the table, only pretending to move the tag guns as they spoke. They had received terribly meager pay yesterday. Their voices were angry and hurt, but their whispers were provocative. "Let's strike," someone said. "Let's go on strike." Immediately the others told her to hush. "We cannot carry out a strike."

With this comment, Hayat, Latifa, and several others shuffled away from the table to the back of the packing room. They spoke in loud whispers that I was not meant to hear. The newest and youngest workers stayed at the table.

One of the younger workers commented, "Everybody is upset today. The pay was not good. Everyone got paid differently, at a different rate."

"Everyone in the factory? Or only the girls in packing?"

"Only packing."

"Was the cost of the equipment subtracted from your pay?"

"No. They will take it out next month. The pay this month was already too low to subtract anything."

I had never been able to get workers to consistently answer my questions about pay. I asked, "Do you know how much you will get paid before you get paid?"

"No, you don't know how much you are getting paid until you get paid. The day you get paid, when you get your money in your hands, then you know."

"Is it like this for everyone? For the sewing machine operators, too?" I asked, still unable to grasp how the pay system worked.

"No. The girls on the machines know what they will be paid." I had heard this said before. The girls on the machines are considered skilled workers in the factory. They earn more, and their pay is more reliable.

I never entirely understood the payment system, and throughout my tenure in the factory, no one seemed able to make it fully clear to me. The workday runs officially from 7:30 a.m. until 5:30 p.m. with a ten-minute break for breakfast and thirty minutes for lunch. According to the administration, workers are paid based on a nine-hour day—the legal limit of the workday in Morocco. By my count, though, the official work hours make for a nine-hour and fifty-minute day, a fact which no ever mentioned. In any case, the day rarely ended much before 6:30, and sometimes it was later than that. Workers were simply kept at their machines and in their places until Sylvie made a decision about the production quotas. Overtime was unmarked and unpaid. Workers were aware of this fact and complained to me about it.

Although workers on the machines seemed to know with some certainty their hourly and monthly salary (hourly salaries based on a nine-hour day), less skilled workers such as the packing workers were not sure of the amount they received per hour. They never knew what they would be paid at the end of the month. When I asked her once, Hayat told me she received five *dirham* an hour; another time she changed the number to three. Either figure is incorrect, based on the amount she received that first month I was there and what she claimed that she would regularly be paid. Newly hired workers often do not know their salaries before they begin and are likely to be paid at half-pay, or even go unpaid for the first several months, as they are considered to be in training. This is true for both machine operators and unskilled workers.

In this factory, the hours worked are marked on small blue time cards, which are distributed to all the workers in the morning and collected by the administration as the day is coming to an end. The workers grab their cards as they are distributed in the morning, and check to ensure that the hours worked the previous day are written in—usually in the form of a number 9, marked in a small box indicating the day on the cards. But the cards are difficult to read. One day I asked Mina, who had been with the factory for three years, to explain how the cards are read. She took the card from her pocket and studied it for a moment and then attempted to explain which little boxes on the card stood for particular days or particular weeks. She could not tell me exactly where on the cards particular days or hours were marked. "Well, sister," she said finally. "I really don't understand these cards. I have never understood these cards. It's good for people to research and understand things, but this I have never understood."

I had the feeling that many of the workers were simply paid an arbitrary amount, based more on the owner's whim or maybe his profits than on any calculation of time spent by the worker in any given month. This seemed to be evident on this first pay day. The veteran packers would have known what to expect after 20 days of work. They were shocked and disappointed by their low rate of pay, but they believed there was no action they could safely take to remedy the situation.

Given all this, I felt certain, throughout my research both inside this factory and with workers from other factories, that I was missing something about the factory pay system. How could workers be uncertain of their hourly rate? How could a worker not know how much she would earn in a given day, or week, or month? After some time, however, I came to realize that the workers' flexible approach to the payment system reflects the fact that they have little power over what they are paid. They have no ability to negotiate their pay and no viable work option other than factory labor. But I began to believe that the workers' attitudes toward pay reflect the fact that they are new to wage labor—as individuals, as a gender, as a generation. These workers, I believe, had not yet begun to internalize that their time was money, that their labor could be meted out in exchange for cash, and that the time they spent laboring could be precisely measured and precisely valued. These workers understood pricing generally to be something that is flexible: most shopped in the local souks, open air markets where the cost of every item is negotiated and nego-tiable. The season of the year, the availability of the product, the relationship of buyer to seller—all these things influence the cost of an item, how much will be paid. From this perspective, then, workers did not necessarily see their wages as fixed and unchangeable, and they could never precisely predict what they might earn in a given hour, week, or month. And so they could never give me precise information.

Eventually I sat down at my own table to make tags. Hayat came over and told me what was happening. "They paid me only 350 *dirham* for 20 days of work. I need to pay the rent. I am working for my parents." Today Hayat was wearing western style clothing and shoes, which made her appear less impov-erished. She told me that she had four young siblings at home who do not work. Her father is old and can no longer work. "I cannot support my family with 350 *dirham*. This is not enough," she said.

And then Latifa came to the table to get tags and tell me her story. She, too, received 350 *dirham* for these past 20 days. "We were crying yesterday, Titia. We cried when we got paid. We received only 350 *dirham*, and that girl in the *djellaba*, who is brand-new and does nothing here, who just walks around, she got 900 *dirham*. We've been here for three years, and she has just arrived." I didn't know who she meant by the girl in the *djellaba*, but I suspected it was Najia, who held an administrative job working in the inventory room and who had brought them the bad news in the first place.

"You cannot even leave this job because there are girls standing at the door this morning," I said. I had seen the crowd of job-seekers at the factory gate that morning, and I knew it was Latifa who had hushed the strike discussion. Latifa had refused to participate in the strike three years ago. Latifa, I knew, could not afford to lose her job.

"Yes, we cannot leave because there is no other work."

"I am so sorry for you, Latifa," I told her. "I cried for you all when I left here last night." And to this Latifa invoked many blessings from God.

"Oh, I forgot to tell you—my little sister sends you her greetings." I sent my best wishes back to her sister.

For the rest of the day I did not participate much in the discussion as I was responsible for putting together 7,000 small white tickets for this run of jackets. Most of the day I felt like quitting. I wanted to disassociate myself from the injustice of this place. And already I could barely stand the tedium of the job.

.

The lunchroom atmosphere was transformed by the fast. Instead of the lively chaos, there was only sluggishness at the lunch break, which had now been reduced to fifteen minutes. Girls crowded together on benches, some laying their heads on the table. In one corner a small group of girls who were not fasting sat together eating as discreetly as possible. They were not fasting because of menstruation, or in some cases, because they were young—and had not yet reached puberty—so were not responsible for fasting. Others who were not fasting but apparently could not bear to separate from their fasting friends were sitting amidst the crowd, sneaking small bits of bread into their mouths. When I entered the room, the question *syama*? (is she fasting?) was whispered repeatedly. Everyone needed to know if the Christian was fasting. I explained to my own lunch group that I was not accustomed to fasting and therefore could not withstand the fast. Many comforted me, urging me to eat. "You must not suffer from hunger," they urged. "Please do eat in front of us. We will not mind at all. This doesn't bother us." Others tried to convince me of the value of the fast. "You see," said Arbea, who had not given up her place as my guardian through the lunch period, "we are not hungry or thirsty. We feel nothing. God sees us through."

But as the afternoon drew on, the toll of the fast was obvious. The fast is difficult, especially for the workers, who cannot sleep through any part of the day's hunger. The girls in packing were counting the hours until the break-fast meal, the ritual meal that would be served when the sun set, to break the day's fast. Tempers ran short. Hannen lashed out at Hayat, accusing her of working too slowly. Later Hannen told Fatima Zahara, a new worker who was constantly being reprimanded for dawdling and arguing with the others, to go up to the factory roof and carry down the jackets that had been washed and left in the sun to dry. She refused to do so, asking, "Who are you to boss me around?" The others had to urge her to cooperate. Eventually she did.

From time to time, when tempers cooled, the workers chatted about their need for money, a conversation spurred on by the recent pay day travesty. "My father refuses to touch the money I earn," Fatima Zahara declared. "He tells me he does not want my money. My mother, however, is always asking me when I will be paid."

Latifa laughed at the possibility of someone refusing her money. "My mother asks me constantly when I will be paid," she said. "As soon as they pay me, she scoops the money out of my hands. I barely see it." Hayat nodded in agreement with Latifa. Mina told a long story about how once her father asked her for money and she claimed not to have any. She was later caught in a lie, for she did have money.

"I would never give my money to my father," said Hannen in response to this tale. "He works. He has his own money. I share my money only with my mother. Is it not my mother who cooks and washes my clothes for me?"

Sylvie's peering at us over the railing put the chatter to a stop. As we fell into silence, I thought about the fact that the most impoverished girls were the most compliant daughters. It was the poorest girls who gave their money, unquestioningly, to their parents. There was no choice. They, too, had to eat. Poverty reduces the opportunities for voicing resistance at home. It helps the factory administration as well.

But resistance to the constant and rigorous control can be expressed in more covert and less dangerous ways than speaking against the line chief or trying to organize a strike. The packing area is darker than the rest of the factory, located below the elevated workshop floor. The finished garments are piled high against the walls of the room, and extra tables and clothing racks are stacked in the back corner. Early in the morning, before the whistle sounds, the packing workers gather in this corner, hidden in semidarkness behind the extra tables and stacks of garments. They store their *djellaba*, shoes, and handbags in this corner rather than in lockers like the other workers. The corner provides a hidden refuge when someone needs to sit to rest her legs, or sneak a snack, or whisper secrets. At the fifteen-minute Ramadan break they move into this corner, turn out the lights, and sit together, recalling the television films they watched late the night before. The corner is a nest soft and dark, protected by piled jackets.

•

We stood around the table in the frigid factory when a woman, fully clothed in a head scarf and *djellaba*, approached our table. The girls greeted her respectfully, calling her Hajja. She watched us work for a while, and then asked the girls, "Are these jackets for boys or girls?"

The girls looked at each other and shook their heads. No one knew who would wear jackets like these. "Ask Titia. She will know," someone said.

"These jackets could be for a girl or a boy. Foreigners make no distinctions. Girls and boys wear the same clothes in France," someone else said with authority. "We don't do that in Morocco. Girls and boys clothing is very separate here."

"Well, not always," said the Hajja. "My daughter wears boys' clothing sometimes."

I shrugged. "It's true. These jackets could be for a girl or a boy." The Hajja just nodded and then walked away, as if to look at something else.

"Who is that woman?" I asked. The girls told me she was the aunt of the owner. She had brought some laundry into the factory, and a factory maid was quickly dispatched to wash the clothing.

"She is wonderful," Alami said. And everyone agreed that she showed them great respect whenever she came into the factory. She never put on airs, they said, or acted as if she were above them.

"This morning she waved at me from her car," someone said as proof of this fact.

•

On a Friday, several days after Ramadan had begun, the girl who acts as Sylvie's interpreter collected the workers together at the noon break and made an announcement. The administration was considering changing the Ramadan schedule on the request of women (meaning married women) who needed more time off in the afternoon in order to prepare the *hrira* (ritual soup) for their family's break-fast meal. The proposed workday would go from 7:30 to 2:30 rather than the previously instituted 8:00 to 3:00, and the administration wanted the general opinion on this change. The crowd—all 150 workers—went into an uproar. Shouts rose, "No, we don't want this. We are all girls [meaning unmarried females]. Most of us are girls. We don't need to cook *hrira*. We are not in agreement with this." Sylvie's interpreter listened to the raised voices and then dismissed the crowd.

The workers moved into the lunchroom to pass the rest of the break discussing the proposed change. Crowded together on the benches, each table counted the number of married women present. There were only three married workers at the table where I sat with some twenty other workers. Their point proven, the girls kept repeating, "We are all girls." Unmarried girls do not worry about preparing the ritual meal, as they live with their mothers who, as married women, take the responsibility for preparing all meals, particularly ritual meals served at religious holidays. They suggested that the few married women present prepare the *hrira* in the early morning hours, so it would be ready when they return from work. Or, one worker joked, "The married women can just get divorced and go home to their mothers for the month."

Once work had recommenced, the decision was written on the blackboard, which most of the workers, trapped at their machines, could not see. One of the packing workers snuck out of the room and came back with the news: as per the wishes of the married workers, the Ramadan work hours would be changed. The disgruntled workers complained bitterly. Much of the joy of Ramadan is in the festivities that occur after the sun sets and the family has broken its fast. The center of Fes springs to life as people stroll the streets in the dark, sitting in cafés and ice cream parlors. Such activities are not available to the workers who live in "popular" neighborhoods, where the roads are unpaved and cafés are strictly the province of men. But even in the popular neighborhoods, young people step outside their homes at night, lighting sparklers and jumping rope in the streets. The working girls cherish the evenings of Ramadan, which they pass eating holiday sweets and watching television films in the company of family, visiting friends, and neighbors.

"With this change in schedule," Latifa said, "we will have to wake much earlier. We won't be able to stay up until midnight. Moroccans," she declared, "are cows," an expression the girls often use to express their general disdain for the system and how they are treated. Despite their complaints about the administration's action, the girls seemed to realize there was little they could do to change the decision. Perhaps they recognized the cultural superiority of married women and the reverence due for the responsibilities of these women—wives—at home. Or perhaps they simply understood that there was nothing they could do about any of the conditions of their work.

Very few married women work in the garment factories: in this particular factory, I could find only three married women out of more than 100 workers. My surveys in other factories reflected similar statistics. Factory owners, in my conversations with them, always claimed that they preferred young, unmarried girls because these girls learn more quickly. This explanation, though, I find unconvincing: at the age of 30, a woman has not yet begun the decline into old age. Her hands have not yet become less nimble and her mind has not begun to falter. And yet I could find very few females over the age of 30 employed in the garment factories of Fes. In this particular factory, nearly every worker was between the age of 12 and 30. The working girls argued that older females would never accept such low pay, but I knew there were many impoverished middle-aged women in Fes who might well have accepted factory work as an alternative to dire poverty.

I believe the reason why no women above the age of 30, and few married women in particular, worked in the factories throughout Fes was simply because the owners would not allow it. In Morocco, everyone is expected to marry, and families work hard to ensure that their daughters are wed by the time they reach 30. Unlike unmarried girls, married women are due some respect. Married women are more legitimate, more "fully human" than unmarried girls. As wives and mothers, they must be accorded deference: to degrade a married woman is to diminish her husband. So factory owners cannot legitimately keep married women at their machines indefinitely or prevent them from returning home to fix the evening meal. Such demands would be an outrage to the men in the community. Thus the factory hours were changed for the sake of the (very few) married women in the factory. Now these married women could carry out their moral duty to cook *hrira*. Local patriarchy—accepted notions of the proper role of woman as wife— conspires with the factory to produce the cheapest labor supply imaginable: young unmarried females.[7]

And so the girls in packing went back to their chatting and occasional bickering. Fatima Zahara kept singing until finally Alami reprimanded her, telling her to stop, and once she had stopped, Alami herself, seemingly infected by the tune, began to hum. Nobody commented. Fatima Zahara then asked Alami if she would teach her how to sew a *djellaba* on one of the machines upstairs after work sometime, and Alami assured her she would be glad to. As the day was coming to an end, the rumor reached us that tomorrow, Saturday, would be a day off. The new shipment of fabric from France had not yet passed through Tangiers and production would be stalled. None of the workers displayed the relief I felt at the prospect of a break in the routine. For them, too many canceled workdays would only mean another month of insupportably meager pay. And the rush that inevitably follows a break in the work pace would surely go unpaid, in the form of unmarked overtime. And so I was careful not to reveal how glad I was not to have to return the next morning.

•

One afternoon early in the month of Ramadan, sometime after the work hours had been rescheduled, Fatima, the manager of line six, invited me to her home to break the fast with her family. Mariam, Fatima's best friend, was to join us on the trip home. Fatima, Mariam, and I gathered at the lockers. We headed for the factory gates, where a crowd of workers stood, waiting and hoping that the factory bus—not always reliable—would arrive to take them home. As we passed through the cluster of workers and out the gates, Fatima turned around and yelled to the crowd, gesturing grandly with her arms, "I am going to 'do the boulevard,' and then go home and make *hrira!*" The workers just looked at her, some smiling.

In Fes, people deride factory girls, saying that they "do the boulevard"—that they stroll freely and unchaperoned through the city streets, wild, uncontrolled females looking for men and other evils. Factory work, it is said, draws young girls from the safety of their homes and leads them to behave in such unacceptable ways. Fatima's call was made only days after the Ramadan work hours had been rescheduled to meet the needs of the married workers, totally dismissing the desires of the unmarried girls who dominated the factory workforce. And thus, I took Fatima's call to be an irreverent mocking of the new factory hours, a repudiation of the social order that reveres marriage and the duties of married women, while denigrating the work of the unmarried girls, nearly all of whom labor for their families. But Fatima's announcement that she was off to "do the boulevard" was also a pretty good description of what she and Mariam planned to do as we made our way home that Friday afternoon.

First, we walked to an apartment near the central train station, where Mariam needed to pick up a package for her aunt. When we couldn't find the apartment, whose address Mariam had scribbled on a scrap of paper, Fatima urged Mariam to ask a gas station attendant for directions. Fatima hung back with a look of daring on her face as Mariam spoke to the young man. When we finally located the apartment, Mariam entered the building alone and came out minutes later with two large packages covered in black plastic. The girls immediately became involved in a discussion as to whether Fatima, dressed as she was in fashionable western clothing, should carry a package. Mariam wore a *djellaba*, with her hair tied back behind her head. Fatima, though, was dressed in a pink wool blazer with high-waisted black pants and a shiny white blouse. On her feet were high heeled plastic black patent leather pumps. Her long curly hair hung loose and unruly and uncovered, in a style that she had once told me her mother abhors.

"Normally," the girls explained to me, "only someone dressed as Mariam is, in a *djellaba* with her hair tied back, would be carrying such ugly packages. A person dressed like Fatima, in stylish western clothing, would not normally be seen carrying such packages." These packages, wrapped in black plastic, tied in string, carrying some sort of food, I was told, were the sort of packages only a country person would carry. Fatima, though, insisted on helping her friend and took a package. I offered to carry a package as well, but this option seemed to be out of the question: I was the guest, and no proper host would allow me to work. What's more, I sensed that allowing a Christian like me, dressed in authentically western clothing, to carry packages such as those would be unthinkable.

Packages in hand, we proceeded through the factory district, toward the Ville Nouvelle, where we would catch the next bus home. Fatima, a large girl with a sense for drama, kept running into people she knew. She waved at the drivers as city buses passed. She waved heartily at a van full of factory girls she recognized from a factory where she once worked. We stopped at a pay telephone shop, where the girls made repeated calls to someone in Rabat, whose identity they would not divulge to me and whose phone was perpetually busy. When finally we reached the next bus station and boarded the bus, I purchased tags for all three of us from the tag sales man. The girls, when they found out, laughed at me: "We never buy our tickets. These ticket collectors are our friends. They always let us ride for free."

We stood as the bus jolted forward and stopped unexpectedly, squeezed in tightly between passengers. The girls flirted openly with the young men who surrounded us. They giggled loudly and tapped their feet, moving their heads to the rhythms of the music playing over the loudspeakers. It was as if we had just arrived at a high school dance and not as if we had just stepped onto an overcrowded city bus. Fatima and Mariam were lower-class girls who probably would not have had the opportunity to attend university. Had they not been factory workers, I knew, they would have no reason for riding this bus, squished between strangers, unchaperoned, unattended, unprotected.

After a half hour of stopping and starting past massive concrete housing developments, we reached the edge of the city, where the uninhabited fields surrounding Fes become visible on the horizon. We had left the clamor of the city center behind us and stepped off the bus, which was almost empty now, into a neighborhood that was quiet. I noticed the silence immediately. The unpaved roads were turning gray in the setting sun, and there were no streetlights to brighten the dusk. Children, most of them boys, played freely in the dirt streets. We started down the street, leaving Mariam at her aunt's apartment, where she lives, and continued on to Fatima's home.

Fatima's house is clean, built of cinderblock which is still exposed and visible both outside and from within. The house, like so many houses in the workers' neighborhoods, was under construction, only half complete. We entered the house through a brightly colored door, the top half of which was covered by a beautifully woven rug, which hides the space where a window-pane will someday go, once the pane is purchased. Through this door we entered the finished portion of the house, which was made up of two large rooms, the cinderblock walls painted a bright white, in which the family lives. I told Fatima that I thought her house was clean and beautiful.

"I built this house myself," she said, "with my own money." Her parents, she went on to explain, had purchased this land in the 1960s, when they first left the countryside for the city of Fes. Shortly thereafter, her father died, leaving her mother alone with three children. Her mother remained, and Fatima has now financed the building of the cement rooms. She is certain that someday she will complete the building of this house.

Now Fatima lives in these rooms with her mother and elder brother, who works at a café in the neighborhood—a part-time job that gives him little more than spending money. Her mother is a part-time cleaning woman for a nearby school. She has a younger sister who also worked in a garment factory until her recent marriage and now lives in the *medina* with her husband. We sat down in the sitting room, and Fatima's mother came in and greeted me. She gestured to her daughter to tie her hair back. Fatima laughed but did nothing about her hairdo. None of her mother's hair was visible, as it was completely concealed inside the tightly knotted head scarves worn by all rural Moroccan women. Most Moroccans of the lower classes argue that the Qur'an instructs women to cover their heads, but Fatima's hair is big and fluffy and flying everywhere. She does not cover it, even when her mother asks.

Fatima went into the next room to retrieve her photo album and began to recount her life history through the photos she had collected. This display of personal photographs is a hospitality ritual among girls in Morocco, at least among those who have been able to collect a set of pictures telling the story of their lives. Fatima left school in the ninth grade to enter a sewing school, which she attended for eight months. She believes, in fact, it is because she was so well trained at the sewing school that she has today secured the position of line manager. After finishing the sewing school, she began her factory career, holding three separate jobs, until her current position as line manager. Her first position ended within a year, due to a factory closing, but she stayed at her second job for four years, at which point she was fired, because "I began to get old." I knew what she meant when she told me this, because I had heard this phrase used often before. Workers who gain seniority are frequently forced out of their positions. Workers reported that this happens consistently, although they had no good reason for why owners would make such a move. Presumably they are forced out before they can start to make demands on the company.

Moroccan labor law does entitle workers to seniority benefits, but such benefits, like nearly all labor law provisions, are ignored in the factories. Why owners would fear repercussions from experienced workers seems inexplicable. And yet, despite the fact that she was forced to leave simply because her tenure at that factory had been so long, Fatima remembers those four years, and even the factory administration, with great fondness.

Nearly all Fatima's photos are of outings with factory friends, some of them sponsored by the factory itself. She showed me pictures of herself at factory parties, pictures of herself on the sewing line, pictures of herself at the birthday party of another worker's daughter. There were pictures of trips taken with co-workers, girls leaning together in the snow of nearby mountains of Immouzer and Ifrane, girls in bathing suits on the beaches of Nador, Fatima with Mariam in a café. (They always slept on the bus on these long journeys, to avoid the cost of a hotel.) "It is good," Fatima told me, "for a person to go out and see things." And as she led me through the photos, Fatima told me that she enjoys not just the camaraderie of the factory but the work itself. She likes the excitement of being line manager—the problems, the arguments, the tension. "As some people like to study," she said, "I like to work. I am always extremely conscientious in my work; I produce the best work I can, every time."

And with this, Fatima's sister entered the room. The young woman and her husband, I was told, had arrived earlier in the day to share the break-fast meal with the family, and they had been sleeping in the next room. Still heavy with sleep, the sister sat silently next to us, as Fatima searched diligently for photos that would help introduce me to her sister's story.

Like Fatima, this sister had worked in a garment factory. But she had stayed there only two years, never liking the work as Fatima does. "I put on the veil," the sister explained, "and soon after that, I received an offer of marriage."

"How did you meet your husband?" I asked.

"My husband owns a gold shop in the old city. One day I entered the shop to sell a bracelet. As I was leaving the shop, he told me that he liked me and that he would like to marry me. So I agreed to allow him to come here, with his mother. They did, right away, and that was all. The marriage was arranged." The wedding, she told me, was carried out quickly and simply. "Because I had already put on the veil, I would wear no makeup or elaborate clothing at the ceremony, so we did not need to prepare. I never went back to the factory." I asked her if she missed working, but she assured me she did not. She never liked the factory, and anyway, "My husband does not want me to work." She gets bored sometimes being in the house all day, but her husband allows her to come visit her mother once a week, which helps alleviate the strain. And now she is pregnant.

Throughout my time in the factory I struggled with the question of whether the factory work is really changing the girl workers, whether the factory routines are shifting the way these girls operate in the world. Fatima is so powerful and certain. She had showed me pictures of her school days, photographs of a basketball team, her at the center. When she left school for the factory, she used her position as factory worker to travel the country, to make friends with people she would otherwise never have encountered, to escape the tedium of the home. But her sister, it seemed, had opted for the best way to get back inside the house: a quickly arranged marriage. Fatima and her sister seem to be very different people. The impact of the factory on their lives has been very different, too.

We then went outside, so Fatima could show me her neighborhood and pass the last hour of hunger before the fast was broken. "I was born here, in this neighborhood. These neighbors are like family to me," she told me. Much of her extended family lived there, both her mother's and her father's brother. We stopped to make a quick visit at the home of her maternal uncle, to whom Fatima is particularly close. "A lot of girls," Fatima told me, "are ashamed to come from a popular quarter like this. They want to leave and never return. But I am not ashamed, I am proud of this place and I'll never leave it behind."

We broke the fast, and I stood to leave. Fatima stood up, too. "I will take you now. I will go along with you on the bus and to your home."

"Oh, no, Fatima," I insisted. "That is not necessary. It is too bothersome for you. I can travel alone." But Fatima persisted and won the argument.

When we got outside and began walking toward Mariam's house, I realized that Fatima had not wanted me to refuse her. She and Mariam had plans for a late-night bus ride, scheduled around the task of escorting the Christian back home. We stopped at Mariam's, and Fatima called from the street to an upstairs window. Mariam came running down from a third-story apartment. The girls began again to giggle. When we boarded the bus, Mariam opened a package of gum and handed us each a piece. The fun had begun. When I left the two, they had started to stroll down the crowded, brightly lit main avenue of the Ville Nouvelle.

Girls, Moroccans say, must respect the boundaries (*hdud*). The boundaries are lines that are invisible to the eye, that control and limit human behavior. Although men, too, must respect these limits, for females the boundaries are particularly physical. The boundaries should curb female mobility. For factory girls who can withstand the work and the confinement within the factory walls, the boundaries are stretched, beyond the home, beyond the factory, to the streets outside.[8]

•

The next Monday morning things seemed to start slowly. When I arrived downstairs, the workers were just beginning to gather around the table. Hannen, having carried the equipment down from Sylvie's office, was consulting Alami on whether it was appropriate for her to start fasting today; although her menstrual cycle had ended, she had not yet been to the public bath to ritually cleanse herself. Alami advised her to begin her fast tomorrow. I asked the girls what they had done on the two-day break. Hayat volunteered that she had visited Moulay Idriss, the mausoleum of Fes's patron saint and the most sacred shrine in Fes. The others had done housework.

Suddenly everyone became quiet. We realized that Sylvie was standing at the railing, watching us from above. The chatter stopped. No one said anything. When it was certain that Sylvie was gone, Alami said with a quiet intensity, "She should never spy on us like that. We should not be spied on."

At 29, Alami was one of the oldest workers in the factory. She was also the most educated. Alami had completed high school and had then attended a vocational school run by the Moroccan Ministry of Agriculture, where she was trained as an agricultural extension agent and researcher. She spent a six-month training period in the countryside, carrying out interviews with rural farmers. After this training, however, Alami could not find a position in the Department of Agriculture, due to the high rates of unemployment in Morocco and, she said, due to the persistent drought in the rural areas. She would continue to try, though, going periodically to take civil service exams. She was saving her earnings, she had told me, to put together the large bribe she felt might help her to secure a government position. Until then, she worked in this sewing factory.

We worked in silence until I questioned Alami about her sisters, having learned that one of them was working on a sewing line upstairs. Alami told me that two of her sisters had worked in this factory, and a third works in a factory nearby. "My younger sister used to have Hannen's job, but she left last year when she married. But my older sister is still here. She's on a sewing line upstairs. Haven't you seen her? She's the cow." Alami gestured to show that her sister was fat. "She is married and has a son. She's working because she wants money, she is crazy for money, she always feels she does not have enough."

Alami scoffed at this. Her sister's husband, she said, was "in education" and was able to support her. "It is she who chooses this work." To Alami, this was somewhat ridiculous.

Hayat agreed that the choice Alami's sister was making, to stay here in the factory after marriage, was questionable at best. She herself would absolutely not work after marriage.

"But, Hayat, why not? Why not, just to earn some money?" I asked her.

"If I am going to work, why would I marry? I might as well stay at home with my parents. If he tells me to work, I will go back home. Better that I give my money to my mother than to a man." Hayat was incensed by the idea of working "for" her husband. She works at all only because her family so desperately needs the money. "I tell you, work in this factory is not clean work. There is no shame in working if you are educated—if I had been educated, and had become an engineer, for example, I would be happy to work, even after marriage, even after children. But a married woman should not work in a factory. This is shameful work."

Still puzzling somewhat over the events of last week, and the changing of the work hours, I asked Alami why so few married women work in the factory: Even married women in Fes were poor, many married women needed money. "Look at these hours we are working," she said. "Girls stop working when they get married because the factory job is from morning till night and there is no way a woman can care for her children if she works in a factory." The girls at the table all agreed with this conclusion. In Morocco, the women who continue to work after they marry and have children are the *muweddaf* (the civil servants, professionals, and office workers). Alami described another sister, who is a teacher. "She has classes one day in the morning and the next day in the afternoon. She comes home to eat her lunch. It is easy for her to care for her children and work." But for a factory worker, who begins work early in the morning and never knows exactly when she will get home, this is impossible.[9]

And with this Naima, whose job it is to check the inside of the jackets for imperfections, announced that she got engaged yesterday. Naima is 15. She is new to the factory, and this is her first job. She works slowly, as if she is always tired. She frequently acts bewildered, as if she is moving inside a cloud. Every day she stands next to Fatima Zahara, and the two seem to be involved in a running argument. Naima reported on her upcoming marriage in much the same way as she operates her life, inconsequentially, with a sense of passive disinterest. "The man and his mother," she said, "came to our house and asked for me last night."

"Who is he? Do you know him?" the others asked.

"I have never seen him before, but they said he had seen me on the street and liked me." Naima said this with some pride. After some discussion with the guests, her father agreed, and they have planned the engagement party for next month. The date of the wedding is not yet determined. Naima displayed no emotional response to the events she reported, as if they were the happenings of a life not her own.

"Do you know how to cook?" Latifa asked Naima, anxiously.

"There are still a lot of things I can't cook," Naima admitted blandly.

"Well then, you really need to stay home now and learn to cook. You cannot get married if you can't cook," Latifa gravely advised her. Naima did not respond. It was clear she did not want to pursue the discussion of her upcoming marriage.

For a moment the table fell silent until one girl volunteered that she had one great dream: "My greatest dream is to marry a foreigner," the girl announced. "Marriage to a foreigner would be better than marriage to a Moroccan." Turning to me, as if to assure me that she understood my kind, she said, "I know how to cook a lot of foreign dishes—like hamburgers, for example."

"Why are you so sure a foreigner would make a better husband?" I asked.

"I am just tired of Morocco. I just want to leave this place."

"How would you even speak to a foreigner? Do you know any foreign languages?" the others asked.

"You only went to school for one year," someone reminded her.

"No, I can only speak Moroccan Arabic. But that doesn't really matter that much." And then she launched into a story that she had recently heard. "There was an extremely wealthy Italian woman who was 100 years old and said that if a young Moroccan man would marry her, she would give him everything. Finally, a young Moroccan man did marry her, and in the end he inherited all her wealth when she died." And to end the story and to convince us it was true, she said, "I swear to you, this is true."

No one argued it. No one said anything. Finally Alami advised her to stop hoping for a foreigner and marry a Moroccan man. "You will never be happy with a foreigner who does not know your language and your customs," she said authoritatively. Alami always spoke as the voice of reason. I seconded Alami.

Later I asked Naima if she was happy with the wedding plans that had been arranged for her. She said, "It is better than this," waving her hands around to signify the factory. These past two months were her first experience with factory work. Naima had never attended school. During the previous two summers she had helped harvest onions for pay in the fields around Fes. Right now, marriage offered her an alternative—her only alternative—to endlessly checking the seams of nylon jackets. I could see Naima's point.

•

The next morning Naima pulled from her purse a plastic book no bigger than her palm, filled with blank white pages that could be locked shut with a miniscule metal key. Her fiancé had come to the factory after work yesterday and given it to her. She considered this a wonderful gift. "It is to write things in," she told us, "such as the day when he came to engage me and the day he came to see me at work."

"But how can you write things in it," one of the girls asked, "when you cannot write?"

"I can write."

But we all knew that Naima had never stepped into a school and that she could not write. At the noon break, she brought the book to Alami, asking her to write things in it for her. Alami used the packing pencil stub to record the day Naima was engaged and the day her fiancé came to meet her at the factory. And Naima took back the tiny book, studied the Arabic script now penciled in it, locked it with the tiny key, and slipped it back into her purse.

Then Hannen asked her if she liked the boy and if they had begun to get to know each other when they spoke yesterday. Naima said that she had not spoken with him yesterday, that she had accepted the gift and told him, "Go and play"—get out of here. Although he wanted to walk her home, she said she told him she would not speak to him until he signed the marriage contract. She said this with pride, knowing that she was behaving as any honorable girl would behave, as her parents expected her to behave. But Hannen reprimanded her. "You must speak to him before he signs the contract, because after he signs, it is too late. If you find you don't like him after that, you will end up divorced. Better to speak to him now so you know now whether you two are compatible." And with this Hannen launched into a story about how she herself once spoke to a boy. Over the course of three months, she walked with him, in the afternoons, on the street, and in this way she learned all she could about him.

In the end, she found she did not like him. "But it is better this way, better than waiting until he signs the act, because then it is too late," she instructed Naima. Naima seemed to listen carefully but gave no response. For a while, then, we stopped speaking of Naima's engagement.

I watched Naima, as she seemed to be absorbing Hannen's words. Hannen was tall and impressive. Her hair was always tied back so stylishly, and she wore frosted pink lip gloss. Next to her, Naima seemed graceless and clumsy. Before these past two months in the factory, Naima had never been a part of a public institution. She had not attended school. As a female from a traditional lower-class family, she did not visit the mosque. There were no libraries she might have frequented or public parks where she might have played. Before becoming a factory worker, Naima had known only her parents, her siblings, her aunts, uncles, cousins, and perhaps her neighbors. Naima's life, until the age of 15, had been played out inside her house and within the boundaries of the urban quarter where she lived. And now, here in the factory, girls like Hannen and Alami, who had been to school and stepped out into the world, were advising her on what to do.

In the lower-class milieu in Morocco, the social lives of young, unmarried girls—indeed, their physical movement—is tightly controlled by the family. Had she not come to work in the factory, Naima might never have heard ideas like those of Hannen and Alami. Together, the packing girls were advising Naima on how to conduct her courtship and ultimately how to involve herself in a marriage. Their recommendations did not conform precisely to Naima's parents' notions of how their daughter's marriage should proceed. Naima's world was expanding beyond the kind of advice she might otherwise have received from her mother and female relatives. For Naima, this factory had become a kind of schoolroom.

•

I was freezing in the factory, and my back hurt. Outside, the Moroccan sun was shining bright and hard, and I wished we could step out at lunchtime to warm ourselves. If a worker wants to leave the factory before the end of the workday, however, she must get a slip of blue paper signed by Sylvie. She must show this paper to the guard at the factory door, and only then will he let her out of the building. If she wants to enter the factory anytime after the start of the workday, she must show the guard a paper excusing her late entrance. No girl can enter or exit this factory outside the regular hours without showing the factory guard a slip of paper. The door is closed and the guard is standing near it. We are locked in.[10]

My mind was wandering on thoughts of the cold and the permission slips and the idea of being locked in and the nature of factory work when Alami interrupted my thoughts. "Titia," she asked, "what do you plan to write in your report?"

"I'm not sure yet. What do you think I should write about?"

"Well," she said, "first let me tell you that you have to be careful, because people lie. I know this, because I used to survey farmers when I was working as an agricultural agent. And they always lied. They would lie about the number of animals they owned because they were afraid that I was a tax agent. So they would lie. People lie. You can't always believe them."

"This is interesting. I think you're right."

"What I think you should write about first, though, is the difference between weddings in the country and the city." I was taken aback. Why does she want me to write about marriage, when I am working here in the packing department, tagging nylon jackets?

"What do you mean?"

"You really have to compare the weddings in the countryside with those in the city."

"But, Alami, I'm not going to have time to go to weddings in the countryside. Just tell me the difference."

"Well, in the countryside girls have to be virgins. If a girl gets married and there is no blood on the wedding night, the man divorces her. I know this is true from my work in the countryside."

"Well, that's not really fair to the girl. What if she was raped or something?" I said this just to hear what Alami would say. This conversation—marriage, sex, blood—was very familiar to me.

"I agree, and people are changing this, but that's how it still is in the countryside. And also, in the countryside, the girl's family decides who she marries, and the girl agrees to it. She has no choice. But in the city, girls see the man on the street and the girl knows before her parents that the man will come and engage her. That's how it is now in the city."

Our conversation stopped when we noticed Sylvie moving our way, and I was left again to my own thoughts. For me, this research was about "work in the factory." But as far as the workers were concerned, it seemed that what mattered most was marriage.

•

Some days later when I arrived in the packing department, the room seemed empty. The lights were out and no one was in sight. The 7:30 whistle had not yet sounded, and as my eyes adjusted to the grim light of the room, I saw the packing girls in the corner, hidden behind tables and brightly colored puffy jackets, laughing. The jackets were puffy because we had begun production of a line of fiber-filled winter coats. In the dark the girls were reviewing the stories all had seen on last night's Ramadan television films. They discussed the woes of Egyptian heroines, women on the television serials who had glaringly blonde hair and who dressed in glamorous clothing and who lived out eventful lives in rooms stuffed with heavily upholstered furniture. But the shows they liked best, it seemed, were the comic routines.

In the one they saw last night, a man who was having mother-in-law problems went to visit the *shuwafa*, a kind of fortune-teller that women in traditional Morocco often visit to help them resolve marital troubles. But unbeknownst to this husband, his own mother-in-law had preceded him and was waiting in the fortune-teller's home before he arrived. When she saw him, and before he saw her, she quickly covered herself with a shawl and pretended that she was the fortune-teller. The son-in-law began his litany of complaints against her until, eventually, he discovered who she was. The girls held their stomachs from the pain of laughter as they remembered the routine. And then the morning whistle sounded.

The tedium of checking seams continued through the morning. As we stood and examined jackets, a small girl came down the steps, into our packing area, to deliver a misplaced jacket. She was a thread clipper who worked on one of the lines of sewing operators. I had seen this girl many times before, and I remembered the evening when I had left the factory with Fatima and Mariam, and the tiny girl had energetically passed us by, hurrying home. Fatima had called out to the girl, "*Syama*?" (Are you fasting?) The girl had said no. Surprised, both Fatima and Mariam had called out, "Why not?" and the girl had said that she had not yet reached puberty, that she was only 13.

Since then, I had noticed this girl in the factory every day. She was always dressed in a long-sleeved striped stretch knit shirt tucked neatly into belted blue jeans. Her body was completely straight and flat, and her hair was always pulled back in a ponytail. After she delivered the jacket to us and went back up the stairs, I commented on how young this girl looked. "She looks so young to me," I said. "All the thread clippers look so young to me."

"They are young, of course," answered Alami. "They are always the youngest workers in any factory. Only little girls do finishing."

"Why?"

"Because the pay is so bad. Those girls are paid next to nothing for a full day's work. Why would a grown woman clip threads?" These girls sit or stand between sewing operators or around a table to the side of the sewing line, clipping the excess threads off garments. "These thread clipping girls have no skills at all."

"Does a girl need to be skilled to qualify for a job on a machine or to work on the training line?" I asked Alami, trying to figure out who gets which job and why. I knew that amidst the lines of sewing operators there is a line of about ten machine operators who are in training. Sylvie had told me she must always have an excess line of workers in training, available to fill positions left empty due to absenteeism. Girls on the training line are usually chosen from the unemployed workers standing at the factory door. They first sew stripes and then spirals on large squares of paper, punching holes in the paper with a machine needle that has not been threaded. They then graduate to sewing the hems on the pockets to be sewn into the jackets being produced.

"A girl who comes here with a certificate from a sewing school is going to ask for a certain wage. She will not work for nothing, and on the training line, you do not get paid."

"Even when you start actually sewing pockets?" I asked.

"Yes, even if you are sewing pockets. You get paid when you learn." But Alami could not specify a time when payment might start.

"One month?" I asked. "Two months? When have you learned? How do they know you have learned?"

"First you get paid a little, and then it grows. Slowly your pay increases." Alami spoke as if the payment system was organic, as if there were something natural about it. Other workers had told me the same thing: workers do not get paid while they are training, even if they are producing for the factory during this training period. No one ever suggested that there was any reason to question this system. Alami seemed to have no problem with the idea that people on the training line, working ten-hour days and sometimes six-day weeks, might not get paid for several months.

Perhaps, I thought, this is part of the way in which Moroccans traditionally think about a craft. In Morocco, people who learn skills do so after undergoing years of apprenticeship. Most Moroccan crafts are produced by males. A young boy's formation as a craftsman requires years in the master's shop, watching the master craftsman. At first he only sweeps the shop and fetches tea; later he does small tasks related to the craft. The boy only becomes a master after years spent training in this way, years in which he will receive a meager pay, if at all. And so, I think, making these kinds of assumptions about skills training, neither Alami nor any of the others were outraged by the lack of pay for trainees in this factory.

In the factory context, however, where the skill being learned is a repetitive task, such as sewing a straight seam, the skill does not take a long time to learn, and the "trainee" can be highly productive while perfecting the skill—as in sewing pockets. The factory is thus able to secure unpaid labor by holding its own standards for when an employee is sufficiently trained—sufficiently trained not to produce, because the worker is already producing, but to get paid.

"Ask Hannen about training, if you want to know," said Alami. "She learned here. They trained her here." And Hannen eagerly recounted to me her work history.

"They taught me to sew right here," Hannen began. (But Hannen had told me earlier that she had attended a sewing school after leaving school in the ninth grade.) "And then I climbed up. At first I worked on the machine as an operator, then I did final control for all the garments on my sewing line, and then they put me in the position of line manager, and then finally they put me down here as packing manager. They trained me, and they have let me stay here for seven years." Hannen was not just proud but grateful, grateful that she had been kept in this factory, when everyone knew so many factories forced employees to leave after three or four years.

"Are you glad they have moved you down here now?" I asked her.

"Well, yes. I myself chose to leave my position as the line manager because of the constant tension. Everyone up there is always fighting. I really think the position of machine operator was the best. There, on the line, you have no conflicts, no tensions. Look at the problems I have now. You can see how I must constantly ask the girls, 'Why did you do this? Why didn't you do that?'" She has to force them to do things, and this is tiresome and difficult. The girls often resist her. Girls are hired because, unlike men, they are believed to be highly amenable to control. But they have ways to refuse, however subtle.

•

At lunch, the girls crowded together on the benches, their heads resting on the tables. The fast is difficult and the workers are tired. Few try anymore to convince me that they feel no thirst or hunger. Instead, they openly talk of hunger, thirst, headache, exhaustion. They talk of how they hate to waken in the hour before dawn for the *sahor*, a meal that is eaten in the early morning hours, just moments before the fast will begin anew. They hate to wake in the dark to *sahor*, but without this meal they would be unable to withstand the hours of fasting ahead of them.

It seems, too, that their concerns about religious duty have heightened. In the afternoon, conversations turned to the kinds of prayers recited at the break-fast meal, with Alami instructing the workers on which were most sacred. When I left at the end of the day, Alami was bending over the packing table using the pencil stub from the equipment box to scribble prayers on the backs of unused tags for the girls to take home and read, or have a literate family member read for them, at the moment before they break the fast.

•

Some days later, I hesitantly asked the girls in the packing department whether they would be willing to answer questions for a survey I had written. I told them I wanted to understand exactly what kind of girls worked in the clothing factories of Fes, where they came from, whether they had gone to school, and where their parents were from.[11] I shyly broached the subject, fearing that my new colleagues might find the idea too intrusive. Instead, they met my request with great excitement. "Start right now, ask us here—at the table—while we are working," they urged me. And so, casually, I began to conduct my interviews as we worked.

As the day was drawing to a close, Latifa offered to stay after work to give me detailed information about her life. And so, at the end of the day, Latifa, Hayat, and I left the factory together. We found a quiet spot at the edge of the factory district and sat on a rock wall. Latifa took the interview quite seriously. As I asked each question, she seemed to concentrate intently, thinking in silence before she delivered her answer, holding up her chin, as if she were speaking important words that would carry in the wind. She articulated each of her opinions and each life experience carefully so that I would understand exactly, absolutely, who she was and how she had become this person. She watched and waited approvingly while I wrote down each answer.

Me: What is your name?
Latifa: Latifa
Me: How old are you?
Latifa: I was born in 1977. I am 18.
Me: How long have you been at this factory?

Latifa: For three years.

Me: What is your job specialty?

Latifa: I am in the packing department. I tag the clothing.

Me: Where did you work before this factory?

Latifa: This is the first factory I ever worked in. I have worked here for three years. This is the fourth year I have worked here, all the time in packing. I was unemployed for the past year when the factory closed. I did not work while the factory was being rented to the other company.

Me: Did you like to stay home?

Latifa: (laughing) It was difficult. I did not like it. My mother did not let me go out.

Me: It is difficult to stay home all day?

Latifa: (laughing) It is difficult to work and difficult to stay at home here. Nothing is easy in Morocco. We have a hard life.

Me: Have you done any work other than packing at this factory?

Latifa: No, they have trained me to put the tags on the clothing.

Me: Have you asked them to train you on the sewing machine?

Latifa: I would like to sew on the machine, but they won't let me.

Me: Why not?

Latifa: Well, they would let me, but then I must be in training, and I won't get paid for two or three or four months, until I learn. I need to get paid.

Me: Did you go to school?

Latifa: I went to the fourth grade. But then I failed the grade, and I could not repeat it because my father was sick. You know he's crazy.

Me: Are you married?

Latifa: (laughing) No.

Me: And you don't have children.

Latifa: (laughing) Of course not.

Me: Where do you live?

Latifa: In Merzouga, near the Macro store.

Me: Who lives with you in your house?

Latifa: My mother's brother and his wife.

Me: I mean, who in your family, your immediate family, lives in the same house with you?

Latifa: Oh, my mother's brother and his wife live on the bottom floor of the building we live in. We live on the top floor. On the top floor with us is my mother, my father—but he is crazy—and me and two sisters.

Me: Tell me about these people. For example, what does your mother do? Does she work? And then your sisters.

Latifa: My mother stays home. She used to clean in a pharmaceutical factory when we were younger. Now she stays home and takes care of the house. My older sister is divorced. She was married to my mother's sister's son, but they did not like each other. Now she works in the Skulli factory. She does not have a skill. She does not work on a machine. And my younger sister works at the factory near us—in finishing. She clips threads.

Me: Are there other members of your family who are not living in the house with you now?

Latifa: I have two married sisters who live near us. One is blind and married to a man who saw her in the street and liked her.

Me: Was she always blind?

Latifa: She was born blind. Her eyes are open. She has eyes, and she looks like she can see, but she sees nothing. (Latifa opened her eyes wide and stared, imitating her sister's appearance.) But she can do everything. She can cook, she can do all the housework, she can live with her husband.[12]

Me: How did she learn these things?

Latifa: She went to a school for blind children for a few years. But she did not learn there. She didn't like the school. She always went into the bathroom and sang. We would go to see her there, and the teachers complained to my mother. She is a singer, you see. She sings. We took her out of the school. She sings for money. She knows how to beat the drums, and she now sings for money.

Me: That is amazing. I want to meet her. Could I?

Latifa: Of course. I will bring you to her house when you come to see my father.

Me: And your other sister?

Latifa: She is married to a boy she talked to in the street. It is no good to meet a husband that way. Now she has two girl children, one six and one two. She works at Asitex and earns a good salary: 44,000 a month [2,200 *dirham*]. Yes, this is a lot of money. She went to work because her husband was a mechanic and lost his job. Now she works for him, and he forces her to give him all her money. He is going to marry again, to take a second wife with her money.

Me: This is not possible.

Latifa: I am not joking.

Me: Well, she should leave him. She should leave with her money.

Latifa: To the contrary, she should not leave that house. If she does, it will only make it easy for him to take the second wife and move her in. He has already engaged the second wife.

Me: That is shameful. Where were you born?

Latifa: Fes.

Me: And your parents?

Latifa: They were born in the countryside, on the route to Meknes, on a farm.

Me: Who do you give your salary to, or do you keep it for yourself?

Latifa: I give all my money to my mother. All of us at home, all my sisters at home, give our money to our mother. I keep nothing for myself.

Me: Do you own the house or rent it?

Latifa: It is our house, both the top and the bottom. We share it with my mother's brother. So we don't have to pay rent, only to buy food. My mother uses our money to buy the food. Our father brings in no money—he is crazy, you know.

Me: If you could choose, at what age would you marry?

Latifa: If I could choose, I would marry now. As long as the boy was a good boy, a good family boy, a boy who has a job. (Hayat nodded her head in agreement to this.) If girls like us had money, you know, we would not want to marry young. We would look around at the world, travel, try to understand things. We would wait until we were 25 to marry so that we would have time to understand things. But we have no money, and we want to marry now, because we are tired of the work, tired of the problems in this factory.

Me: Do you want to marry in the traditional way, or would you rather meet the man in the street and come to know him before the wedding?

Latifa: I want to marry in the traditional way. I want the boy to come to my house and ask for me. That is all. I do not want to marry the way my sister married, to a man who she had been speaking to in the street. Once the boy comes to engage me at my house, then I will be willing to go out with him to walk in the street or to sit in a café. But not to his house. I would never go to his house. But I would talk to him to make sure we are compatible and understand each other. But first he must engage me. Then we will talk. Not before.

Me: Do you want to marry a boy from your family, a relative?

Latifa: No, definitely not. My sister married my mother's sister's son because my mother and her sister got together and decided that their children should marry. (And here, Latifa imitated women gossiping.) But my sister did not like the marriage, and now they are divorced. Nothing but problems will come from marriage to a boy in the family.

Here, Latifa paused, and we were silent for a moment. And then she started talking again.

Latifa: I used to go out and walk with our neighbor, a boy who lives near us. For two years, we would walk in the streets and talk about things. He is in the university, but his family is poor. But then I told him not to walk with me anymore.

Me: Why not?

Latifa: Because he started to go walking with other girls. I saw him walking with other girls and told him, "No, do not come back here to walk with me." But he came back and wanted to walk with me again, and I didn't let him, not when he likes other girls. But boys from the university are like that. They want a lot of girls.

Me: Is this when you put on the veil?

Latifa: Well, yes, it is around the same time. I put on the veil after that.

Me: Why?

Latifa: Because I was fed up with the whole world, tired of the way things were. And some girls who live next door to me wear the veil and read the Qur'an. And they began to read to me and teach me. They taught me that people who wear miniskirts and who leave themselves naked will go to hell. And things like that.

So I put on the veil. And now, no one in the street talks to me. Boys do not bother me. I take only the straight path. I don't dil-lydally in the streets.

Me: Do you work only because you need money, or do you work because you like working?

Latifa: I work only because we need money, not because I like to work.

Me: Does your mother approve of your working? Does she like that you work?

Latifa: My mother lets me work because of the situation. We need mon-ey, so this is not a question. My sisters and I must work.

Me: Do you think it is good that girls work nowadays, whereas they did not work in the past?

Latifa: It is good that my sisters and I are working for ourselves since our father is sick. It is good we can take care of ourselves.

Me: But if you had enough money, you would not work outside your house?

Latifa: If a girl or a woman is rich, she should not work. She should study or do handicrafts, like embroidery or sewing in the house. Perhaps she can have her own store, a sewing store or a boutique of her own. But above all she should stay inside; she should not go outside. (Hayat again nodded in agreement.)

Me: But what if a woman is educated to do a particular kind of work, or if she wants to work?

Latifa: This is very different. A woman should work if she is educated; she should be a doctor or a teacher. But this is different because it is good work. It is good work; therefore, it is not shameful. But to be a factory worker is weak work, not good work. (Hayat nodded agreement and added, "Factory work is not clean work.")

Me: Should a girl have freedom to come and go as she pleases, or should her parents control her?[13]

Latifa: A girl should not have freedom. Because if she makes a mistake here in Morocco, she will not be forgiven. It is not like what you have. It is good what you have. [She is referring to what she presumes is sexual freedom in America. Latifa is being polite to me here.] But here in Morocco if a girl goes with a boy and she makes a mistake, she will not be forgiven. He will not marry her, and nobody will marry her. So a girl should be controlled.

Me: But, for example, what about that girl who left the factory with us and stopped and spoke to that boy on the Moped? Was this bad?

Latifa: Oh, no, not at all, because that boy is like her brother.

Me: He is related to her?

Latifa: No, he used to work with us in the factory, so he is like our brother. It is all right if you greet and speak with people who are like your brother.

Me: And a married woman, should she have freedom or be controlled?

Latifa: There is no way a wife should have freedom either. She should respect her husband. She should do everything by her husband's *idn* (permission). She should ask him everything and get permission from him for everything she does. A man rules a woman. But, you know, even boys and men should not have too much freedom. It's not just girls or women.

Me: What do you mean?

Latifa: People just cannot have too much freedom. They will take the wrong path if they don't have the law. They should only have a little freedom. But women should have less freedom than men. (Hayat nodded.)

Me: If your husband told you you could not do something you wanted to do, what would you do?

Latifa: If I had a husband and he told me I could not do something, I would not do it. That is all.

Me: In your family, do men and women mix at parties, or do you stay in separate rooms? And if a man you don't know comes into the house, do you and your sisters sit with him?

Latifa: In our family, men and women do not mix at parties. Each one sits in their own room. And if a man comes into the house, then my mother and I will leave the room unless it is my uncle or a friend of my father's that is very close to him.

Me: Who does the housework in your family?

Latifa: My mother does most of the housework, since we are all working, but we also help. For example, in Ramadan we take turns, each one helping to prepare the food on different nights.

Me: Would you be happy if your husband helped you with housework?

Latifa: I would be very happy if my husband did housework. However, it would be shameful if he did certain things.

Me: Like what?

Latifa: He could not wash dishes or wash the floor. He could not do the laundry unless we had a washing machine.

Me: What could he do?

Latifa: He could help in the cooking, cutting vegetables.

Me: Who is the person you are closest to in your family?

Latifa: My favorite person in the family, who I am closest to, is the wife of my mother's brother. She took me and reared me from the age of 2 to 15—she has no children. I lived with them first in Ourzazate for four years, then east of Fes. We just returned recently to Fes, and only a few years ago I moved upstairs to live with my mother. I prefer my uncle's wife to my mother, and my mother prefers her other daughters to me. My mother does not really like me. She is jealous of my relationship with her brother's wife.

Me: Is this true?

Latifa: Whenever I go downstairs to talk with her, my mother says, "Why are you talking to her?" She is jealous.

Me: Who is more important in your family—your father's family or your mother's family?

Latifa: They are the same, because my mother and father are cousins through two brothers. But really, we have no family. We have a small family. My father used to have a brother, but now, since he has gone crazy, the brother never sees us anymore.

Me: What do you think is the difference between yourself and your mother?

Latifa: The difference is that my mother did not study at all, and she does not know things.

Me: If I were to write a book about you and your life, about factory girls and their lives, what would you want me to say about you?

Latifa: God have mercy on me. Send me a good boy, a family man, to marry me and work for me and to let me stop working. And God make it easy for us. And God do not let me and my sisters keep working. And God look down upon us.

I thanked Latifa for the interview, and she, squished between me and Hayat, thanked me. I told the girls they had better hurry home, because their parents would wonder where they were. "This is not a problem," they quickly responded. "We'll tell our parents we were forced to work late."

And then Latifa volunteered, "The owners of this factory are very good people." Hayat agreed, and both girls, to my astonishment, began to praise the factory owners. "The man who ran this factory before, before this owner came in to manage it, was an evil man," Latifa said. "He was a womanizer. He would choose a beautiful girl and ask her to go out with him and tell her if she refused she would be fired."

"Did anything like this happen to you?"

"When I began working here, three years ago, before last year, that is, Alami's sister who at that time was manager of packing, told me that if he approached me I should turn away. This was before I was veiled, and I wore kohl on my eyes. So soon after I had come into the factory, he came down to the packing area and asked, 'Who is the new girl?' I turned my back to him. After that, he never bothered me."

"But these owners are different," Hayat began. "For example, once, when we worked overtime, late into the night, the owner drove each of us home and waited while each girl got into her house. These owners are not like most rich people in Morocco."

"Rich people in Morocco do not care at all for the poor people. The poor people are ants, they are flies. They can be stamped on," and Latifa imitated a person stamping on an insect, rubbing it with her foot into the ground. "This owner told us that he himself used to be poor," Latifa continued. And so both girls agreed that they "have not yet had enough of these owners," that they "have not yet grown tired of them." And that is why they do not want to work at another factory, even though they earn so little where they are. The owners are good people.

"Money is meaningless. Money goes away in a day. It flies away. It does not stay with you. It is the people you know who matter," Hayat asserted. "And that, too, is why we cannot ask for more money from the owners. Because the owners are good to us, so we are ashamed to ask for more. The owner has said to us, 'If you need something, tell me and I will help you.' But we are ashamed. It would be shameful to ask him for anything. So we ask him for nothing."

"Perhaps you should ask him to pay you more," I suggested. They did not respond.

I was bewildered by the conversation. Perhaps, I thought, these girls don't trust me. Perhaps they think I am going back to the owner with what they say. But the girls' delivery was so heartfelt, so impassioned, I felt it was somehow genuine. I believe that at that moment the girls were expressing real loyalty to the people and the organization they had served for almost four years. And their willingness to provide their service as loyal clients to a patron upon whom they depended is a cornerstone of the factory's power over its workers. Workers envision the factory as a family and often speak of the owner as a father figure who is eager to protect them. Factory owners play this role: they provide bus service to take the girls from their homes to the factory and thus prevent them from moving through the streets. In this factory, shortly after our interview, the owner instituted a ruling that prevented any of the working girls from leaving the factory on foot: all workers would be taken home in factory transport. This edict was the result of rumors, I was told, that many of the factory girls were dallying on the streets outside the building after work, speaking to boys. The owners are fathers, and the workers are daughters and sisters to each other. In this way, the factory makes sense.[14]

We continued to sit as the sun was beginning to set. My friends did not seem to want to leave. So I asked them another question. "I have heard that in some families, the parents do not let girls marry because they want their earnings from the factory. Is this true?" Both girls said this often happens.

"Sometimes," Latifa explained, "the parents make a deal with the boy, saying, 'We will give you this girl if you let her continue to give us part of her salary.' And sometimes they just refuse to let the girl go, and the girl keeps quiet because she knows she must help her parents." Sons, they said, will not help the family like this. They are not like daughters.

More time passed, and I told the girls they must get home before dark. Hayat and I separated from Latifa, whose home was in the opposite direction from ours. Before Hayat and I parted ways, she burst out spontaneously that the problem in families is the boys. "My brother," she said quietly and bitterly, "just left his job. He quit because he had a fight with his boss. We have been begging him to go back, but he won't go. We need his help. But this is how boys are." This outburst was fast, immediate, and when I questioned her on the situation, Hayat did not want to pursue it. We came to the place where the road to our homes separated. I wished her good night and thanked her for helping me. "*Denia hniya*," Hayat replied, a phrase she used all the time, which means something like "The world is good."

•

It was a cold Friday morning and when I arrived at work, I found the packing workers huddled in the corner, where they sat every day, waiting for the 7:30 whistle. I joined them there. Sylvie does not like them to be there, they told me. She wants them to stay in the center of the room, where they can be seen. But they don't always obey.

With the sound of the whistle, they dragged themselves to the work table, where they carried on conversations, punctuated by giggles and sporadic silences made interesting by someone's soft singing. The comfortable chatter was silenced only by the occasional realizations that Sylvie was near, or standing at the railing, staring down at us. According to factory regulations, workers are forbidden to speak while they are working. Latifa and Hayat told me that before the factory had closed for a year, policy was that they suffered a pay deduction if caught talking. Often after I had stood for hours listening to their conversation, one of them would politely say, "Excuse us for bothering you with our talk. We talk to make the day pass. If we do not talk, the day gets longer and longer." The tedium of standing for ten or more hours, checking seams or ticketing jackets is, for me, unbearable. I know that they suffer this tedium as well, for every few minutes someone asks Mina the time. Mina is the only one in packing who seems to have a watch.

Eventually, as happened so often now, the conversation around the work table turned to Naima's betrothal. Since she had announced her sudden engagement, Naima had decided that she was, in fact, too young to marry. Her father, though, had given his word—he had promised Naima to another man, or more specifically, to the son of another man—so Naima would not tell her father that she did not want to marry. She planned to get married to keep her father's commitment and to protect his good name.

Naima's co-workers were distressed by this situation and were pleading with her to reconsider her actions. Hayat was particularly perturbed. "If a girl is going to get married, her father must ask her, 'Do you want this or not?' If she does not want the marriage, she must say very clearly, 'No, I do not want this. I do not want this marriage.'" She repeated this several times, earnestly, emphasizing her words for Naima's benefit. "The father must ask, and the daughter must tell him what she wants. Naima must tell her father. Because she will marry, and it will soon become obvious that she did not want to marry, and she will not like him and will soon be divorced." Hayat turned away from the work table, frustrated at her inability to convince the stubborn Naima. "How many boys came for me when I was younger," she told me, "and each time my father asked me, 'Do you want this marriage or not?' And each time, I said no. I refused marriage more than three times because I knew I was too young."

Hayat then began to tell the story of her sister, as a kind of cautionary tale for Naima.

"Look at my sister, for example. She is only 17, and six months pregnant. She will not even know how to care for her baby. She will not know how to raise a baby. She is too young."

"But didn't your sister want the marriage?" I asked.

"Yes, she wanted to marry. My father asked her, and she said yes. She was only 16, and she wanted to marry." And Hayat made a sign twirling her finger near her head, indicating she thought her sister was crazy. Hayat's sister, I knew, had worked in a sewing factory since she was 12. Perhaps, I thought, she is not so crazy. Maybe she, like Naima, had figured on marriage as a way out of the factory.

And then the subject of Naima's national identity card came to the fore. Naima's birth, some fifteen years ago, was never officially registered. As a result of the engagement, her parents had begun the paperwork to secure her a national identity card so that she could legally marry. Alami had a suggestion which would allow Naima to avoid this marriage and at the same time protect her father's honor. "The courts will not let you marry if the card shows your proper age, you know. One has to be at least 16 to marry in Morocco, and you say you are only 15." Her parents planned to register her as older than she is, in order to facilitate the marriage. "Fifteen years old is too young to marry," Alami insisted. "You must not allow them to revise your age. If the state knows you are only 15, they will not permit you to marry. And then you can avoid this marriage without causing your father any shame."

Everyone at the table agreed with this plan. Naima listened quietly, showing no reaction. And Alami launched into another short lecture. "Naima must not get married now, because when a girl marries so young, it is like her life is over, lost. She gets very old very quickly. She starts having children. She gets locked in the house. Her husband watches her, and she cannot move. She can no longer go out. She can no longer experience life. Naima will have no experience of life if she gets married now."

And Alami was motivated to tell a long story about her own life and how she had always preferred other things to marriage. "When I was young, my mother always urged me to think of marriage. But I could think only of becoming a doctor or perhaps an engineer. I thought I would work, not marry. And when I went to the agricultural school and began to work with the farmers, I never thought of marriage. I adored this work. Only now have I begun to think of marriage. Only now, and only because I am working in this sewing factory."

Naima listened to Alami and to this story, which reflected a life so unlike her own. Again she said nothing.

•

The next day we in the packing department were in crisis. After having packed one thousand jackets in boxes to be sent out by 2:00 p.m., Hannen discovered that she was still holding thirty-six size 6 tags, which meant that thirty-six jackets had not been tagged. Hannen was panicked. We all knew, as Sylvie had often reminded us, "The shipping deadlines are death." Like the others, I was terrified. It didn't matter that I didn't really work here. We began furiously opening boxes and looking at all 1,000 jackets, while Hannen reviewed her lists. Shortly before 2:00, we found the carton of mistagged jackets. We retagged them.

When we could relax, the girls looked at me and said, as if proving a point, "And now you see, don't you, what we mean when we tell you we have problems here. These are the kinds of problems we have. Do you see how hard this work is?"

And Hayat said that in the past, it was even worse. In the past, the trucks would come and go constantly, shipments all the time. "This is nothing compared to how it used to be. It used to be even harder."

•

I had begun to ask workers at the lunch tables if they would be willing to answer my survey questions. The next evening, as we exited the building, girls began to crowd around me. Everyone had heard about the survey and all of them were eager to tell me about themselves. It was as if they wanted to hear themselves speak about who they were and have this information committed to paper. Hayat pushed through the group to bring me a young girl who desperately wanted to be interviewed. She was 15, very tiny, and very excited to speak with a foreigner. I went down my list of questions, and when I asked her if she was married, she said, quite proudly, "No, I have a boyfriend." The crowd around us giggled. "Please come with me," she continued, "to meet my boyfriend. He is waiting for me now, on the main road." She thought I might be interested in meeting him, because she had heard that foreigners always have boyfriends.

"No," I told her. "Not all foreigners have boyfriends. Anyway, you are still too young. You should not have a boyfriend now." Everyone in the crowd was listening carefully to my response. I knew I should not be telling her what to do, but I could not stop myself. She was such a small girl. It was no good for her to have a boyfriend. On hearing this exchange, Zaynab volunteered to the crowd that she would marry this summer.

"Do you want to marry?" I asked her.

"No, it is my father who wants this."

The crowd rose in discontent. Everyone admonished her, much as the packing girls had told Naima, "You do not have to marry against your wishes. Your father cannot force you!" Finally as the girls began to disperse, a small and dirty girl waited until the others had disappeared. She was anxious to speak with me alone. Her name was Sama, and she was one of five workers who had answered my survey questions in the lunchroom. For some reason, when she spoke, everything she said seemed to make the other girls at the table laugh. When I had asked her if she was educated, she said that she had left school in the sixth grade. Now, alone and without an audience, she wanted to explain to me why she had left school. "I left because I saw other girls who worked in factories, and I wanted to work to buy clothing and lipstick." She said, "My father begged me not to leave school. Soon after I left, he told me I could return, that he could get me a doctor's note explaining my absence, and I could go back. But I didn't want to go. And then, a year after leaving school, I regretted this decision terribly. I wanted to go back to school, but my father said to me, 'Daughter, I cannot get you a doctor's note for a year. It is too late.'" Now she was terribly regretful. She wanted me to know this.

We walked together to the bus stop.

.

The next morning, both company transport buses broke down en route to the factory, and workers came dragging in an hour late. Before they arrived, Latifa, Hayat, and I stood alone at the packing table, folding jackets. Another packing worker, Ilham, sat in the back corner, doubled over in stomach pain. Ilham asked me to go find Sylvie and to tell her she was ill. Normally, Hannen would speak for her, but Hannen was not there yet. I went to Sylvie's office and Sylvie followed me back to the packing room, yelling. She berated the girl, "Why did you even come here if you are really sick?" Then Sylvie yelled at me, saying I should know that Ilham needed only to come to her office to get permission to exit the factory. Sylvie had never liked me, and she seemed to be liking me less and less as the days wore on. I told Ilham she needed to go to Sylvie's office, and she followed Sylvie back upstairs.

"Sylvie will never believe Ilham is sick when she is wearing clothing like that," Hayat whispered as the two walked away. Ilham was wearing fancy western clothing—tight jeans and a brightly colored shirt. Latifa agreed.

"She should have worn a *djellaba* and head scarf today," she said. "That would have been a more convincing outfit for a sick person." I did not know if Sylvie would have felt more sympathetic toward Ilham had she been wearing a *djellaba*.

•

I knew that Sylvie no longer liked me or my presence in her factory, and I could not bear her demeaning treatment of the workers. "I don't like Sylvie at all," I admitted out loud.

"She was worse before, when we were here before the factory closed," Latifa said. "She used to scream like crazy. And she used to take our fingerprints when we talked and then she would take money away from our paycheck. Everyone is afraid of her. Even when they are sick, they are afraid to go to her office."

"We are cows here. We have no value," Hayat said. "People can just yell at us; they can do as they like to us, like Sylvie does. We have no value. If we were *muweddaf* (civil servants, professional workers), we would have a value, but they give us no value here. We bear this only because we have to. We are not educated. That is why we are here."

The other workers had finally arrived and joined us at the table, and the girls started to talk about why they work. Hayat said, "Titia, I was *glesa* (sitting, unemployed) for a year and four months, and that time felt like a week to me. I stayed at home and did the housework. I loved it. I work here only because of our situation. If I could, I would stay home. My mother does not yell at me like Sylvie does."

Hannen disagreed vehemently. "Listen, Hayat, even if a girl has enough money, she cannot stay home. If you stay home, you soon become the maid for the entire family. In the morning you are cleaning floors, and at night when people come home you are still doing housework."

"Is this why you are doing this job?" I asked Hannen, who had mentioned to me several times that her family did not need her money.

"Oh, yes," she said, "but also I need money. It is not that I don't need money.

My family would never give me money to buy nice clothing or gold, or to shop around town, to buy clothes."

Mina, a girl who rarely said anything, spoke up. "I cannot stay at home all day, because the situation there is too difficult for me to bear."

"What is the problem?" the others asked.

"I am less than my siblings. I feel inferior to all my sisters and brothers. My parents, I know, prefer the others over me."

"How could this be?" I asked her.

"This is because I wasn't raised there. When I was little, they gave me to my father's mother. I lived in a small village to the north of here. I only came here to live with them four years ago, when my grandmother got ill. My parents feel like I am not really their daughter. But still, they won't let me go back to see my grandmother now, because they know I will stay there if I return to her."

The conversation dwindled. And then a few moments later, Alami, who had not yet said anything, said, "Wouldn't it be wonderful just to stay at home all day and do housework? I would wake in the morning, leisurely eat my breakfast, listen to music as I cleaned the floors, cook lunch, and in the afternoon, after sleeping for a few hours, I would get up and make pancakes and something light for the evening meal."

"I would always make couscous for lunch on Fridays and lentils on Saturday," Hannen joined in. And then the girls began to trade recipes and discuss cooking methods, a topic they so often arrived at, a topic that helped them, I think, remember that they are not really factory workers, they are first and foremost Moroccan girls, on their way to becoming Moroccan women—wives and mothers.

At one point, Hannen needed extra packing boxes and she sent Naima and Fatima Zahara to the basement to carry some up. The girls looked at each other and dashed from the table, racing each other to the basement. When they returned, Hannen reprimanded them for their silliness. I was sent with them on the next trip to prevent any misbehavior. So many of these workers, I was reminded, are almost still children.[15]

The afternoon passed. In the evening, when the factory group dispersed, I found Sama again waiting to speak with me. She wanted to tell me more about leaving school, but this time the story was different. "The truth about me leaving school is different from what I told you before. What happened is that my father came to me and said, 'My daughter, you now know how to read and write. You can write a letter, and you can read signs. You know enough of reading and writing, and you know enough French to speak to a foreigner'"—and here she gestured to me, indicating she was communicating with me, a foreigner, although we were speaking in Moroccan Arabic. "And he said, 'So please, daughter, you can see the situation we are in. Please can you now leave school and try to get work to help us?' I could see the situation we were in, and so I left school. He gave me the choice," she assured me. "This is how he spoke to me. But I knew the situation." Sama wanted to be certain I understood that her father did not force her to leave school. He had offered her a choice—a choice which we both knew was really no choice at all.

She spent three months looking for a job. She only looked in this factory district, as she lives nearby, and the other districts are too far from her home, and the bus fare is too expensive for her even to go there to look. Finally, they allowed her into this factory. She is clipping threads.

"I am only a girl," she said, "and I am carrying all the weight in our family. I am the one who worries about buying the wheat and the oil." Sama was aware of her poverty. I asked her about her father and the older brother I knew lived at home. "My father can only find work occasionally, and my brother spends all his earnings in cafés and on hashish. The boys today are no good."

"A lot of the girls tell me this."

"Listen, I know I am the first girl to tell you the truth about things. The others say, 'You must work, so don't complain, don't talk about it.' But you should know exactly how it is for me."

We arrived at the bus stop, and Sama urged me to join her family for the break-fast meal one night soon. I looked at her in her filthy clothing. She looked worse than most of the other workers, as if she could not afford to buy soap to wash. I suddenly felt very tired. I assured her I would come soon. This was the gracious response required of a polite invitation.

•

The next morning work was slow. Several lines had come to a halt, and few jackets were making their way to the packing department. We stood at the table pretending to be busy, checking the seams of the same jacket for minutes at a time. The factory had begun producing big, bright, puffy, fiber-filled snow coats, and they were piling up all around us. Down in the packing department the girls were taking turns sneaking away from the work table, posing amidst the jackets, lying on top of the jackets, pretending they were being photographed. From time to time someone would run behind a pile of jackets and pretend to hide from Sylvie, sending ripples of hushed laughter across the table.

But soon the fun was ruined by the sound of Sylvie's screaming coming from her office above. The workers knew already what had happened. "A girl is being told to leave the factory," they told me. "Yesterday she slapped Absellem, the manager of her sewing line, in the face." Apparently the worker had asked the line leader for permission to go to the bathroom, and he refused to give it to her. She left her seat anyway to head for the restroom. When she stood up, Absellem slapped her. She slapped him back. Now she would be fired.

"This is terrible," I said, and the girls agreed it was terrible that he hit her.

"There used to be other managers who hit the workers, before the closing of last year, but they are all gone now," Latifa said. Almost every girl agreed that if Absellem had hit her, she would certainly have hit him back. And, they agreed, it was shameful that this girl was to be fired because of the incident. To explain why the girl now had to leave, Latifa said to me, "We have strange customs. In Morocco, a man can hit a woman, but a woman must never ever hit a man. Even if he hits her, she must never hit him back."

"But things are changing," someone said, "due to the king, Hassan II. He has given women their rights. He has made laws so that a man cannot simply introduce a second wife but must get the permission of the first wife. And he has changed the divorce laws, giving women more rights in divorce." No one responded to this.

Hayat did not participate in this discussion at all. This incident was not to be taken lightly. It bothered her. "This woman is married," Hayat said solemnly, shaking her head. "This woman is a married woman. She is married." For Hayat, this fact changed everything about this incident. "She is working here only for herself, for her own benefit. Her husband told her she does not have to work. She works to buy gold and clothing. And now this terrible thing has occurred: she has been hit by a man and she has hit him back, all because she is working in this factory." And Hayat went on, "This woman should not complain about being hit. If she wants to work in this factory, she works here because she must work. That is all. So she should just be quiet and not complain about things. She has to bear it." Hayat put an end to the discussion.

For Hayat, the incident was shameful. But the shame rested not so much with Absellem, the man who hit, but with the woman herself—not necessarily for hitting back but for choosing factory work in the first place, when it was not necessary. Hayat, I felt as she spoke, was reflecting her own personal humiliation attached to working in the factory. Workers had told me that girls in the factory are treated like "cows," like "dogs," like "maids," that they are not respected as professional working women—bureaucrats, teachers, doctors—are respected. Hayat frequently said that the factory was not a "clean" place to work. No one, in her view, should choose work such as this. Such "unclean" work is entered into only out of absolute need, like her own.[16]

Marriage should put a female in a position where she has a husband to support her and thus automatically should relieve her of this sort of work. This woman's error, then, for Hayat, was that she chose this work. She chose to transgress the rules of marriage, in which the husband should support his wife. This woman chose to tamper with the proper gender arrangements, and she suffered the consequences. As Hayat had once told me, "I would never marry if the man expected me to work in a factory. Why should I? If my husband asked me to go to work, I would go home and work for my mother and father." By definition, marriage should relieve the girl of factory work—of the need to support herself or anyone else.

The conversation ended and the day wore on until finally the dismissal bell rang. I collected my jacket and joined the stream of workers headed for the door. There was chatter and confusion as to whether we would work the following day, a Saturday. Finally, just as we passed out the gate, the news that the factory would be closed the next day spread through the crowd. The blinding afternoon sun hit my face and I breathed a sigh of relief.

•

The next workday began with the girls bickering amongst themselves. Hannen instructed a young worker to move a pile of coats from one side of the room to another, and the girl refused. Even Hannen's threats to tell Sylvie that "this girl does not work at all" did not motivate her. Finally Alami gently reminded the girl, "She is the manager here," and the girl relented. Her resistance spurred Fatima Zahara, who then refused to carry jackets down from the roof, where they had been hung to dry. Latifa stepped in to soothe Fatima Zahara and urge her to cooperate, which eventually she did. Workers comply immediately with Sylvie's demands and reveal no emotion. But with the floor managers, who are closer to peers, the workers often argue, expressing anger and defending their work. Ultimately, though, they understand that they must comply, and they do.

It was not long before the bickering subsided and we settled into a quiet mood. Inevitably, conversation began, and our topic turned quickly to marriage. Alami told a story she had recently heard about a girl living in the town where her sister teaches. This girl was raped. She brought her attacker to court, and he was forced by the law to marry her. The girls heartily endorsed this course of events, as they all agreed that the rape had destroyed her chances for marriage to another man: she was "lost," "wasted." No man but her attacker would be willing to marry her.

And then everyone complained about how nobody could find a husband anymore. Hayat and Latifa together argued that this is simply because men are poor and unemployed and therefore unable to pay the bride price. But Hannen asserted that they were wrong. "The problem today is that girls nowadays go out with boys and do everything with them, and so why should boys marry girls? Girls are available to boys without marriage. This is our problem."

Hayat did not see it this way at all. With great intensity she asked Hannen, "How many boys are there who want to marry, but they can't? They can't set the engagement because they have no jobs." Hayat's voice was hushed for fear of Sylvie, but impassioned. Poverty—not the bad behavior of girls—was preventing them all from marriage, she was certain of this. I knew that Hayat had three older brothers who were jobless, destitute, without prospects, and of the proper age for marriage. I knew Hayat was arguing for them.

•

Today, because the truck with the imported fabric was delayed on the road, the factory could not continue production. The packing department alone was told to report to work to catch up on garments produced but untagged. We arrived at 7:30 and the factory was quiet, dead. Sylvie did not arrive until an hour later, so we could not begin working until then as the packing equipment was locked in her office. Nobody complained about this fact, even though the pay cards would be marked with an 8:30 start time.

Hannen had brought in more photos of her sister's wedding. She showed us the pictures of women dressed in glamorous caftans against the backdrop of a large and luxuriously furnished house, certain we would be impressed. Hannen said her father was rich, that he worked in metal and made a lot of money. The girls gathered around the album, expressing admiration for the beauty of the wedding. Some got up and danced, imitating wedding dances. They tried on each other's *djellaba*s and giggled. The general silliness continued even after Sylvie's arrival, due in part to her lack of surveillance on this day when so few workers were present.

In the quiet of the factory I surveyed several more workers. After helping me with Latifa's interview, Hayat had invited me to her home so that I could interview her mother. When we finished the work, the packing group left the factory together. The girls strolled through the factory district, leaning on each other, giggling in the streets. Alami and Hannen walked slightly ahead of the group in keeping with their status as managers. All were heading toward the public bus stop because the company bus was not provided today.

As we strolled, a young man pedaling a Moped somehow ran his vehicle right into several workers, whose arms were locked together. This set the group into giggling hysterics. The man moved on, and the girls, in a fit of silliness, waved at two young men on another Moped, who honked back. With this, Hayat became annoyed. "Stop laughing," she said. "Don't laugh in the street. It is not right to laugh in the street." She was wearing a scarf that completely covered her hair and obscured her face, in the style of a *hijab*. Normally her head was bare, even in the streets, although I had noticed that she seemed to be covering it more during Ramadan.

"Why, Hayat?" I asked. "Why can't they laugh in the street? Is it because it is Ramadan?" My very question set the others into a fresh fit of giggling.

"No," said Hayat, "not just because it is Ramadan. It's just not right for girls to laugh in the street. Girls should go straight. Look at me. I look straight ahead, I don't speak with boys, and I don't laugh and talk in the street." Hayat had separated herself slightly from the group in delivering this speech, which only I was still hearing. We soon said good-bye to the rest and headed through a nearby popular neighborhood toward her home.

We walked down a paved road, lined with large, expensive houses, and Hayat pointed to a grand villa. It seemed to rise up out of the dusty road, with bright green tiles covering the roof and a wall that hid a garden. This, she said, was the home of her mother's sister, whose husband was the wealthy owner of a shoe factory. I was stunned by the sight of this house. Hayat, I knew, was poor. Why didn't her family get help from this branch? "Why doesn't your brother—the one who just left his job—get work in that shoe factory? Surely they would hire him?"

"My brother is a bookbinder. He has a skill; he does clean work. To work in a shoe factory is dirty. It is filthy work, and he would not want to do that. Not when he has the clean kind of skill that he has." Hayat, I thought, has no control over her brother. So I made no more suggestions.

The paved road soon gave way to the dirt roads that predominate in the interior of the popular neighborhoods, and we began to pass the houses. Some were in process, large gray concrete structures whose top floors were empty shells yet to be built. Some seemed impermanent—shanties patched together with wood, sheet metal, and other materials. "The government is slowly moving people out of houses like that," Hayat told me, "and giving them land to build on."

"Why can't your family secure some land from the government then?" I asked her directly. I knew that Hayat paid rent.

"My father does not have any idea of how to work with the government," she said with frustration and what I detected to be disgust in her voice. "He is not savvy at all." She seemed unwilling to explain any further. And I thought, Hayat has no control over her father. And once more I stopped asking.

Finally we arrived at a large bright blue metal door and passed through it into a dirt yard littered with scrawny trees and small concrete boxes, which were one-room houses. Children in small groups were running around the enclosure. To the far right, against the concrete wall that surrounded this enclave, was the single concrete room that Hayat's family inhabited. It had a bright blue lean-to built against it, made out of a heavy plastic tarp held up by and sticks, which was used as their kitchen. Against the concrete wall there was a chicken pen, and sitting next to the pen, peeling large green beans and throwing the skins to the chickens, sat Hayat's little sister, Wafa. The rent for this little patch of housing, Hayat told me, is extremely high—500 *dirham* a month—more than either she or her sister earns in a month at the factory. For those who had not secured a piece of government land, life is particularly expensive.

I walked over to the chicken pen, not because I wanted to see the chickens but because I was not sure where to look at the moment. Hayat encouraged me. "Look carefully. Take a good look at the chickens." She then led me, holding on to my elbow, around the dirt yard, so I could look at the other houses there and the toilet used by everyone in this compound. Hayat's mother, who had seen us enter the yard from inside their room, called out, "Hayat, what are you doing? Where are you bringing her?"

"I am showing her the yard."

"Why?"

"Because she needs to look. She needs to see. She is doing research." When Hayat had invited me to her house, she had said, "This way, you can see how we are living." She was determined to be thorough. Hayat had an intensity that I admired.

We returned and entered the room. Hayat's mother sat at the end of the room, rubbing the back of the infant she cares for, the baby of a neighbor who works in a factory and whose husband is unemployed. Hayat's elder brother sat in the center of the room binding books. Wafa finished peeling the beans and followed us into the room.

The family comes from the countryside far to the east of Fes, close to the Algerian border, near the city of Guercif, a region devastated by drought. They came to Fes some ten years ago, after selling off what was left of their sheep. Drought had killed much of the herd and rendered their land infertile. They came to Fes in search of work. They retain hold of their land in the east, which is useless because of persistent drought.

Now, living in this single room, are the father, who is too old to work, the mother, who has never worked outside the household, Hayat's elder brother, the bookbinder who had recently left his job, a younger brother apprenticed to a bookbinder, 14-year-old Wafa, who works in a garment factory, and a 10-year old boy who is in school. There are two married sisters who live with their husbands' families, and two more elder brothers, unmarried, who live and work in other cities.

Hayat had told her family about me and how I liked to interview people. Her mother was eager to tell me the story of her life and she launched right in. Throughout the afternoon, the elder brother interrupted frequently, rephrasing his mother's words, adding and correcting information. Always, when he spoke, his mother and sisters stopped speaking, and we all listened to him.

Hayat's mother quickly told me she had borne twelve children, all in the house, without the help of a doctor. "At 16 I was married to my father's brother's son, when I knew nothing." The man was twenty years her senior. "Immediately, I began to have children. I had twelve in all. Three of them died. But I was strong then."

"And we knew nothing then," interjected the brother. "We knew nothing because we lived in the countryside." He seemed to think he needed to explain the number of children or perhaps their deaths. He needed, too, I thought, to reassure me that he himself was far more urbane. He was not a country person, in the same category as his mother.

"My sisters had already come into the city," the mother explained, "but we remained on our land. Back then I really knew nothing. I was afraid to go outside."

Hayat and Wafa now supported the family. They gave their earnings to their mother, who then paid the rent and utility bill (there is a television and an electric light in this room) and to buy food. The elder brother, having left his job, had no earnings, and the two younger brothers earned no money. The two older brothers lived in the north of Morocco and supported themselves, but they could not contribute much. As Hayat and her mother explained, "Boys must prepare their own futures. They must save their money for themselves, to prepare for their own marriages. Boys are not like girls." The father was old and so did nothing. "He is too old. He has only a few teeth left in his head. He has nothing left," said Hayat's mother, brushing her hand to signify nothingness.

"Look at the way we are living," she said. I felt, as I so often did, as if they thought I could save them, that I could save this family who had so little hope of something better. When Hayat showed me the interior of their makeshift kitchen, she followed us in. "This is not clean, you see," she said. "We have not always lived like this, you know." She assured me they had been in this single room for only six months. They had spent several years living on the ground floor of a villa under construction, as guardians of a vacant structure being built by her sister's husband's son. They had moved about frequently in Fes.

We talked late into the afternoon. And finally, when I was going to leave, I asked Hayat and her mother, "Do you think it was better, in the past, when the girls did not work in factories?"

"Definitely not," Hayat responded immediately. "It is better today."

"Yes," her mother said. "It is better today because in the past, women did not go to the *hammam* (public bath). They bathed at home. Today they can go to the *hammam* and to the doctor. And this is better."

"How has the factory work changed your daughter?" I asked. "I mean, what is different now about Hayat? What is the difference between you two?"

"Hayat knows how to go places. My daughter knows how to walk in the streets," said the mother.

"My mother does not like to go places. She cannot go to the market alone. She doesn't like to walk in the streets alone. She is afraid. If she goes to the market, she must take only one street—she knows only one way to the market— and if she takes another street, she will immediately be lost. And if she is in the streets and it begins to get dark, she will immediately get lost. Even if she is on the right street, she will not know how to get home, and she will become too frightened."

"I am from the countryside, you know. Women there do not go out," the mother tried to explain.

"When we first came here to the city," the brother added, "my mother was frightened to go into the streets. She was so frightened that when she went out of the house into the street, her knees would shake. She would say that she was ashamed, that she felt everyone was looking at her."

"Still," the mother said, "even today, I cannot speak to anyone in the street.

I am too embarrassed to speak in the street. Even if I see a member of the family, even a kinsman, I cannot greet him in the street. I am too embarrassed to speak in the streets. And when we go home, back to the countryside, I do not go out. I just stay at home. There, women don't go into the streets. It is too shameful. And so the real difference between me and my daughter is that my daughter is smart, she is awake, she is aware. She knows how to walk in the streets. If she gets lost, she knows how to ask people questions in the streets. She does not feel shame in the streets."

"I am not afraid," Hayat said. "I go to work, and I come home alone. If it gets dark and I am still in the street, I am not afraid. I know how to walk home."

"It is much better to be like Hayat than like me," said her mother. "My daughter is better. She is smart. It is not good to spend your entire life in your house. Hayat is better."

"It is better this way. People should go to school, so they can read the numbers on the bus and read the signs on the streets. People need to go out. They need to read," Hayat added, stressing each phrase, as if she wanted to teach me this, convince me of this.

When I asked Hayat what she would say in a book about factory girls, she said immediately, as if she had planned her response, "I want to live well and to get a good clean apartment, to get it well furnished and to make life good for my family, to live well with my family, before I marry."

I felt amazed by Hayat, how she was so fierce and determined. I thought about how we had walked here and how the others were laughing in the streets, but Hayat would not laugh publicly. She would not risk drawing attention to herself. She does not want that kind of shame. She knows how to move through the streets, and she takes this responsibility seriously. Every day she travels back and forth to the factory, without fear. She has learned a skill—she knows the work of the factory. Hayat seems to understand that this is not quite enough, but she knows that it is something.[17]

•

The next day, Hannen started giving me directions the moment I arrived. "Titia, go to Sylvie's office and tell her that you want to know what we should do with these other jackets that are left." There were hundreds of jackets piled everywhere. "Tell her," Hannen instructed me, "that you are wondering what kind of tags we should put on these jackets. Don't tell her that it is me who is asking. Just act like you want to know." Since my arrival, Hannen had increasingly been trying to force me to intercede with Sylvie for her. I had taken on the job of collecting the packing equipment every morning to alleviate some of the girls' fears of Sylvie. But Hannen was constantly pushing me to talk to Sylvie whenever we ran short of tags or when she had any confusion over the correct method of tagging the inventory. And I, fearing Sylvie myself and not wanting to become so involved in the running of the packing department, found myself constantly resisting her.

I didn't want to confront Hannen, because I knew I needed her support. We worked around that table, all of us together. If I was not cooperating with Hannen, I suspected the others would not approve. But neither did I want to deal with Sylvie. So, to delay things, I said, "Hannen, why don't you first count all of your tags, and then I will go and ask." Hannen consented, and ultimately my delaying tactics worked. By the end of the morning, I had placed myself in a position where I had little, if any, responsibility for the packing. Hannen kept telling me to count boxes as we were packing the export, and I kept saying, "Okay, but you better count again yourself, Hannen, to be certain." Finally I felt she had gotten the message.

CHAPTER 4

Final Days

On Monday, I woke up feeling ill. I was too sick to stand up and did not go to the factory. On Tuesday, I took myself to a doctor in the center of Fes. When he heard that I had been working in a factory, he told me that the factory was what had made me ill. The factory, he knew, was damp and drafty. "The cold has gotten into your body in that factory," he said. "It is as if it cannot escape." There was little I could do about it now, he told me. "Now you are sick." On the walk home, I ran into a worker I had met months earlier, who was employed in a factory in the center of the city. She said she was not surprised to see I was ill. "The sickness," she told me with certainty, "is from the atmosphere in the factory. You are inhaling tiny particles of fabric, which is making your eyes ache and giving you a cold. Girls always get sick when they begin working. You will get used to it," she said, and she encouraged me to endure.

I stayed away from the factory for a week, tired and sick and, as the days wore on, increasingly dreading my return to the monotony, the endless standing, and the cold. I thought about how I hated the work in the factory. On Sunday night it rained, and the rain turned to sleet for a few minutes. I thought about how cold the concrete floor in the factory would be. On Monday, I got up and went back to work.

•

I took my place at the table downstairs in the packing department. No one at the table was speaking, as if the cold which made their fingers less nimble had frozen their thoughts as well. As we began checking seams, we watched as one line of machine workers, slightly visible to us, stood up and walked into the lunchroom. No one knew exactly why the sewing line had moved like that, and no one seemed particularly interested. But I had never seen the routine stop so abruptly, and I needed to know what was happening. I snuck up the steps to watch.

The fabric had not yet been cut for assembly, and several lines of machine sewers had been sent to the lunchroom to wait for the fabric for their lines. During my week's absence from the factory I had had time to worry about whether or not my research was going as planned. I had been able to experience factory labor, to speak endlessly with workers, to get a glimpse into their daily lives. But I did not have enough hard data on the makeup of the factory population. Where did these workers come from, as a group? What kinds of families did they come from? How many siblings did they have? How many really were married? How many were poor, and how poor were they, compared with others in the city of Fes? I knew I needed to survey as many of the workers as possible, in a consistent manner, but as a worker myself, I had had very little chance to do so. During my week off, I began to wonder how long I would be able to stay at the factory—how long could I, weak and spoiled as I was, bear this factory labor? And how long would Sylvie tolerate my presence? Over the weeks I had noticed her remarks to me growing more snide, more clipped, and nastier.

Here was my opportunity to complete my survey. At least two sewing lines were seated on the lunchroom benches. The workers had nothing to do. Some were idly chatting, while others were resting their heads on the tables. They would not be paid for this time, but they were not permitted to leave the factory either.

I carefully approached one table of workers, almost tiptoeing for fear that Sylvie would spot me out of my assigned position. "Would you mind answering some questions for me?" I said this shyly, never having met this particular group, fearing their reproach, uncertain if they would be willing to speak with me, not wanting to put them at any risk with Sylvie. "Of course," they answered, with the usual Moroccan politesse. "This would be no problem. You are welcome here among us."

I stepped away then, heading for Sylvie's office. Although I knew she would disapprove, I thought I had better clear my actions with her before I began. I knocked softly and stepped inside. She raised her head, looking up at me over some plans, impatient and surprised to see me, "The owner told me," I started to remind her, "that I could interview the workers. Remember, that is why I'm here. I see the workers seated in the lunchroom, and I would like to give some of them my survey now, while they are not busy. And it isn't busy in the packing area anyway."

Sylvie stared at me with her small blue eyes. "Are you planning to start a revolution?" she said without a hint of a smile. I laughed, acting as if I assumed this was only a joke, although I was quite certain that it was not. Then she told me I could go ahead.

I went back to the lunchroom and approached one table of workers who were sitting close together on the benches. I explained what I was doing and why I wanted to interview them. Most had already seen me, and some had spoken with me at the factory gates. Leaning against the lunchroom wall, underneath the high factory windows from which the sharp Moroccan sun was streaming in, was a large, dark-haired woman. She was stout and looked powerful. She spoke to me in a harsh voice, and as soon as she started, all the voices in the lunchroom abruptly hushed. "I will happily talk to you about this work," she said, "because I fear no one but God. It does not matter what happens to me. We working girls used to have rights, but no longer."

I became frightened. Here was the revolution that Sylvie feared. I had no intention of leading a labor revolt. In fact, involving myself in local political affairs, I knew, could land me in a Moroccan jail. Even if I had wished to become a martyr, I knew well that labor actions had so far done nothing for these workers: factories were shut down when their workers went on strike, only to open days or weeks later with the same conditions and newly hired workers. Anyone who attempted to resist factory power simply lost her job and often even found herself blackballed—unable to find work in other Fes factories.

I was alarmed by this woman's talk because I feared it could harm her and the workers surrounding us. I knew I could offer these workers no help: I was powerless to change the conditions of their labor. I knew I would never be able to return the kindness they had extended to me, their welcome and their willingness to share their thoughts and stories. At least, I thought, I would not harm them. And yet here I had started this woman speaking in a loud and dangerous voice. And I could not tell her to stop.

This woman was confident and determined. I was thrown off by her fast response, and the seated workers seemed stunned. She continued, and we all listened. "It used to be that when a woman was pregnant, she got to stay home and have the baby. She got money for this. But now there is nothing for pregnancy. And they used to have sickness insurance. If you became ill, you got a paper from the office and you got money to help you pay for the sickness. If your tooth hurt, they gave you money to fix it.

"But now everything has changed. We have no rights. We work for nothing; we do not get paid well. We leave our houses in the mornings and have no idea when we'll return at night. We just walk out of our houses, saying to ourselves, 'Maybe I'll come home tonight, or maybe I'll sleep at the factory.' We work at night; we have no choice. But it didn't used to be like this. We used to have better working conditions, before the strike of 1990, before all the factories closed. Now there are hardly any factories left in Fes. The factories have closed, and we have nothing."

We were all sitting in silence, our faces turned toward this woman. No one responded, but everyone knew about the general strike that had occurred in December 1990. Although the government had successfully kept the details from the press, everyone in Fes had a tale of the violence that had ripped through the city. On one auspicious morning, I had been told many times, factory workers and students had refused to board city buses and report for work or school. These workers and students then united in destroying factories, hotels, even cars, in protest of the ever worsening poverty of the city's lower classes. It was widely agreed that these strikes had forced at least one-third of Fes's factories to shut down, some permanently, some moving to safer cities. And ever since this general strike, everyone agreed, with far fewer factories operating and ever increasing numbers of hungry workers, working conditions had deteriorated even further.

I looked toward the steps, hoping Sylvie was not witnessing this demonstration. The woman, though, was not searching the stairway in fear of Sylvie, and she went on, unprompted. "I used to work at the government-owned sewing factory, and let me tell you, we were comfortable inside that factory. We worked well there; it was nothing like this place is now. Here, you must work, work, work. You are pressed and stressed for days. And then, suddenly, there is no work at all. Then, for days, for weeks at a time, you have no work at all and no pay. At the government factory, we just worked every day. There was steady work. We worked regularly. We were relaxed with our work. But that closed four years ago. Let me tell you that four years feels like forty years to me. Four years has been a whole lifetime. That is how bad work has been since then." She paused for a minute, and then she started again. "I am telling you, it would be better to return to that government factory and clean the toilets than to sew in the factories that are operating now. That is how good it was to work there. But now so many of the factories have closed their doors and the work is much, much worse. We have no rights, we have nothing . . ." And she trailed off.

She seemed to have come to a stop. Sylvie had not appeared. I had heard about the closing of the government factory where she had worked and had never understood why this factory had closed, and so I asked her, "Was it the general strikes of 1990 that closed the factory where you used to work?"

"No, not really," she said. "For a while there were new factory managers every week." And here she listed the names of well-known factory owners in Fes, family names that everyone in Fes knew to be the wealthy oligarchy of the town. "And then finally it got to be the time of the Great Feast, and usually we were given money to purchase our rams for the feast. Every year they gave us a bonus at this time. But that year they told us we would get nothing. The manager said the coffers would be empty if they gave us the money for the holiday. So we workers went to the union with our problem, because there we had a union. And then we just stopped working; we all walked out of the factory in protest. And once we walked out, the factory just closed its doors. They would not let us back in. We lost our jobs, and then the factory just shut down."

There was silence. The workers listened intently, although everyone knew this story. But this time the woman leaning against the wall did not speak again. Slowly the chatter resumed in the lunchroom. This fearless worker sat down at the end of the table, near where she had been standing. I moved over to sit near her. I had been standing at the opposite end of the table and now was glad to be seated, glad that we were all seated, as if we could hide better this way. The worker's name, I learned, was Sala, and the women clustered around her were also original employees of the government-owned factory of which she had spoken. This factory had been one of the first large garment factories in Fes, the first state-owned and state-run garment factory in Morocco.

Sala's talk had encouraged her friends and co-workers to describe to me the difficulties of their work conditions. Following her lead, they spoke freely of their anger. "You know that we will not be paid for the time we are sitting in this lunchroom." Any work slowdown that might force the sewing line to become unoccupied would not be marked on their blue cards. "We don't get paid the minimum wage on the sewing lines. We don't even get paid near the minimum wage." They are often forced to remain at the machines indefinitely, if an order must be completed. Sometimes they stay at the machines sewing until late at night. On the other hand, there are times when the orders are complete, and they are simply sent home, without pay, to wait indefinitely until the factory needs them again. They cannot leave the factory during the day; they cannot step outside on their lunch break. Their trips to the bathroom are restricted and counted. Even speaking to each other is prohibited during the work hours on the sewing line. They have no sick pay, and if they leave the factory due to sickness, they may not be permitted to return. Eventually the workers themselves grew tired of telling of their outrage, and the subject changed to more ordinary concerns, such as household finances and cooking.

I moved to the next table. One of the workers from the first table moved with me. She was young, much younger than the former government employees. She watched quietly as I spoke to workers at this new table. After I had interviewed a few girls, she whispered to me, "I need to ask you something."

I turned to hear what she had to say. "Don't worry," I said. "Just ask me. What is it?" She had a heavy, curly kind of bang of hair hanging over her left eye. She lifted this bang to show me that, underneath it, a large part of her head was hairless. And the skin around her eye, which had been covered by this hair now lifted away, was rubbery and burnt looking.

"Is there any drug in America that could get my hair back?" she asked me.

I looked at her, somewhat puzzled. "No," I said quietly. "I'm sorry, but there is no drug that can help grow hair. They have not yet made a drug to do that." I was fairly certain of this, as I had already given it some thought. A balding man had asked me if I had a drug to cure baldness, and I had thought about this issue again with Zaynab and her hair loss.

And then she put her head on the table, cradled her head in her arms, and began to weep. "You don't have to cry," I said to her. "You are still beautiful. It doesn't show." Others at the table stepped in to tell her that her hair looked fine. "Your wounds do not show," they kept repeating, but this did not seem to help her. When she did not stop crying, they reminded her that there were worse things, that other people had more difficult problems. And when still she would not stop crying, they told her that she needed to stop the crying. "That is enough," they said, like I have seen Moroccan women do among themselves, reminding someone that there is only so much sorrow a person is permitted. So finally she sat up and began to tell the story of how this had happened to her. I had the feeling that the others had heard it before and that this rendition was for me.

"I was a little girl," she said. "I was running into the kitchen, and I slipped. My shoe slipped. And I fell into the pan of frying fish. My parents didn't take me to the doctor, though, because it was Sunday, and the clinic was closed. My mother put bleach on the wound, and I stayed in the house until Monday, when they took me to the doctor. And when we got there, the doctor said, 'You should have brought her earlier. You should have brought her earlier.' It was too late."

She spoke with immediacy, as if all of this had transpired last week. But she was a child when this happened, and now she was about 15, she believed. "I think about this every day. It is all I think about. I can think of nothing else," she said. "This is why I started working. I heard there was a doctor in Casablanca who could do an operation. And so I am working to earn the money for this operation." And having said all this, she quieted down. No one spoke; each girl listened. There was nothing for any of us to say.

And so I went on with the interviews, speaking then to the next worker at the table. She, too, said she had something to say. The tone had been set, and I feared another story of horror.

"My father's retirement check," she said, "is being pilfered."

"How could this be?" I asked. Her father, she explained, had been a soldier for the French government. He had always received a retirement check, which was a major portion of the family's income. He died one year ago, and now the check that they were receiving was far smaller. The family is certain that the French government is sending the correct amount but that the Moroccans are taking away a large portion of it. This I could not understand. I just wrote down what she told me.

Eventually I moved on to the next table and surveyed the workers sitting there. When I had finished, a conversation about Islam was begun. I was not sure whether or not this conversation was for my benefit, but it started quickly and, like all conversations about Islam, took off like a wild fire. A black woman, fat and married, led the discussion. "We should all be veiled," she wanted me to know. "In reality, according to Islam, we should all be veiled. We should listen to our husbands. We should not step out into the streets. We should not really even be speaking with you. We should not wear this western clothing that we wear. We should not even be working. In the past, even if people were hungry, the women did not go out to work. But now everything is different. All the women are out in the streets, doing the things that Europeans do. But Islam is not like this. Islam does not allow this." And with this, the workers at the table began to speak about heaven and their possibilities for getting there. "We do this work instead of doing something more evil to get money," the fat black woman continued. "We are straight, and we are honest. This is not good work, but this is honest work. At least we are not doing something bad for the money we earn." With the words "something bad," this woman implied prostitution. This was something no workers ever spoke of as an alternative to factory work.

Everyone was nodding in agreement now, and someone declared that everyone in this factory ought to be veiled (in the form of the *hijab*), according to Islam's dictates.

"But many of the companies do not allow the workers to veil. They won't even let veiled women come in," someone else said, as if to defend herself.

"Why is this so?" I asked.

"The companies want everyone to wear makeup and dress nicely."

"But why?"

"Because they say that the Europeans do not like to see all the women veiled." Later, in packing, I asked Hayat if it was true that veiled women were not let into some factories.

"It is true," she said with certainty. But when I pressed her on this issue, she had no answers. She said she did not know why this would be so.[1]

•

The next day everyone in the factory was back at work and the factory was running at full capacity. I stood in my place at the packing table, listening to the talk. Early in the morning, the rumor reached us downstairs that something had been stolen. Something had been taken from the factory, but no one knew what had been taken. Some said it was a pair of scissors that had gone missing. Others were saying that a piece of sewing machine had been taken. Something had been stolen, and all lockers would be inspected.

We watched from our table below as, one by one, workers stood up from their seats at the sewing machines and walked across the workshop floor to the locker area, where Sylvie stood with the line chief who acts as her interpreter. As these two watched, each girl opened the lock on her locker door and displayed her locker's contents. The packing workers were quietly tracking the process, "Now it is Absellem's line," they would say as they caught sight of girls they knew crossing the workshop floor. "Now it is Fatima's line." A quiet fear had settled over the table as the girls watched their peers walk to the lockers.

As if to reassure themselves, the packing girls kept repeating certain phrases: "Those who do not steal have nothing to fear." "Those who are honest and straight have no reason to be afraid." But these assertions could not eradicate the fear in the air. It was as if each of us was guilty of something. The girls kept their hands moving, checking seams that they did not really seem to be seeing. They were completely preoccupied with what was happening upstairs. The locker inspection went on throughout the morning, and the packing girls had no other subject of conversation. They knew there was always the possibility that somehow they could be falsely accused. "It is true that sometimes girls plant things in the bags of workers they are jealous of," one girl commented.

"They do this just to make trouble or maybe to get a girl they do not like forced out of the factory."

Mina admitted to her fear. "I have a piece of elastic in my purse," she said, fright palpable in her voice. "But it has been there for such a long time. I got it here. I found it here in the factory. But I was just using it as a hair tie. They have noticed this elastic in my purse before—at the search—in the evenings. They have seen the elastic and have never said anything about it. They simply left it in my purse." Now Mina was frightened. She kept talking about the elastic, and no one said anything to comfort her. "I hope they won't now accuse me of stealing it," she said finally.

And with this, Hayat turned to me and said, "You see, this is not a clean job. We are all treated like thieves. Look how we will all be searched now, because one girl has stolen something. Now we are all thieves." Hayat almost spat as she spoke, as if she could taste her humiliation. The others agreed.

"A professional woman, a teacher or a secretary, would never be treated like this, like a thief," someone said.

"A professional woman is never searched at her work," someone else added. "No one ever assumes she would steal something." And now the fear was turning to anger.

"This locker inspection is necessary because all those girls *upstairs* are probably thieves," Hayat announced, jerking her chin up. And the others agreed, saying that when they worked here prior to the one-year closing, the packing department was kept completely separate from the rest of the factory. At that time, the packing girls had had no lockers assigned to them, and they never mixed at all with the girls upstairs. This, everyone agreed, was the way it should be.

The packing girls were aware that they were distinct from those who worked on the machines—the girls upstairs—due to their lower status (as defined by skill) and lower pay. And yet I had never heard them distance themselves so strongly from the others. Perhaps the fear of being accused caused the girls to highlight their separation from the other workers, thereby reinforcing their own feelings of group solidarity and marking themselves off as a moral community of good girls within the wider factory world.

And then Hayat began to recount a story her sister had told her. "At a factory where my younger sister works, a girl was caught stealing fabric. She stole five meters of fabric, which she rolled up and tried to hide in her *djellaba*. She did not get caught at the search at the factory door that was done at the end of the day. But as she was stepping out of the factory gates, the guardian of the building asked her what she was carrying. 'It is only my *djellaba*,' she told him. So the guardian grabbed this from the girl, by force, and he shook it until the five meters of cloth flew out. The factory owners called the police and the police came and took her away. She was sentenced to three months in jail for this crime. She was married, but of course her husband divorced her for her crime. He has since gone crazy. The incident drove him mad. He has lost his mind."

"That's such a sad story," I said. "I feel sorry for this girl."

"Oh, no," Hayat responded immediately. "There is no pity for her. She stole. She should be put in jail. Three months is actually a light sentence for her crime." Latifa agreed that it was.

Eventually the packing girls were called, one by one, to open their lockers. They all survived the inspection. We left the factory that night not knowing what had been stolen and whether it had ever been retrieved. No one seemed to know, and the incident was soon forgotten—or at least it was never mentioned again.

•

Ramadan ended, and we had several days off to celebrate the break of the fast. The weather was slowly turning warmer, and a sense of the reprieve from the cold that spring would bring was in the air. The day before we were to return to the factory, I was walking down a main thoroughfare in Fes when the factory owner passed me in his car. He stopped, rolled down the passenger window, and leaned over to tell me that the factory would remain closed for an additional three days because of a delay in a shipment of supplies. I thanked him for telling me and breathed a sigh of relief that there would be more vacation. And then I wondered how the others would find out. Most of the workers I had visited had no telephone. But everyone knew someone else, and it seemed no one ever appeared at the factory, ready for work, on a day when the factory was shut. Word of mouth in Morocco is very effective.

When we finally did resume work, there was little actual work to do. In the packing room we continued to process jackets, but most of the sewing line workers spent their first day back in the lunchroom, sitting, waiting for fabric to be prepared, not being paid. I snuck back to the lunchroom to do more surveying of the workers. And there I ran into Salima Bendoun again. We had met early on during my time in the factory before I was transferred to the packing department. Salima Bendoun was generally viewed by the other girls as being quite scandalous in her speech and behavior. It seemed pretty clear that she chaffed at the social mores imposed on Moroccan women.

The workers who had spent the morning in the lunchroom, watching the strange Christian interview them, were told to go home and return to work tomorrow. Much of the day had passed, and they had done little work. They would receive no pay for their efforts. Salima Bendoun asked me to come along with her and her best friend, Fouzia. They were close and always left work together. Today they would have extra time for a stroll in the city. I walked out of the building with the girls, and we slowly walked to the central bus station. Salima seemed desperate to go somewhere. "Let's go to see Lahlou, the line leader who was sick today," she said. She got no response from either of us.

"Whatever happened to Saudi?" I asked. I knew they had been friendly and wished to know what had become of her and her child.

"It is likely that she has left for good. She was absent so much," Salima replied. "Let's go visit her. I know where she lives. Do you want to visit her?" Again she got no reply. I did not want to walk in uninvited, unannounced, on Saudi.

"How about let's go to Sidi Harazem or to the *medina*. Let's just go somewhere."

"No," Fouzia said. "Absolutely not. I go straight now, you know that."

"This girl," Salima explained, "has signed her marriage contract. They have not done the wedding yet. She has not yet slept with this man. But the contract is signed." And the girls laughed. "She used to go around with me," Salima said, acting angry at Fouzia, "but now she won't come with me any longer. She is officially married, so now she takes the straight path. From home to work, work to home. That is all she does." They agreed that it is okay for an unmarried girl to stroll around town, to be free, but "once she is married, that is all over."

So Salima Bendoun, I could see, had lost her companion and now wanted me for company. As we strolled down the factory street, a man driving his car slowed down and then pulled over to the side of the road ahead of us. This meant that if we were interested, we could get into his car. He might drive us somewhere. "Do you want to get in the car?" Salima asked me. Salima was laughing, and I was not sure if this was a dare, a challenge, or a serious proposition.

"I don't think I really do," I said. "I really don't want to get into his car. I have no idea who he is."

"I agree," said Salima. "I would never go in a car with a man I do not know." I felt certain, from the way Salima was behaving, that had I not been there, Salima might have had her day out. As we continued onto the main thoroughfare, Salima greeted those who passed us, especially the young men. Fouzia spoke to no one. I don't know if she would have been greeting these strangers if she had not signed the contract. But today, as a married woman, she was silent in the streets.

And so, preferring not to walk down the street like a political candidate on the eve of the election, I asked Fouzia, "Why did you sign the contract if you have not yet planned the wedding?"

"With the act signed," she replied quickly, "no one will talk. No one can say anything about us now. If I go out with him, walk on the street, go to a café, anything, no one will say a word. He is my husband now. We can do anything together." I asked if they would sleep together. "Yes, we can. We can sleep together, but there must be blood at the wedding."

At this Salima joined in this conversation. This was, I knew from the past, a constant concern of hers. "Oh, the blood is not so important these days. Not anymore. People really don't worry too much about that." Salima, I sensed, was speaking mostly to reassure herself. "Anyway," she continued, "you can always do the operation. And this would only cost you about 300 *dirham*."

"If the man is smart, he will know. He will know you have done this," Fouzia said, and Salima did not argue.

"I used to have a lot of boyfriends," Fouzia told me. "There was a man, who was married to a friend of my mother. This woman had done my mother a lot of favors—she had helped my mother out a lot. And the man—the woman's husband—was far younger than the woman herself. He used to come to my house and he started to really like me. He would take me out in his car and we'd go out driving on long rides. Finally he told me that he liked me and wanted to marry me. I told him I liked him, too, but I began to weep, really to cry hard. In the end, I told him, 'We must stop this driving around. I cannot do this to your wife, because she has been such a good friend to my mother over the years.' He just did not like his wife, because she was older than him and very ugly.

"After that, I had boyfriends, lots of boyfriends. I went out with a lot of boys. Only one at a time, though. I never had more than one boyfriend at once—not like Salima. She has lots of boyfriends, this one, all at once." I did not know what this meant precisely, but I could not interrupt the flow of her conversation. "But then, finally, my husband saw me and wanted me. We got engaged. And then he wanted to go out with me, to stroll around, but this time I said no. I told him, 'Let's not *shab* (make friends). Let's not be friends. Let's just wait.' I told him this because he was a friend of my brother's. I knew that my brother did not want this." And then she launched into a long story about how once, when she was out on the street with a boy, her brother saw her and he became furious. It was this incident that had led to her current engagement to her brother's friend. How exactly the engagement came about I could not catch, because the noise of the cars whizzing past us was making it extremely difficult to follow the long and convoluted tale of her past transgressions.

Fouzia was dressed in a long skirt with a blazer. She wore giant earrings that stuck out from her thick black hair, which she let hang down her back and which was cut in the front, fashionably winged to frame her face. She knew something about fashion, it seemed to me, and she dressed in a way that would call attention to herself. She looked modern and independent and free. But she was decidedly not free any longer. She no longer passed her afternoons strolling through the city with Salima.

As we walked, Salima trailed slightly behind us. We were on a busy thoroughfare, and men in cars and on foot called and gestured to us as we strolled. Salima was answering some of these calls. She was waving at the cars as they passed and seemed to know many of the people who passed us by. Finally she caught up to us and joined in the conversation. Perhaps, I thought, she is tired of all that now. She was eager, though, to tell of her own lost loves.

"I am now seeing a man who is married," Salima Bendoun began. "I see him on the street, almost every day. He has a lot of problems with his wife. He tells me about them all the time. He likes me a lot, and I like him. We go out together."

"Where do you go with him?" I asked.

"We go to cafés."

"You go to cafés with men?" I asked, surprised, for this is a rare activity among factory girls. A girl socializing with men in a café is highly suspect among people of the factory class; in fact, a girl in a café with a man might automatically be considered a prostitute.

"Oh, yes, I do, of course I do," Salima said, quickly, almost defensively.

"But most girls don't do such a thing," I said.

"I am free," Salima said fiercely. "My brothers don't control me."

"Why not?"

"Because my father worked in France for a long time. He had an open mind; he had the French mentality. And my mother is educated. Well, not exactly— she did not go to school—but she knows things, she understands things. My siblings are all educated. They all went to school, except for me. I am the only child in the family who was not sent to school. My brothers even got as far as university. And so they don't control me because they are educated."

After Fouzia boarded a bus for home, Salima was eager for companionship, so I went with her to shop in the *medina*. She was looking for a new skirt and sweater. We stopped in shop after shop, and Salima tried on clothing. She joked with the shop owners, as if she knew them well. One even "helped" her by measuring her hips while she laughed. All the while, she greeted these men with typical Moroccan politesse, thanking them by asking God to bless their parents, invoking God to help them and protect them. We passed some women on the street dressed in a form of Islamic veiling rarely seen in Morocco. The women were covered completely in flowing black gowns, and even their faces were covered. "That is how we should all be," she pointed to me. "That is what is necessary in Islam." Watching Salima, I could see that, at least for now, veiling would not really work for her.

"I'm not sure that's true," I said.

"No, it's not. It's what is in your heart that matters." Salima responded with this quickly, and I was not sure which statement she truly believed. "God doesn't look at your clothes. He looks into your heart. He can see what's in your heart."

"In my opinion, Salima, you are right."

Salima didn't buy any clothing that day, although she told me she "eats money." She had paid for my bus fare and had bought me a sweet donut from a street vendor, despite my insistence that I would pay for her. The excursion had cost her 12 *dirham*, which a girl like her—a girl with no education, from the lower classes—surely would not have had, had she not had a job in the factory. And so perhaps to some extent, what people in Fes say about the factory girls is true: sometimes they work for themselves, to buy things they want to buy, to get out of the house.

When we left the *medina*, Salima headed back on foot to the factory district from which we had come some hours earlier. She would meet her best friend, she told me, at the Tazi factory, which was located behind our own factory. Salima would walk the distance, some three miles at least, to save money on the bus fare. "My best friend," she told me, "is very beautiful. We do everything together. Just this past weekend we went to Sefrou together. We got a ride there from three men—one was a doctor, one a pharmacist."

"Who were these men?"

"These men were friends of my friend. Believe me, we just went to Sefrou for the drive. That is all. There was nothing between any of us. But my friend and I, we like to do things like this." And with that, Salima and I parted. And I thought about other things that people in Fes always said: Factory girls did not respect the boundaries. Factory girls were uncontrolled. Factory girls had no virtue. But the line between some freedom and no freedom is very stark.

•

Today I went to the factory at 11. I was late. I intended simply to keep interviewing the workers who might be sitting in the kitchen. Since our extended vacation, the work routine had been broken. Workers were being displaced from their lines because little work was available. They were spending much of the day sitting on benches in the lunchroom, waiting to be called. When I arrived at the factory, I found a few workers left in the kitchen. Most had been called back to the line. Still, the factory was quiet. Work was very slow, and the sewing lines were not running at capacity. The girls in the packing department told me there was hardly anything for them to do. They just stood at their table, waiting for things to inspect, or tag, or pack, laughing and giggling all the while.

Before I began my interviews with workers waiting in the lunchroom, I walked up the stairs to the factory office. I was looking for the owner, wanting to tell him that my work at the factory would end now with this work slowdown. I had decided I would no longer spend my days around the packing table, but I would like to continue talking to the workers.

The owner told me that the truck had come in yesterday, bringing with it from France the order to be sewn. But there was very little work this time. "My buyer in France has no orders. No stores in France are buying his goods. And so now, suddenly, we have no work. The work has disappeared." We talked for a while, and the owner seemed very unhappy. When I asked him how his holiday had been, he said it was not good. "There is no money," he said. I was surprised. I knew this family to be one of the wealthier families in Fes.

And then the owner asked me about my research. After our first few attempts at English lessons during my first week of work, the owner had never spoken to me again. He seemed not to care about my presence in his factory. I had assumed that because he was young, he was savvy, and he understood that I could and would cause him no real political trouble. My study, I thought he understood, would only be published as a book about an anonymous factory in an anonymous place. I thought he knew that no harm could come to his business from me.

But today, rather suddenly, this owner was uncomfortable with me. "Have you done any studies in other factories?" he asked. I told him about other factory visits I had made. "Which factories have you visited, exactly?" I told him. "How many more interviews will you need to do here?" I sensed that this man regretted things; he had begun to wish he had never allowed me into his factory. But he remained polite, never forgetting the rules of hospitality, treating me still like a guest. He did not wish to tell me directly that I should leave now.

"You know," he said, laughing with a sound that was not really a laugh, "you could make this all up. You don't even have to do these interviews. It would be just as easy to make the stuff up." I was certain, then, that he did not want me there and that he was sorry I had ever come.

And with this Sylvie walked into the office. "Bonjour," she said in a harsh voice. "This one," she said loudly, pointing at me, "I saw walking yesterday with the girls from this factory. I saw her walking on the street with the girls. I didn't know she had even come here to work yesterday, and then later in the afternoon I see her in the street with them." Sylvie was mad. And she frightened me. I struggled to put some words together, although I didn't know exactly what my crime was.

"I did come to work yesterday morning, but there was no work. And so I spoke with the workers in the lunchroom, and then I left. I walked out of here with some of them. And then today, as soon as I arrived, I came here to this office to speak with the owner." I added that I had looked for her as well, which was a lie.

"Well," she said, "I am always here. I am always in this office, especially when a new shipment has arrived." She was getting madder.

I was alarmed. These people, I thought, seem to be connecting me with their work slowdown. Are they thinking I have connections in France, that I have caused them to lose work from overseas? The owner was just sitting in silence, but Sylvie stood looking at me, enraged, it seemed, by the sight of me. Don't let her intimidate you, I said to myself. If these people don't want you here, they can just tell you to leave. Why don't they? That is all it would take.

And I thought back on the past few weeks and my most recent encounters with Sylvie. At the start of my tenure at the factory, I used to stop at Sylvie's office to tell her I was there in the factory. She would always respond curtly, "It does not matter. You do whatever you want," confirming the fact, I thought, that she did not want me there. The last time I had stopped in Sylvie's office to report on my presence was after I had been absent for several days due to illness. At that time, she had purposefully ignored me and had behaved as if she could not see me. After that, I decided not to report in. I actually stopped going in her office for the same reason the girls avoid her office: I did not want to deal with her. I assumed she had just figured she could not eliminate me, that I was there on the whim of the owner, and she would not bother herself with my presence. But now it seemed that Sylvie could ignore me no more.

Sylvie walked out of the office, and the owner told me that he might have to stop work completely by Monday. He might get some work from another factory owner in town, a friend who had a large order and would subcontract some of this order out to him, just to help him keep his factory running. And then our conversation ended. It was as if the owner did not understand that he was in control. He could have told me to leave his factory. He could have told me never to come back. But he didn't. He just said good-bye, and I walked out of his office.

·

I returned to the lunchroom. I had not been told to leave, and I was eager to finish my survey, so I simply decided I would not take a hint. If they wanted me out of here, they would have to tell me to go. There were only two workers left sitting in the lunchroom: Fadela, the round, slow sister of Zaynab, and another girl who looked as disheveled as Fadela. The two seemed to be wrapped in rags. I sat down next to them and learned that the second girl, like Fadela, was a factory maid.

Fadela and I began to chat. She knew I was conducting a survey and had already answered my questions. Now, it seemed, she had decided to offer me some new material. "Do you know, Titia, that I run contraband down from Al Hoceima?" Perhaps I had not heard her correctly. I looked at her, confused.

"She doesn't understand what you are saying," the other maid said, nudging Fadela with her elbow. "She doesn't know the word *contraband*."

"Oh, yes, I do," I replied. "I understand contraband. I know what that means." Everywhere in Fes, men set up blankets on sidewalks, selling goods illegally brought in from Europe. During lunch break in the factory, workers often walked among the lunch tables, displaying necklaces or watches for sale at a cheap price, items that likely had been smuggled into the country by their brothers or fathers. This was contraband.

"But do you know what kind of contraband she runs?" the second maid asked, as if eager to see my reaction.

"Clothing?"

"No," said the second girl, while Fadela sat staring at me, a slight grin on her face. "She runs hashish."

It was quiet in the lunchroom. All the workers still needed in the factory were at their places. I looked at them both, my mind moving fast, trying to ascertain whether they were playing a joke on me. I had been asking questions in Morocco for a long time. I believed that people always told me what they believed to be true. But I also knew that these truths were slightly mutable, depending on who else was listening to the conversation, how much they really wanted me to know about them, the point they wanted to convey, or even their mood at the moment. Truth shifts in this way everywhere. These workers, I had come to realize, were young girls who had a flare for the sensational. These girls were gifted storytellers, able to relate minute details of an incident in a way that could captivate their audience. Perhaps now they were just having some fun with me.

"Fadela," I repeated the sentence, to be sure we were clear. "You run hashish down from Al Hoceima?" Fadela nodded. The other maid nodded as well.

"Well, tell me then, Fadela, how did you get involved in running contraband?"

Fadela was only too happy to tell her story. "It started when I got an inheritance from my grandfather. Twenty thousand *riyal* is what he left me, and so I started in the business. When I got this money, I took it to Al Hoceima and bought some hashish. I carry the hashish down south, from Al Hoceima, and sell it to clients."

"Who are the clients?" I asked. It was jarring to hear Fadela speak of "her clients," as I knew her only as the younger and more destitute-looking sister of Zaynab, a girl who was not even able to secure a job on the factory line but instead had been consigned to wet-mopping the factory floors. Now, it seems, Fadela had clients.

"Oh, clients can be everywhere," she said. "When you travel around Morocco, and you tell people you are from Fes, it is likely they will say, 'Fes is very close to the north.' When they say this, you know that what they really mean is, 'you live near where the hashish is.' And so that is how you can get clients. That is how I have gotten a lot of my clients. If you go to Marrakech, a lot of people will ask you about 'the north.' I have clients in Marrakech, especially at the hotels. They want my business."

Fadela did not come up with this idea for a business on her own. "I got this idea from my cousins—my father's family. They are involved in the business, and so when I got this inheritance, I began to do it, too."

"But aren't you afraid? What if you get caught by the police?"

"I am not afraid," Fadela said defiantly. "I am not even afraid of jail. There are other girls who do this, you know. I do this with other girls." I asked who the other girls were, and Fadela obscured the point. "I work with two other girls right now. They are not family, just friends. They are not in this factory, though. No one else in this factory does this work. Really, it is extremely rare to find girls who do this.

"Girls don't get caught when they run contraband," she continued. "The police never expect a girl to be committing a crime, so they never check a girl. Once I went to Al Hoceima with my uncle (my mother's brother), and we both brought a lot of hashish back with us. We had hashish tied to our bodies, strapped onto us." Here Fadela gestured to her stomach to indicate where the hashish was hidden. "My uncle sat in the front of the bus, and I sat in the very back of the bus. The police boarded the bus, and immediately they checked my uncle because they know people traveling out of Al Hoceima are likely to have hashish. They frisked him, and they found the hashish on his body. So they took him away, and they put him in jail. He just got released from the jail this summer. He had spent two years in jail. Now he has just been caught again, and he's back in jail. But they never frisked me—not that day, not ever. The police are just not likely to suspect a girl. They won't frisk girls. So why should I be afraid of jail?"

I knew this question was rhetorical, so I didn't try to answer it. I sat in slightly stunned silence.

"I do this for the money, you know," Fadela said. "At this factory, I will make about 250 *dirham* a month. That is nothing, and that is all I get, working every single day. So the contraband money is so much better. You know, I don't want to work in this factory—spend my whole day just sweeping this place. The only reason I do it is so that the neighbors won't ask, 'Where does she get all her money? Why does that girl have so much money?' This factory job is just a cover for my real job, which is running contraband."

While Fadela paused, I recalled what the owner had said to me: "You don't really have to do this work, you know. You could make this up."

"Could I have made this up?" I wondered. But I did not have time now to pursue this thought.

"Fadela," I asked, "do your parents know what you are doing? Aren't they worried about you?"

"My parents do not fear for me," she asserted. "They know I won't get caught. I go to Marrakech, to Al Hoceima. I go with other girls. I go alone. When I'm going to make a trip, my mother will ask me where I'm going, but she does not fear for me."

Fadela could see that I didn't understand how all this could be so. "Listen," she said, "I started this business four years ago. My parents know they did not educate me. I would not need to do this business if I were educated. Yes, I'm an aware person. I'm awake to what is happening in this world. But I am not educated. We have ten children in our family, and only two of us went to school—Zaynab went to the fifth grade, and my little brother is still in school.

My parents know they didn't educate their children. Moroccans just don't educate their children. The families are too strained. They're too poor. If they send one child to school, they know they won't have the money to send the others to school. So no one sent me to school. And now I am doing this."

Fadela was working to make me understand the logic of her life. But she was not defending herself. Although she understood that running contraband was illegal, she perceived it as a legitimate economic choice, especially given her situation. "I bought my own house, you know, with the money. Well, actually, my father has contributed some, but I have bought a house. It's right near where my parents live. Just this past Ramadan I bought it, and now I've moved in. I left the family and moved into my own house."

I asked, "Why did you want to leave them, though? Aren't you afraid to live alone?" I knew Fadela was only 20 years old, and it is unheard of for young Moroccan girls to live alone.

"Why would I be afraid? What would I be afraid of? I had to leave the family house. There was way too much trouble there. They are constantly fighting. My brothers live there with their wives. One wife does no housework, and the other complains she does too much housework. There is constant noise in that house. So I left. Now I go home from work at night, buy some lentils and bread from the store on the way home, get home to peace and quiet, and cook my food. It's better this way. I'd rather be alone."

When I made no reply, she said, "Why don't you come over some time? You would be welcome to see both houses."

.

The next day I returned to the factory, but few workers were left. Several of the sewing lines had been sent away. Some workers said that they had been told a new truck would come in later in the week, and they should return on Friday. Some said they had been told to come tomorrow, in the morning, to receive their pay. Others said they were told to come in the afternoon. It seemed that the factory was on its way to closing. Everyone knew this, but no one knew how long it would remain closed.

Downstairs in the packing department, puffy snow suits were piled everywhere. The truck carrying the cartons for packing them had never arrived. Only a few girls were left. Hayat, Latifa, and a few others stood around the table, still inspecting jackets but now in a leisurely way. I knew that this would be the end of my stay in the factory. With no workers to observe, there would be little reason for me to remain. And so I asked them a question I had thought

I would answer by working in the factory, a question whose answer still re-mained somehow elusive. "If a girl starts earning money by working in this fac-tory, does she get to control herself? I mean, if she is earning money to support the household, does that mean she can make her own decisions? Especially if her father or brother is unemployed, and she is taking care of them financially. Will she get to take charge of at least herself?"

"Oh, no," they answered, almost in unison. "Absolutely not," said Latifa, to the end eager to make me understand. "There is no way. It does not matter if the girl is supporting the whole household. She does not rule herself. Always, no matter the situation in the household, her father and her brother have the right to tell her what to do. They control her even if they are unemployed and she is supporting them. They still have the right to tell her what to do. She can-not defy them, even if she is supporting them."

"So," Hayat chimed in, "if a girl wants to go to a café, even if she is earning money, her brother will say no. And he has the right to do this. She will not defy her brother or father. She won't defy him openly. But what she might do is to go to the café secretly."

Ilham, a young worker who was usually silent, seemed to be an expert on this. "That girl will go to a café if she wants to, but she will hide. She'll be afraid that her brothers will see her. So she'll go secretly, and she'll lie about it. She'll never tell her parents."

This was the answer to my question. Even Latifa, honest, virtuous, seri-ous, had told me, when she was giving me her interview late into the evening, that she would tell her mother she had been delayed by work. Even Latifa! The power structure in their households remains largely unchanged, but these girls do gain some kind of autonomy. They don't get much authority, and their brothers—even younger brothers—can tell them what to do. But they must go to work, and no one in the family really knows what time they need to be there and what time they might be sent home and who they might meet along the way.

And so I asked about money, another issue I had thought I would figure out just by being present in the factory. "Do you ever fight over the money you bring home?"

"No," everyone agreed. "We don't fight about this."

"But," I said, "if you want to buy something and your mother says, 'No, give me the money,' what happens?"

Without a moment's hesitation, they said, "Well, then you hide your money. You tell your mother you only earned seven thousand that month, when indeed you earned ten thousand. And then you take the money you have left over and you buy what you want."

"For example," another one said, "if you want a dress, you can buy it with the money you have hidden from your mother. The problem with this is that your mother is going to see that dress. And she will know that you bought it. And she'll ask you about it. So there really is a limit on this. There is a limit on how much money you can keep, how much stuff you can buy."

Most of the factories, I knew, paid the girls with cash, so it would not be hard for a girl to sequester some money. The girls admit that they do not fight with their parents over the money. They don't openly defy parental authority; they just hide what money they can. But I remembered how, before Ramadan, so many of the workers were talking about needing wheat and oil and other food supplies for the holiday. In the face of that overwhelming need, many of the girls, I was sure, did not sneak away with much of their salaries. Just like their parents, and the brothers and sisters they were helping to support, they, too, would need to eat.[2]

And then I asked them if they believed that they themselves had been changed by their work in the factory. "Well, yes," they answered, although at first they seemed unsure of the question. "We have changed. We used to be ashamed of ourselves for working here in this factory. When we first started working, we thought this was so shameful. People say, 'You are only a girl of the factory' and 'Factory girls are not good girls' or 'A girl of the factory is a girl of the street.' But in the end we changed: we got used to this work; we got used to the factory. And we don't bother much anymore with this talk."

"But," I said, "are you different from girls who stay at home? Has the factory made you different?"

"Oh, yes," Latifa answered. "We are girls who hear a lot of talk. We hear the talk of this one and the talk of that one. A girl who stays at home listens only to the talk of her mother and her father. That is all she will ever hear. But here in the factory, we hear everything."

And so, I wanted to ask, is that a good thing or a bad thing—hearing all this talk? But the conversation changed, and I stopped asking questions.

•

I never did get to ask them whether they thought that hearing all this talk was a good thing or a bad thing. The next morning when I arrived at the factory, it was locked. The previous day the owner and Sylvie had approached me at the end of the workday and told me they would prefer I not come back to work.

They said I could come back over the lunch hour to finish my survey, and I had gratefully accepted their offer. I felt now that they somehow connected their business collapse with me. But, of course, I had no proof of this and would never know with certainty why they decided I should go.

When I arrived, the gates were closed tight and I was certain that no one was there. I was puzzled, as I knew that work had come to a crawl, but no one had told me the factory would be shut. I went home, wondering how I would contact my friends. I decided to telephone the factory office, and Amal answered. She told me that, in fact, they were open today; girls were inside working. I told her I would be back tomorrow. I wondered why the factory was shut so tightly. I imagined that it had all been a ploy to keep me out.

The following day I returned at noon, determined to complete my survey. I found that the factory gates had been shut tight the day before because the import truck had come in and was full of goods. The gates had been shut to ensure that no passers-by would see them empty the truck—not to keep out the American. Now work had begun again. When I arrived, just a few workers remained seated on the benches in the lunchroom. There had been many girls sitting there throughout the morning, they told me, but now they had slowly been called back to work as the new order was set in motion.

By now I had interviewed most of the workers in this factory, over lunch breaks and during work slowdowns, as well as after work in the streets and in their homes. I sat down and asked the few remaining girls whom I hadn't spoken with if they would be willing to speak with me. "I am sick. I can't speak now," one said. "I am eating, and then I am going to pray," said another. "No, I don't want to take your survey," another said blandly, the first bald-faced refusal I had ever received in Morocco. These were the few workers I never succeeded in interviewing. It was likely that, from the start, they simply did not wish to speak with the foreigner. I repressed the thought that they, too, believed I had caused the work flow to stop. I stayed on while the workers were assigned their tasks, speaking with those who wished to speak with me. And then, as the lunchroom emptied, I took myself out the factory gate.

·

My tenure in the factory was done. While I had learned much about the workers from inside the factory walls, I knew there were facets of their lives I would never glimpse from the confines of the workplace. I began devoting my days to visiting with workers and their families, inside the workers' homes.

PART III

Inside the Home

CHAPTER 5

Introductions

Nadia never worked in the factory where I worked. I met Nadia in the factory named Couture, during a rainy spell in late November, when the factory owner (who, incidentally, believed I was a CIA agent) allowed me to survey his workers. Some days after our initial meeting inside the factory, Nadia came to my apartment with a co-worker, and they graciously answered my interview questions. At the end of our visit, Nadia told me that, at one time, her sister had cleaned house for a German, and this German had visited her family many times. Her family was open-minded and eager to welcome foreigners, and she invited me to come and meet them.

One week later I made my way to Ben Souda to visit Nadia and her family. It was the first of many visits. Over the course of the year Nadia became my close friend, and I came to know her family well. During the winter months when I was working in the sewing factory, I had fewer opportunities to visit with Nadia. But before the start of my factory job, and then in the spring and summer after my factory tenure had ended, I spent many afternoons visiting with Nadia, her mother, and the women of her extended family. I liked sitting and listening to them talk.

But this is not the reason I have chosen to detail the story of Nadia and her family. Nadia's story is important because I was able to spend the better part of a year with her as she lived through a very typical cycle in the life of a factory girl. While I knew her, Nadia endured the sudden closing of her factory, months of waiting for the factory's promised reopening (which did not occur), a frustrating and prolonged job search, the securing of another position only to see this position disappear, and renewed unemployment and job hunting. Over the course of this cycle, Nadia spent time at home with her family, and with typical Moroccan cordiality, they welcomed me. Although I met Nadia because she was a factory worker and our friendship was established by my interest in her work, at home—as in the factory—Nadia and the women surrounding her did not speak much about work in the factory. Instead, they spoke of marriage, pregnancy, children, and family.

Nadia lived with her mother, her three older brothers, and her sister-in-law. I frequently encountered these family members on my visits. She had an older sister who was divorced, but she did not live with them. I was told that she sold bread in the market and stayed with an uncle. Nadia's sister visited the family household every Thursday afternoon. On the rare occasions when I encountered her, she ignored my presence and fought viciously with her siblings. This is all I came to know of her. Nobody in the family wanted to talk with me about her whereabouts or activities.

Nadia had a father whom I also never met, although his situation was freely discussed. Some years earlier, late in the marriage to Nadia's mother, Nadia's father had taken a second wife. He lived several blocks away from the family in a separate house with his new, younger wife and the baby girl from that marriage. He appeared from time to time in Nadia's household, and his visits apparently precipitated terrible fighting. I came to fear an ill-timed visit when I might run into him. Fortunately this never occurred, although once I stepped in just moments after he had stepped out.

Nadia also had a cousin, Aisha, a married woman with six children who lived several blocks from Nadia's house. This cousin and her children were an integral part of Nadia's family life. Nearly every time I called on Nadia, we would stop in at Aisha's house and pass much of the afternoon with her in her sitting room. And so Aisha became a central part of this story.

Over the course of many afternoons spent in Ben Souda, I met many people, most of them women, whose formal relationship to the family I never fully grasped. We would hear a pounding on the metal front door, and one or another wrinkled woman, covered in heavy, worn-out robes, her head wrapped in voluminous scarves or perhaps draped in a bath towel, would waddle in and ease her heavy body onto the banquette, groaning as she bent her knees. The woman would sit and speak and listen and pass some time and then just as suddenly get up and leave. Nadia, it seemed to me, would always identify the woman as her "aunt," saying she was her father's sister or perhaps a wife of her father's brother. Sometimes the woman would be described as Aisha's in-law. It was clear that these women were related in some very complex and specific ways; the precise connections, however, eluded me.

After my initial struggles to identify how, exactly, these people in the neighborhood were tied to Nadia and her clan, I began to accept her designation—aunt. I knew that in Morocco, family members are often connected in multiple ways. People keep close to their siblings, to their cousins, and to their aunts and uncles, and when possible, they try to live near one another. In Morocco people freely marry cousins—and the in-laws of cousins, and the friends of cousins—because they believe that relatives—or the relatives of relatives—can be trusted in the risky and important business of marriage. This is why multiple aunts, or women who are referred to as aunts, pass through this story.

Finally Abdul-Haq, or more accurately, Abdul-Haq's voice, reappears in this part of my narrative. My tutoring sessions with him came to an end in midwinter. But Abdul-Haq had foreseen, it seemed, the discussions I would have with people in the industrial districts of Fes. The Morocco he had chronicled in his language lectures came to life in the sitting rooms of Ben Souda.

•

I always traveled to visit Nadia in Ben Souda by public taxi from the Ville Nouvelle, squeezed between the driver and two other passengers. I was always given this place in the front seat by the taxi driver, who wished to award the front seat privilege to me—a foreigner. I never refused the offer of this seat, wishing to repay this hospitality with a show of gratitude for the honor. But each time I rode in fear, for I believed that a quick stop would surely send us all through the windshield.

The industrial district called Ben Souda lies on the road running around the southern edge of Fes. The garment factories sit at the very edge of Ben Souda, and beyond them is barren, hilly land and sky. The vacant hills beyond the factories are spotted with what look like olive groves. Ben Souda is not made up just of factories, though. At its center is a sprawling development of yellow concrete buildings, tanning in the dust. Here live the poor and the lower classes of Fes: the factory workers, the mechanics, the men who sell fruit from carts. At the center of the district, the buildings are as high as four or five stories, with the top floors often unfinished. The side streets are lined with much lower concrete structures, two to three stories high, which are also half-built. The skyline is peppered with metal poles, the frames of the buildings into whose walls concrete has not yet been poured, buildings whose hopeful owners slowly expand upwards, adding concrete as the money is gathered.

The central streets of this urban suburb are paved and on the pavement donkey carts mix with cars and small trucks. Dirt streets spread out from the center, and old men move along them on donkeys, steering around the puddles that lie at the center of the roads despite the absence of rain. Children, sent out by their mothers, stand at public water spigots holding plastic containers to await their turn for water. Many houses in Ben Souda do not have running water. Some do not have electricity.

People are everywhere. The women wear *djellabas*, the men polyester pants. Some look neat, clean, middle-class, but many look tattered and worn, as if they have just come in from the dusty hills. Children are everywhere and they too look like they have only just arrived from the countryside: boys with their heads shaved close, their hair only a black shadow on their skull, girls with their hair held back tightly with a piece of string out of which knotted strands explode.

On the first day I visited Nadia she met me at the public taxi stand in the center of Ben Souda and helped me push through the crowds, women pulling children and carrying buckets filled with towels, on their way to the *hammam*. She led me down a wide dirt road and then down a twisted narrow dirt alley to her house, a two-story concrete building, connected to all the others on the block. I looked closely at the residential section of this factory district because, although I had visited some of the factories here, I had never seen the houses. Many workers had told me they lived in Ben Souda and that they had used their wages to build homes here, on land their parents had received from the government. These were their houses, I thought.

We arrived then at Nadia's house. Rashida, Nadia's mother, greeted me loudly at the front door. She was broad and short, and her white pantaloons billowed out below the robes she wore. Her head was covered by two scarves, one wrapped tightly and tied at the top, another more colorful cloth covering this, knotted loosely at her chin. Her face was fleshy and full, and her nose with broad nostrils seemed to cover much of it. As soon as she was done greeting me, Rashida disappeared up a concrete staircase just inside the front door. Throughout the visit she remained upstairs on the flat roof of the house, where she cooked pancakes over an open burner. But I would only later learn of Rashida's rooftop retreat.

Nadia led me into a hallway with a concrete floor, pitted with use. To the right was a small room—the kitchen. On the left was a door that was shut. The hallway extended just a few yards longer and emptied into two separate rooms. To the left, the hallway led into a small courtyard, open to the sky, whose high walls were constructed of unfinished cinderblock. A tiny turtle lived in the corner of this courtyard, faithfully fed vegetable bits by the family. To the right, the hallway ended in a compact sitting room, where the painted walls were lined with banquettes. The banquettes were focused on a television connected to a VCR, both resting on a low table. Light streamed into the room from the one window to the courtyard; otherwise the room would have been dark. And in that room sat Jamila, Nadia's sister-in-law.

Nadia's complexion was uneven, and her nose was very pointed and sat crooked on her face. Nadia often wore western style clothing, and on this day she was dressed in a heavy acrylic sweater and skirt, which looked worn and somehow uncomfortable. Nadia was a practical person, articulate and open, eager to speak and capable of speaking forcefully. When I first spoke to her in the Couture factory, she answered my questions freely, without hesitation. She did not murmur or whisper, even though the line manager was watching. Nadia did not hesitate to speak her mind.

Jamila, Nadia's sister-in-law, who was waiting in the sitting room for my arrival, was a very different sort of person. This I could tell immediately. Jamila was hesitant and quiet. She had thick straight black hair knotted at the top of her head in a big puffy bun. Jamila was pale. Her skin looked damp and it was unflawed, and she had bright black eyes in an even oval face. Her nose was small and unnoticeable and it sat perfectly in the middle of her face. She wore a loose black gown embroidered with gold thread around the neck, a traditional kind of gown worn by women in the home. The black cloth at her neck and the black hair on her head made her face look whiter and her eyes brighter. When Jamila spoke, it was with little force, and she laughed quietly. She did not have Nadia's opinions. Or if she did, she did not lift her voice enough for them to be heard.

I sat between Nadia and Jamila, and they offered me tea and warm pancakes. We ate and drank, and they soon put the videotape of Jamila's wedding into the VCR. This tape, I guessed, had been selected in advance for my entertainment. But before anyone pushed the play button, they needed to go over the events that had culminated in the ceremony that would bind Jamila in marriage to Nadia's brother, Yousef. Jamila was eager to recount the tale of her recent marriage.

"My sister," Jamila began before the video was set on play, "had already married Nadia's cousin. One day I was visiting my sister, and Yousef came over to visit this cousin. And he saw me."

"Immediately Yousef was struck by her beauty," Nadia said. "He wanted to marry her the minute he saw her. So quickly, in early March, our families agreed upon the engagement. They signed the marriage act and in early April the wedding was held." This had transpired almost two years ago, although they spoke as if it were yesterday. And then Nadia looked at Jamila, laughing, and added, "The betrothed did not speak to each other before the wedding, but they wrote love letters to each other. They wrote letters that began '*habibi, habibi*' (my sweetheart, my sweetheart). Nadia was mocking now. "Everyone knows this." Jamila just looked down at her hands in her lap.

"You did not know each other much before the marriage?" I asked Jamila.

"No, after the marriage, we came to know each other," she said. And within minutes of our meeting Jamila told me her central story, the story she would repeat for me over and over throughout the course of our friendship, the story she could not resolve.

"I have borne children over these past two years since the marriage," she said. "The first baby came out of my stomach after nine months, dead. The doctor examined me with a machine and knew the baby was dead. So he removed it. And then, a few months later, I became pregnant again. But that baby, too, was taken from me. That baby was removed after six months."

"What happened?" I asked.

"This last time, the baby was ground up, like it had been put through the wheat mill. That's what the doctor said after he removed it."

"When did this happen?"

"This last baby was taken just this month—at the start of this month it was taken. I am still suffering from this. The doctor has warned me not to become pregnant again—not yet. He has prescribed birth control pills for me. He is testing my blood to see what is wrong with me." Nobody had yet pushed play on the video. Jamila was determined to give me this information. She needed me to know this. She spoke in the same matter-of-fact tone other Moroccan women had used to recount their tragedies. Jamila was not crying as she told me these things. These were just facts about her that I should know.

And then, having gained my rapt attention, Jamila proceeded to tell me more about her reproductive past. "I *tuwahem*ed intensely when I was pregnant," she went on, "especially in the first three months."

I knew this term from other conversations. *Tuwahem* is a verb that does not translate into English. In Morocco, it is said that pregnant women *tuwahem*—which sometimes mean they crave things. They can crave particular foods, such as expensive white bread purchased at a store rather than the less refined wheat bread baked at home. But *tuwahem* is a verb that can mean more than just craving. A pregnant woman might desire to have a beautiful child, so she may *tuwahem* by staring at a beautiful child. The power of her staring combined with her desire might reproduce such beauty in her own unborn child. And in yet another sense of this word, a pregnant woman might become supremely sensitive and irritable, so that she may feel herself unable to bear the presence of others around her, including (and perhaps particularly) her husband. I listened with interest to what kind of "madness" Jamila's pregnancy had brought upon her.

"I threw up everything I ate, and I fought constantly with Nadia. I fought with Aisha's youngest daughter whenever she came into the house. I fought with Yousef when he came home after work at night. I could not bear to have anyone near me, not even to have anyone sit close to me, like this," and here she gestured at me for I was sitting next to her on the banquette, our bodies touching as Moroccans sit, even when there is sufficient room to separate. "I could not even bear to sleep near Yousef and forced him to sleep downstairs so I could sleep alone." Jamila seemed proud of the intensity of her feelings, as if they marked her in some way. "Yousef," she assured me, "just laughed and let me sleep alone. He knew this was all part of my condition. No one was angry, not even Nadia, because they understood it was just part of the pregnancy."

With this Nadia hit the play button on the VCR. We watched Jamila, the bride, as she sat motionless, looking stunned, in a chair made to look like a throne. We watched her throughout her wedding night as she appeared and reappeared in seven bridal outfits, each one more elaborate than the next. And then as the light began to fade, I got up to leave. Rashida appeared suddenly as I was walking out the door.

"You must return," she said. "We like *benadem* here." *Benadem*, I knew, meant people. The children of Adam. Human beings—all kinds.

The darkness settled as the taxi took me home. I didn't know it then, but the themes of this first visit—Jamila's marriage to Nadia's brother, her tragic pregnancies, and ultimately, the extended family's disapprobation of the courtship—would slowly reveal themselves. But I never left Nadia's home without Rachida reminding me that they liked me, that they accepted me, and that I was welcome to return.

•

I returned some days later. This time Rashida remained with us in the small sitting room. It was now her turn to talk. And in this way I began to fill in the pieces of Nadia's family history. Nadia's father was gone from the house, having taken a second, much younger wife. Rashida spoke bitterly of her marriage to this man.

"My husband," she announced with no hesitation, "was a drunk who chased women. He beat me. He beat me often. My eyes would be closed from the punching. These eyes," and here she tapped my arm to make sure I was paying attention, and pointed to her eyes to be certain I understood, "would be black from him." Nadia's father left when Nadia was nearly 14, which was Yousef's last year in high school. It was for this reason, both mother and daughter agreed, that the beloved son and brother never completed his schooling, destroying all chances for him to attend university. "That same year the man married again," Rashida spat. "He took his second wife. And this woman—this wife—he met in a bar."

"She is trash," said Nadia.

"He left us no money when he walked away. When he left, I began to sew slippers. I did piecework, getting paid for each slipper I could sew. But after a while my eyes would not hold out. My eyes would not let me do such fine embroidery work—not with all the beatings I had taken to my head, beatings from him. That is why Nadia went to the factory."[1]

The two complained bitterly of the little support this man provides. Although he left her to marry the second wife, the man did not divorce Rashida. She remained his legal wife, and therefore, by law, he owed her financial support. He owned the house where the family continued to live, and he allowed them to live there rent-free. He owned a shop, and two of Nadia's three brothers worked there, taking their living from this occupation and using their earnings to contribute to the household expenses. But the father did not provide Rashida or her daughter with any cash. They believed that as a husband and father to an unmarried daughter, he owed them that—he owed them more than he was willing to give.

But this marriage between Rashida and her husband established other permanent links, ties that would not be broken by bitterness. Many years ago, Rashida had arranged for her own niece, Aisha—the daughter of her sister—to marry her husband's brother. Aisha—Nadia's cousin—was thus also her aunt—in English terms. Aisha and her husband had settled in Ben Souda two dusty blocks away from their close relatives. Rashida was the midwife for all of Aisha's six children. Rashida pulled the third daughter out of Aisha (right arm first, Rashida said), and Rashida fed the last baby bits of bread soaked in olive oil when Aisha had no milk to nurse her. Aisha's children called Rashida "mother." They often came to sit with her.

I listened carefully in the sitting room. We drank tea and watched television. As night began to fall I got up to leave, and Nadia joined me on my walk through the center of town to the taxi stand. "How are things going at Couture?" I asked her.

"I hate that job. I cannot tell you how much I hate it. I am leaving there at the end of this month. There are fourteen days left until we are paid, and then I'm going."

"What's happening there?"

"Last week we worked until 8 p.m. On some nights we have to stay until 10, even. And then what do we see? The owner drives up to the factory with a brand-new car. A beautiful new car. And we are working into the night." Nadia was outraged. My friends in the factory where I worked would never express their outrage so fiercely.

In the early fall, when it was still very hot in Fes, I had visited a small and old factory. When I walked into that factory, the heat of the workshop floor slapped me in the face. The air was so thick I felt I could not get a breath. The workers were dressed in sleeveless housedresses, as if they had stripped down as far as they could, and their dresses were wet with sweat. After the floor manager had very pleasantly showed me around the factory, he brought me to the office of the owner so that I could speak with him. The owner opened the door of his office and a blast of frigid air hit me hard. The owner's office was air-conditioned. Really, it was refrigerated. At that moment I wondered what the workers thought of this, for they knew how they were suffering from the heat, and surely they knew how cold that office was. And now, hearing of Nadia's outrage, I felt I knew with some certainty what those workers thought about the air-conditioned office.

.

Other visits to Nadia followed. One afternoon Nadia announced: "Aisha wants to see you. She is desperate to have you visit her." I had met Aisha only briefly thus far, when she had passed by the house with her daughter late one afternoon. And so I did not sit down on the banquette in Nadia's sitting room next to Jamila as I had on earlier visits. Instead, Nadia and I left the house, left Jamila in the sitting room, and headed down the dirt alley to Aisha's house.

Aisha's house was the upstairs portion of a two-story building. Downstairs was a shop that sold video cassettes, a shop frequented only by men, a shop that I never entered. The whole building was owned by Aisha's husband, although a tenant ran the shop. We entered near the shop and climbed a steep cement staircase into Aisha's house. We walked through a large, empty, tiled foyer to

Aisha's main sitting room, which was bright, because there was a large window on the wall facing the street.

The room was lined with banquettes that were crowded with women. Rashida was sitting there, and sitting next to her was an aunt I had already met, a squat, old widow with a round brown face who seemed always to be stopping in at Nadia's house but who said little. Aisha's 16-year-old daughter, Saida, tall and thin with wiry hair, was squeezed among the hefty women on the banquettes, her eyes swollen, crying visibly.

In the center of one banquette sat Aisha. Aisha was a large woman with a strong, loud voice. Her face was bold and round and well defined. Her hair was completely hidden under a scarf tied tightly around her head. The robes she wore had a sparkly thread running through them, a golden thread that matched her dangling earrings. I did not know Aisha yet, but I would soon learn that she was a commanding personality. She rarely got up from her position on the banquette. Instead, her daughters would carry tea and snacks in and out of the room, as she directed them. Aisha was always the center of attention. She liked to joke and watched to see that people laughed at her jokes, which they did, because she was funny. With time, though, I would come to detect a current of anger under the surface of her humor, an anger that frightened me, even though I had no reason to fear Aisha.

When I walked into the room, Aisha greeted me loudly, introducing me to the group of women, delighted that I—a foreigner—had come to visit her in her home. I quickly realized that I had stepped in on a funeral. "The woman who raised Saida," said Nadia, pointing to the thin teenager weeping on the banquette, "died two days ago."

"Who was this woman?" I asked, grasping to understand how I had been so desperately needed at this funeral.

"When Saida was born, Aisha was unable to nurse her, so she gave Saida to this woman, when she was just an infant. The woman nursed Saida and kept her. She took care of her until about four years ago, when Saida returned to Aisha."

"Where did this woman live?"

"She lived here, nearby, in the neighborhood. And although Saida had returned to live with Aisha and her siblings, she often stayed with this woman at night, keeping close to her." Nadia was bringing me up to date as we squeezed onto a banquette.

The women on the banquettes were quiet, mostly. They looked at Saida and reached out to touch her and used words to assure her. "You need not cry. This woman who has died, she was not really your mother." But these women could barely be heard, because the loudest voice in the room was Aisha's. Aisha was making fun of the fact that Saida had cried throughout the night. Aisha threw her head back and opened her mouth wide, imitating her daughter's weeping. The women watched her and said nothing, occasionally reaching out to Saida and otherwise just allowing Aisha to distract us all with her antics.

And then, almost as if she had decided to change the form of entertainment, Aisha turned to me. "How do you people manage your funerals?" she asked.

"We cry," I said. "We weep. We take our dead to the cemetery. We bury them in a casket."

And here Nadia's aunt, the stout, brown-faced widow who was sitting next to Rashida on the banquette, cut in, giving her own account of a French funeral she had once witnessed. With her thick rough fingers she daintily grabbed a cloth napkin from the coffee table and coyly held it to her face, covering only her mouth, whimpering softly. "This is how the French girls we knew cried at the death of their father," she said. "For three days the man's body was left out, unburied, and the French people looked at it. And then they put the body in the middle of the car and drove it to the cemetery. They wore black clothes and black veils on their faces and cried quietly and used handkerchiefs to cover their faces." With muted and controlled gestures, she again whimpered, imitating for us the sound of the French girls crying.

We all watched and listened. And then Aisha began to instruct me in the etiquette of Moroccan funerals. "In Morocco," she said, "the funeral is three days long, but the person is buried immediately, before the sun has set on the first day." She touched my arm as she instructed me on the finer points. "Now, if the person dies after the sun sets, they don't have to be buried until the next day, but the men will still try to bury the person immediately, even in the dark. Women, though, would not try, because women are afraid. Women wash the body of a woman who has died. If it is a man who has died, they will hire a man to wash the body, for a fee."

She continued: "And they don't bury the body in its clothes. They sew a cloth on the body to cover the body. And they never look at the body if they can avoid it. They cover the face of the dead person until the time comes to kiss the person. This time is right before the moment of burial. Then they lift the cloth off the person's face and kiss the person. And if the dead one is a virgin girl, they cover her body in a special way and put kohl on her eyes and *swark* (a twig that reddens lips) on her mouth.

"And then, they read the Qur'an at the cemetery, and they continue to read the Qur'an in the house for three days. Usually the *fqi* (Qur'anic teacher) comes to read the Qur'an, and the women all cry." At this point Aisha, who was completely engrossed in her own dramatic description of how funerals are conducted, began to demonstrate to me the precise sort of crying used to express grief appropriately. "This is how I cried at the funeral of my brother," she said, and she spread her legs out with knees bent, as if to brace her large body, and she began to throw her head forward and back forcefully, chanting in a loud and rhythmic mantra, "*oh hoya, oh habibi*" (oh my brother, oh my sweetheart), and she kept repeating these words of endearment and praise for her brother, over and over, slowly and rhythmically while moving her head, as in song. The sounds Aisha made were beautiful. This was the same kind of rhythmic repetition of phrases I had heard old women chant, although more peacefully, to rock babies to sleep.

And then, so completely swept into the drama of death, Aisha showed me how her own mother had mourned at her brother's funeral, reenacting for me the mournful cries and wails. "My mother," she said, "was destroyed by my brother's death. My mother lost five children in all." And with this, Aisha picked up the pace, moving her head more determinedly, more fervently shaking and singing phrases to her dead brother. At that moment she seemed to be reliving the loss.

And then Aisha pushed back her head scarf to show me how some women pull out their hair and scream and yell and flail their arms and use their entire bodies to express their grief. "It is necessary to do this at a funeral," she said. "Why don't you people do this?"

"I don't know." I could not explain.

"In Morocco," she said, "you must do this to show how much you loved the person, to show that you are sorry he died. If you don't do this, people will talk. They will say that you did not really love the person and that you do not miss him. For example," and here she pointed to the stout brown-faced aunt on the banquette near Rashida, "she did not cry loudly at her husband's funeral. She wept quietly. When I saw her just sitting there, crying that way, I went over to her sister and said, 'This is terrible, we must begin the crying. . . . People are saying that she does not really care that he is dead.' And then I said to her sister, 'You begin it.' And her sister said to me, 'No, you begin.' And so I did. Someone must begin the wailing, and then the others will follow."

"You see," she said, "as soon as you hear the wailing, you too will cry. It will make you cry just to hear it, and soon everyone in the room will be crying. This must happen at a funeral. Everyone must cry loudly and with feeling, or else it will be said that the person was not loved." And then Aisha showed me how she began to move her head and wail for the husband of the brown-faced aunt. "But I was not really crying for him, you know. I was crying for my own brother, who I told you had died years before. No one in the room is really crying for the dead person. They are really crying for their own dead. Everyone knows this. And this is good."

And the brown-faced aunt nodded her head, in complete agreement with Aisha's assessments, not for a moment offended by Aisha's admission that she had not really been crying for her husband. Aisha, it seemed to me, liked funerals. The very idea of a funeral seemed to please her in a very practical way.

Aisha finished eventually, and the conversation subsided. We drank tea and ate bread and I got up to leave. Aisha stood to walk me through her front foyer to the top of the steps. She stopped to point out a picture of her brother, for whom she retained so much grief. "He died at the age of 24 in a motorcycle accident. There was a girl with him at the time, but she did not die." The young man's picture, framed and large, was hanging high on the wall of the living room, although I had not noticed it before.

And then, as we were walking together to the taxi stand, Nadia told me that the boy in the picture, Aisha's brother, had wanted to marry her. "Nobody knew of this plan. It was still only between the two of us. Nobody knew that we had discussed this. Even today, nobody knows that we had planned to marry. That was four years ago, when he died. And when he died, I ate nothing for three days."

I could not think of much to say. It was too late to comfort Nadia on this loss, a loss that had happened so long ago. I wondered who the girl on the motorcycle had been. And then I squeezed into the taxi that would take me home to the Ville Nouvelle, and I decided that I understood Aisha's penchant for funerals. I was beginning to feel that there were a lot of things here to cry about.

CHAPTER 6

The Women in the Sitting Room

One afternoon I went to visit Nadia and found her ill. It was cold outside, and she was lying on the banquette in the chill of the sitting room, covered in a blanket, in pain. "There is something wrong with my uterus," she told me, and almost immediately Jamila rushed into the room, carrying two large X-rays which, she said, were pictures of Nadia's uterus.

"Nadia," Jamila excitedly began to explain, "is getting her period two times a month." And with that Jamila left the room, returning with her hands full of small bottles. These were the drugs that Nadia had recently purchased.

"We took Nadia to my specialist last week—the same doctor who treated me," said Jamila. Just last week, Nadia had taken the day off from work to seek medical help. She and Jamila left the house early in the morning and walked from Ben Souda to the doctor's office in the center of the *medina*. "We waited in the office from 8:00 that morning until it was time for lunch. The office was filled with people. And around noon, they sent us out—they told us to return in the afternoon. And so we came home."

"Why didn't you just wait in the *medina* and have lunch there?" I asked. The walk from Ben Souda to the center of the old city was long, I knew.

"We can't afford to eat in restaurants," Jamila answered quickly. "It's too expensive. So we just walked home, ate, and then walked back to the office in the afternoon. And then finally, at 4:00, they let her in to see the doctor."

The doctor had advised Nadia to get the X-rays that I was now being shown. This had forced her to stay home from the factory on yet another day—more loss of pay. Ultimately, Nadia was told to purchase the selection of prescription drugs that Jamila had brought out for my review. Nobody knew what the problem was, only that it concerned her uterus, which was now supposedly visible in the X-rays, which Jamila was displaying to me as proof of something conclusive and yet bewildering. Somehow buoyed by these developments and this contact with the medical profession, Jamila began to urge me to go visit this doctor. "Really, you should go," she said in a hushed voice. "You are married. You were married last summer. And you have no children yet." I expressed polite interest and waited for the conversation to change.

And soon Jamila returned to the discussion of her own lost children. "I have already had two," she reminded me, "but they both died. The second one was completely smashed up, as if it had been ground through a wheat mill. They did not know if it was a boy or a girl." And again I murmured words of sympathy, stunned by the matter-of-fact way in which Jamila kept telling me of this.

Nadia rested on the banquette throughout our visit, a blanket over her legs. Her mother, Rashida, sat next to her. At one point, Rashida leaned over her daughter and the two quickly kissed, saying nothing. When it was time for me to go, Rashida hit Nadia on the legs and told her to get up and walk me to the taxi stand. "You need to get up, you need to walk, it's enough now. You have been sick long enough."

More and more I could see that sickness seemed to surround us. But Moroccans accept sickness like they accept sadness. There can only be so much of it, and then it must be left behind.

.

Nadia went back to work at the Couture factory. She had not taken much time off for her illness—only the two days needed to visit the doctor and take the X-rays. The next time I saw her, she told me the girls at the factory were up in arms. There were only nine workers left now and very little work to be done. The factory owner left town for three days, leaving the floor manager in charge, and this had produced near chaos. "This man treats us like dogs," Nadia said. "He turns the lights off on us. He makes us work till nine at night without even letting us stop for food." The girls decided to take action.

"We planned to speak with the owner. We figured we'd get to him as soon as he got back. But, when he returned, he stood in front of us, in front of the line of machines, and told us to stop working, and he said, 'Shame on you,' and he began to lecture us. It seems that the floor manager had got to him first." "That's too bad," I said.

"Well, when he finished, all the girls stopped and got up and walked into his office and complained to him. He listened to us. He said to us, 'Speak one by one,' and so one by one we all told him about the horrible things the floor manager does to us. And the floor manager was standing there, with his head hanging."

In the end, Nadia asked the owner for her paperwork, telling him she planned to leave the job. He begged her to be patient, to stay with him. He told her that the floor manager had asked him to fire all the workers, but he had refused—he would never do this—he would never fire them. So Nadia stayed on at Couture for a while longer and nothing changed. The floor manager continued to berate and insult the workers.

I remembered how one factory owner had told me, in an interview, that he was always kind to his workers. He allowed the floor managers to be "strict" and "harsh" with the workers, in order to frighten them and compel them to work. He told me he stayed off the factory floor so as not to come into daily contact with the workers. But when he did confront a worker, he always treated her with kindness and respect, he said. In this way, he thought, he would make his workers feel loyal to him and to the factory. This seemed to be what the owner of Couture was doing. But I remembered this interview and what this owner had told me only after Nadia and I had separated that afternoon. I never bothered to tell her this owner had said that. I don't know if it would have mattered.

•

Ramadan had begun and I went to celebrate the break-fast meal with Nadia's family. Nadia had continued feeling ill and complained of getting her period every seven or fourteen days, despite the purchase of all the prescriptions the doctor had ordered. "I have spent close to 1,000 *dirham*, [which is more than the pay of even a good month in the factory] and have not even bought the renewal of these prescriptions. This doctor has done nothing for me. He is no good," she said. Rashida was certain that her daughter's illness was caused by the stress of her factory work.

"My daughter is a good girl, isn't she?" she asked me, to make a point.

"Of course she is."

"She works hard. She makes no trouble. My daughter is straight. So why do they cause problems for her?"

Rashida, too, had been ill. For two days she had been unable to stand up, so weak were her legs. She made a visit to the *fqi,* who wrote a verse from the Qur'an on a piece of paper for her. She soaked the paper with the holy phrase in water, although she was unable herself to read the words, and drank the water down. "I am healing now," she told me, "thanks to this cure." As soon as we finished dinner, Rashida disappeared from the house. She had hurried off to get more healing from the *fqi.* I thought of Abdul-Haq. He would not approve.

Then there is the fqi. Women go to the fqi a lot. They spend a lot of money at the fqi. Why? The reason is psychological. Again, women spend their time at home. They cannot go out. They are forced to stay home and think of their problems. If they do speak, they speak to other women, perhaps in their apartment building, who tell them to go to a fqi. For example, if a woman is jealous of her husband, or if she has some deformity and looks in the mirror and sees this deformity, she is afraid he will marry someone else. So she tells her neighbor and her neighbor eggs her on, saying, "Yes, I am sure your husband has another woman. I have seen him with another woman." And the neighbor encourages her to go to the fqi. She says, "I know a fqi who freezes water—that is how powerful this fqi is." So the woman goes to visit the fqi.

A fqi is completely different from a doctor. Why? The doctor is dressed in city clothes, he has a clean office with a telephone, and he writes things down. He is completely different from the woman herself and what she knows. But the fqi is exactly like her. He wears clothes like the people she knows wear. The doctor has a pen, but the fqi does not even use a pen. He uses an instrument fashioned out of wood, and he does not even use real ink. The fqi is completely and totally different from the doctor, and people like him for this reason.

The big problem with the fqi: He gets women to waste their money. Women waste tons of money at the fqi. Once they begin to go to a fqi, it is like a drug they cannot stop. So the woman becomes a slave to that fqi. She will do anything he tells her to do. He will say come back tomorrow, come back tomorrow. He will keep telling her to come back, and she will keep coming back. She puts all her faith in the fqi and has no faith in God. For her the fqi is like a god.

And the fqi helps women poison their husbands. The fqi writes spells with that special pen; three times he must write something. The first time he will write something with that pen and then tell the woman to soak the paper with the writing on it in water and give the husband the water to drink. In this way he will ingest the words and ingest the spell. And then perhaps the fqi will tell the woman to feed her husband the tongue of a donkey. The fqi will get her the donkey tongue at an exorbitant rate. Ultimately after three or four years of ingesting these poisons the man will become extremely ill. His hair will all fall out and his skin will turn yellow. So the problem with the fqi is that he helps women poison their husbands.

So, not all people like the fqi. Except for women.

Encouraged by her mother, and her mother's apparent cure, Nadia also made a visit to the *fqi*. He wrote godly words for her as well, which she began to wear under her shirt, words on a small piece of paper tied with a scarf to her waist. She had quickly noticed an improvement. "A *fqi*," she told me, "is better than a doctor. The medicines the doctors give never work and are far too expensive."

Jamila, too, complained of her health problems. Although it was now February, she said she was still suffering from the miscarriage she had in November. "I know," she said, "that my uterus is not in the right place. My nose bleeds at night, and my head gives me horrible pain. When I was pregnant, I could barely walk. Even after only two months of pregnancy, I found it hard to move." She went on to ponder why she suffered so from her childbearing. "Quickly after marriage," she said, "my sister had three children. My mother had eight children. No one in my family has had children who have died. Except me. I am the only one with this trouble." She shook her head as if bewildered, sounding almost annoyed.

And then she told me of a plan she had devised: she would take the birth control pill prescribed to her every other day, rather than every day, during Ramadan. This way, she believed, she would put off her menstruation through most of the month, and would be able to fast nearly every day. "Last year," she told me, "I was able to fast only about five days during Ramadan. Because of the miscarriage and the illness it caused me, I had to eat all the rest of the days of that month. And so, over this past year, I had to make up 25 days—25 days I had to fast alone, all by myself. This is too difficult."

I listened to Jamila, and I said nothing. I thought to tell her that this was a bad idea. I worried as she spoke that maybe she would become pregnant again, so soon after the last disaster. I started to tell her that she should not risk another pregnancy now. But I stopped myself. Almost as I started to speak I realized that she would not listen to me. Jamila would have children at any cost. And at the moment, I felt I was surrounded by people who were overcome with inexplicable, incurable ailments, illnesses I knew nothing of and could not make better. Just the day before, I had gone to visit another factory friend, and in her home I had been introduced to her niece, a 6-year-old girl whose face was blue. "There is something wrong with her heart," my friend had explained. "She had one operation already, but it did not work. She needs a second operation." As Jamila spoke, my mind was on this child. I had no remedy for Jamila or for any of them.

I just sat and talked of other things with Jamila. She seemed always to want to sit next to me. Whenever I entered the room, she moved over slightly on the banquette and gestured for me to sit close to her. And then in a soft voice, as people moved in and out of the room, she would tell me things. Perhaps it was because I was from the outside—I was not her in-law—Jamila felt safe with me. Or perhaps Jamila liked me simply because she knew I wanted to hear what she said. This time, just to move the subject away from her dead children, I asked her whether she had ever worked.

"Oh, yes, I worked. I worked for six months in a garment factory in Casablanca."

"What did you do there?"

"I wrote things down. I worked in the administration. I had been to high school, you know, so I could write. I was there for six months and then left."

"Why did you leave?"

"There were constant problems there, constant fighting among the girls. I couldn't bear it, so I left. And after that, I married."

No one was in the room. Nadia and her mother were in the kitchen, making preparations for the break-fast meal. I wanted to ask Jamila how she could stand it—how could she stand her marriage—sitting in this room, day after day, preparing meals, washing clothing, never leaving these rooms. But I was afraid to be so rude, so direct. I tried my way around the question. "Do you like Fes?" I asked her. "Is it hard to be here, away from your family?"

"No, it is not hard to be away from the family so much. But it is hard to come to a new house." But that is all she would say. And then she repeated the story of her wedding, a story she had already told me. "When they brought me into this house, I cried and screamed hard, so hard that Yousef had to hit me, and only then did I stop. It is hard, marriage—a new house. I am still shy here. I am still shy in front of Yousef."

"Do you go out?" I asked. Thus far, I had never seen Jamila leave the house. She never accompanied us to visit Aisha. I had to know if she ever got out. Perhaps, when I was not there, she was outside dancing in the streets.

"Yousef does not want me to go out. Sometimes he takes me to the *medina*." Jamila said this with no feeling. This was not voiced as a complaint. The sitting room was getting darker as the sun sank in the sky. The call to prayer sounded, and the three brothers walked into the room and assembled around the table, which had already been set for the break-fast meal. Nadia and Rashida came in quickly with the *hrira*. The soup was passed around quickly, and the room became silent except for the sounds of slurping.

We ate what was on the table, and as soon as it was cleared, the brothers abruptly stood and went outside to smoke cigarettes. They returned, and we ate a second meal—dinner. When this was complete, the three men left the room and did not reappear that evening. We women sat in front of the television, watching Egyptian soap operas interrupted by loud commercials. And then Nadia and I stepped outside into the dirt square in front of the house.

Children were dashing about, waving sparklers made of ignited steel wool on sticks, running, calling to each other. A girl appeared with a long rope and suddenly a large gathering of girls, women, even old ladies, emerged from nowhere. Nadia knew all these girls—they were neighbors living in the houses surrounding her own. I had never before seen any of them, although I had walked the neighborhood streets many times. In the safety of the darkness they began to jump rope, and Nadia and I joined in. We jumped and talked, the girls laughing, shameless in the dark. And while we played, Jamila stood in the shadows of the doorway of the house watching. I went to stand with her. "Why don't you join us, Jamila?" I asked.

"I cannot jump rope. I don't know how to play outside," she said, matter-of-factly.

I looked at her quizzically. "Really, though," she said, laughing, "when I was a child, I was afraid of the little girls in our neighborhood and never went outside. I stayed inside always, near my mother." Jamila's tone suggested to me that she was proud of this fear and of her proclivity to remain inside. This idea—that the street is unclean and unfit for nice girl children—was a theme I had heard voiced by Moroccans, so it did not surprise me. "Anyway," Jamila continued, "Yousef does not want me to go outside. He doesn't want anyone to see me."

"But don't you want to go out?" I asked.

"No, I really don't like it out there. I'd rather stay inside."

And so I left Jamila in the shadows of the doorway where she stood and joined the girls jumping rope.

•

Sometime in the middle of Ramadan, the workers at Nadia's factory received their pay for the month. The pay was short by 100 *dirham*. Without reason, without warning, the workers had received 100 *dirham* less than usual. "The factory just took 100 *dirham* from our pay," Nadia told me, outraged. "Now we are angry. This time we are really going to walk out. But we're waiting for the owner to return from France. He went there to meet with a client. But this Monday—or maybe Tuesday—whenever he returns, we're walking. We've had enough. We work into the night, you know. It's Ramadan, and we work into the night. And this is what we get."

The workers waited a few days, and then finally the owner returned. They were ready to confront him with their problems, but again the floor manager got to him first. And again the owner told them they should be ashamed of themselves for their improper behavior. This time, though, they did not get the opportunity to speak with him directly. "We just collected our advances—we are being given a small advance on the next month's pay—and we left. We're not going back—but we haven't told the owner that." The way Nadia spoke, I thought that she was describing a worker action. I thought there had been some kind of revolt; that amongst themselves the workers had decided that they would refuse to return when they were called.

However, as Nadia continued to explain, there was no work available at the moment anyway. When the workers walked out they were told not to return the next day. They would be called back as soon as a new shipment of cloth from France arrived. When I heard that the factory was shutting down, I realized that this was not a worker action at all. I could not label this a wildcat strike or a work slowdown. It was simply a factory closing. The closing was supposed to be temporary, but this was a closing nonetheless. The agreement the workers had made among themselves, the agreement to refuse to return when the owner called them back, was an attempt, it seemed to me, to stand up to the cruel floor manager and the manipulative owner. It was the workers' attempt to grasp some control, some retribution for the injustices they had been dealt. But really, it meant nothing, because the factory had shut down.

·

Ramadan was nearing the end. The next time I visited Nadia, nearly all the furniture had been removed from the inside of the house and stacked up in the courtyard. The rooms were being painted. Rashida took the opportunity to give me a tour of the house—I had never seen the upstairs. We crept up a narrow cement staircase to a second floor, where Jamila and Yousef's room was located. The walls of their room were unpainted cement, but the room was filled with massive faux mahogany furniture—a dresser, a wooden headpiece on the bed, a wardrobe—furniture that looked anomalous against the unfinished cement walls. From the second floor we climbed to the roof, where a chicken pen housed chickens.

"This part of the house is not finished—we have never completed building—because of my husband," Rashida said. "We planned to build another room here, on the roof, but now, since he took that other woman, this won't be possible. Or it will take a long time. We have no money."

I couldn't stand the bitterness, somehow. I was growing weary. I had been working in a factory for weeks now and had heard worse stories. "Well, thank God, you do have the house. You have no rent to pay."

"Thank God," Rashida nodded, and she quickly returned to her usual attitude. "We have no rent. Thank God for that."

We broke the fast together and then ate dinner. But this time we were not going to sit. Nadia was eager to go to Macro, a giant, newly constructed superstore on the outskirts of Fes. We were heading to Macro to see what products they might have to help in Nadia's restoration project.

"I am desperate to get this house fixed up," Nadia told me. "It is my idea to get this painting done. I've wanted to do it for a long time. But Yousef just doesn't care."

"Can you come with us?" I asked Jamila as we prepared to go. She did not budge from her place on the banquette.

"No," she said. "I did not tell Yousef. He has already gone back to the shop. People like to buy food in the evenings in Ramadan." And so we left. We left without Jamila.

On the way to Macro we stopped at Aisha's. We had gotten the word that Aisha wanted to see me. "Aisha wants to see you" was something I would hear over and over in my visits to Nadia's house. Aisha, I knew, liked the entertainment my presence provided. When we arrived that early evening, perhaps because the subject of Nadia's recent renovation was in the air, Aisha gave me a tour of the finest room in her own home: the bedroom of her firstborn child and her only son, Si Muhammad.

I had already met Si Muhammad, a tall and handsome young man of 21, who stopped in often to see Rashida and his cousins. Si Muhammad had not completed much schooling and had just recently been brought into the family's shopkeeping business. Si Muhammad was a dandy, always dressed in the best European style—leather jackets, white track sneakers, and bright, silky shirts. When he stopped for a visit, Nadia would admire him, flirt with him, and tease him about his fashionable clothes and his many girlfriends. The last time I had seen Si Muhammad, he told me that he had had an offer of marriage from a European girl—"a European like yourself," he had told me. He claimed that a girl from Spain was interested in marriage, but his mother had forbidden him to entertain this idea. I liked Si Muhammad for his verve and his sense of style. Si Muhammad behaved as if he owned the world.

Now Aisha was proudly leading me into his bedroom, which was located off the empty tiled foyer in Aisha's house. I had glanced into this room before, in passing while moving through the foyer into the sitting room. I had always assumed that this room was the master bedroom, where Aisha and her husband slept. But it was not. This was the room of Si Muhammad. It was a large room, at the center of which was a giant bed, covered with a satiny white cloth. Over the bedstead hung a large framed picture of Si Muhammad himself, a portrait of just his face, in which he looked strikingly like the eldest son of the Moroccan king, the heir to the throne. Opposite the bed, on a dark wooden dresser sat a large television, and next to this television hung a giant framed mirror. All of this for Si Muhammad.

Such an elaborate private bedroom for one person was a strange phenomenon in Ben Souda. Moroccans in the lower classes do not usually strive to provide their children with fancy, individualized bedrooms. But even stranger was the room next to Si Muhammad's. Next to his bedroom was the bedroom of Aisha's five daughters, girls ranging in age from 6 to 20. This bedroom was a tight, dingy sitting room, lined with banquettes that the girls slept on each night. It housed no dresser, no television, no mirror, no photograph. Nothing but banquettes.

Sons, I knew, are dearly valued in Morocco. But daughters are dearly valued, too. Everyone knows that daughters love their parents until the end. One day when a factory girl and I passed an old man begging in the market, the girl told me, "It's likely that old man has no daughters. That is why he's forced to beg."

So when Nadia and I left Aisha's house, I said, "Nadia, Si Muhammad's room is so beautiful. And the girls have nothing. How can this be so?"

"You know, Titia," she said, "here in Morocco we say that the girl is not important. The boy is important because he will stay at home after he marries. But the girl will leave."

"Yes, I know, but—"

"Aisha really wanted more sons. Each time she was pregnant, she would say, 'It's a boy, it's a boy,' and every time, after the birth of Si Muhammad, it was a girl. Five girls after Si Muhammad." I thought about Aisha and all those daughters as we tripped in the dark on the dirt path alongside the highway to the superstore.

Nadia was happy. The trip was exciting. "You know, Titia," she said, "I saw my father here once, buying beer." She looked, I think, for my reaction. I had none. "I once tasted beer. I like it. I really do. I think it's okay to drink a little beer—with some food."

We entered Macro, where the entry doors are automatic and the fluorescent light casts a gray tone on the products lined up on shelves in the massive building. We walked up and down the aisles. Nadia touched the products on display. Soda glasses, china tea pots, glazed figurines, little spice containers. She turned things over, looking at the tags, which I knew she could not read. She talked about her goal to make her house beautiful. "Whenever I come to Macro, I just die to have money. I want lots and lots of money. I need money when I come here. I like everything here." And we laughed.[1]

"You know," she said, "if I had been working for myself—if my father had not left us—I would have gold up my arm. I would have been able to buy an armful of gold, if I had just been working for myself all these years. But everything I earn is for the house. So I have nothing. No gold. It's because of my father." And we continued to look at the treasures in Macro. We walked down the aisle where china dishes sat displayed on shelves, and the aisle where clean boxes of crackers were stacked on the shelves, and the refrigerated sections where hundreds of tiny containers of yogurt were on display. And then we went back out into the darkness.

But the trip to Macro had moved our minds to other places. "You know," Nadia said, "I have a cousin who has gone to France. He told me he would marry me and take me there, as soon as he gets a house."

"Would you want to go there?" I asked. "Wouldn't it be hard for you to leave your mother?"

"Its true, you're right. My mother and I are tied to each other. When my mother goes to visit people, and they tell her to stay, she says, 'No, I can't stay. I have Nadia at home.' And she always says, 'Nadia, when you get married, bring your husband to live here with us.'"

"She's right," I said. "When you marry, you should try to stay near her."

"Yes. But still, if I could go to France, if I could get away from this life, the troubles in my house, I'd do it. I'd do anything."

•

Some weeks passed. Late one afternoon I arrived at Nadia's to find Rashida resting on the banquette with Aisha's youngest daughter curled in her arms. Hassan, Rashida's second son, sat near them. The three were watching a black-and-white American movie dubbed in French. No one could understand the words, but with great interest they were discussing the clothing the actresses wore. I noticed that Hassan seemed particularly interested. When the movie ended, Hassan announced that he was going to the *hammam,* and he left.

On my previous visit, I had arrived to find Hassan in the kitchen, washing all the utensils in a large bowl of soapy water. Another time, I found Hassan helping Rashida with laundry. Once when we were eating in the sitting room, we heard a knock at the door and Rashida instructed Hassan to get up and see who was there. All of these were tasks for women, but Hassan happily carried them out. Most Moroccans say that it is inappropriate for a man to do women's work. Surely, if a man finds himself with no female assistance, he might prepare tea or cook something light. But it is shameful for a man—surrounded by women—to do laundry or heavy housecleaning. Nadia's other brothers were rarely even at home. Her eldest brother, when not working at the shop, spent his time and wasted his money in cafés and restaurants, Nadia said. Although Yousef sometimes sat at home with Jamila, he too limited his time spent in the sitting room. But Hassan was often at home. Hassan did women's work.

Hassan was the only one of Nadia's three brothers who did not work in the shop. He caused too much trouble, I was told, when he was there. It seemed to me that Hassan did not work at all. He remained comfortably at home. From time to time he sat with us and contributed to conversations, even conversations about such things as wedding clothing. He was thin and kind and sweet. He had a strange way of speaking. I could not figure out what was going on with Hassan. Nobody would tell me.

Almost as soon as Hassan left the room, Nadia returned. She had been out visiting her friend with whom she was planning to start a new job the following week. Couture had called Nadia back to work.

"I told them I'd be back. But I'm not going," she told me. "I'm not going back there. I will only work for a good factory—a really good factory this time." She had begun to hunt for a new job. In the early morning hours she would walk to Sidi Brahim with her friend Amina, a veteran worker. Amina had a contact in a new factory that would open next week. Nadia was fairly certain they would start work there the coming Monday—or maybe Tuesday—when this new factory was set to open its doors. She would not return to Couture.

I had been absent for over a week. The agency funding my research had organized a conference in Yemen, which I had been invited to attend, and I had now returned with gifts of cloth which the family had asked me to bring. With some embarrassment, I presented the gifts of cloth and scarves that I had brought, feeling it was not enough. Throughout the afternoon, Nadia studied with delight the heavily brocaded fabrics, saying how she would use them to make beautiful gowns. One piece of cloth in particular would be perfect for her wedding day. Again and again she modeled the scarves I had brought. And then she left the room and came back with a *djellaba* with an elaborate machine embroidered design. "This *djellaba* was sewn by my father's second wife. It is too small for her, and she is trying to sell it now," she said. And then she left the room again and came back with a pile of small towels that the second wife had embroidered. "This is what I am going to do, as soon as I get back to work. I am going to buy towels and embroider them, and buy napkins and a tablecloth, and embroider all of them, in preparation for my wedding." I knew that Moroccan girls traditionally put together a trousseau of finely embroidered linens for their wedding. "I have not yet done anything like this because I always thought that I would wait until a man came and asked for me. But now I'm going to just start—I'll do the work, so that if a man comes, I will be ready. And then I'll use the money he gives me to buy a washing machine instead of buying this kind of stuff."

"Good idea. But why a washing machine?" I had never been inside a house in the factory districts with a washing machine.

"Because I hate to do laundry. When I do laundry, I get dizzy and I feel like I am going to fall down, and when I raise my head, it hurts and I feel sure I'm going to fall. I do all kinds of housework—I can do everything—but not laundry. So I'll buy a washing machine with the money he gives me. And I'll already have embroidered all these other things I need. Because if a girl does not have these things at her wedding, people will say she has nothing."

•

The family—or at least the women in the family—had recently been to visit a saint at a nearby shrine. They assured me that they had wanted to bring me with them. They had telephoned me, but I was not home. I knew that this was a lie, but I thanked them for thinking of me. I felt that this little lie marked a kind of transition in our relationship. Now, maybe because of the cloth from Yemen, they were going to let me know about their shrine visitations. In Morocco, many women, especially poor and uneducated women, visit the shrines to ask saints to intercede with God on their behalf. The educated and the modern classes scorn such behavior and consider it forbidden by Islam. Many men consider it an expression of women's folly. For this reason my friends would not readily admit that they persisted in such outmoded and demeaned practices. Abdul-Haq had strong opinions on the visitation of saints:

The thing that is important about saints is that they have baraka. They have baraka which is a grace, a holiness that comes from God. Moroccans say, for example, that there is baraka in sharing food on one plate. That is, if there is only a little bit of food in a plate, and many people share that small amount of food, they will feel satisfied, they will feel full. That is because there is baraka in sharing the plate of food. And if a man works and has to give his salary to his family if he only earns a little bit of money but must divide it many ways to feed his wife and children, the money will suffice because there is baraka.

Now saints have baraka. It is often women who go to visit saints. They go there, meet their friends, visit, talk. Women particularly go to saint shrines because whereas men have a lot of work to do and are extremely busy, women must stay inside the house all day, left alone with their thoughts. They cannot talk to other women, they have no one to share their thoughts with, so they go to visit the saint.

A man works all day, and on Sunday, his only day off, he gets up, goes to the hammam, does the shopping and in the afternoon, he wants to go to a café. If he is single he will go to the movies, but if he is married, he will just go to a café, as this is the only cheap alternative. A man has no time in his active and busy life to go to a saint shrine. He has no time for thoughts like women have.

Why do women visit saints? They go when they fear their husband is going to marry someone else. They look in the mirror and the mirror tells them they are old and ugly but the saint tells them they are young and beautiful so they go and tell their problems to the saint. Or, they go when they cannot bear children. First, they try herbal treatments. Then, they eat seven mice fried in oil. When these things do not work, they go to the saint and ask him to give them children. They swear by the saint, in the name of God, that if he gives them children they will sacrifice something to him—a chicken, or a cow, perhaps.

They might go to a saint for something as simple as having their son pass an exam or get a driving permit. Or if they are jealous of another woman with their husband. This is why women go to visit saint shrines.

I knew that they had visited a shrine at least once before that year. One day, shortly after I had first met the family, I dropped by in the morning for a visit. I found the women gathering up bags, putting items together, preparing to go out. I heard the word *chicken*, but this was before I knew that there were chickens living on the roof, and I was sure I heard the word *blood*. But the women were behaving secretively, as if I had caught them at something. They very politely offered to make tea and made some gestures toward greeting me as a guest, but I knew I had interrupted them, and I lied about being on my way to somewhere else. They did not insist that I stay. I left. I was sure they were going somewhere with a chicken, somewhere they did not wish me to know about. I assumed that they were headed for a saint's shrine, where the chicken would be sacrificed. Where else would they be taking the chicken?

Now, some months later, they would tell me about their most recent visit to the shrine. "Originally," they said, "we thought we would stay there, at the shrine for five days. But in the end, we only passed the afternoon there, and then came home."

"Why did you come home so quickly if you had planned to stay so long?" I asked. This made no sense to me.

"People often go to this shrine for an indefinite amount of time. They go, and they plan to stay there. They stay until they are healed or until they get the message to leave. Usually they just cannot leave until they are healed. People go to this saint to have children, to get cured, for many reasons," Nadia said. "For example, there was a man there who just cannot stop speaking. It is as if he has no mind, as if he is crazy. He has been there for months. He cannot leave the shrine, he just stays there." They had seen many awful sights at this shrine, and Nadia seemed eager to tell me all about them.

"And there was an older woman there, a grandmother, who was a Berber, but who spoke Arabic. And she had with her a little baby girl. This girl was her granddaughter. The girl already had her teeth, but she could not walk. The girl's hands were all curled up, and her feet were straight and stiff, and she couldn't move. Her mother had already had a second baby, a boy, and he was already walking. But this baby girl could not move. The father had spent two million on her at doctors, with no results. They were very wealthy; this was obvious from the way they were dressed. The old woman was very clean. The baby girl spoke Berber to her. She had a beautiful face, but she just couldn't move. It was terrible." Rashida kept nodding as Nadia spoke. This sight bothered her.

"And there was a girl who had a spell placed upon her. She had been engaged to a man, and she had already received many wedding gifts. Everything was prepared for the marriage. Everything was purchased, the furniture for the couple, everything. But then a spell was placed on her, and the wedding plans came unhinged. The man refused to marry her. And now, every time a man comes to marry her, to ask for her, he comes to her house and then discovers that he prefers one of her sisters, and he takes a sister instead. So far, two of her younger sisters have been married, and she has been left behind. That is why she was at the shrine. She was weeping pitifully there."

"Why did *you* go there?" I asked, although I already knew.

"We went for Jamila, for her to have children," Nadia began.

"But she is still taking the birth control pills," I said, "How will she get pregnant?" I knew she had changed the dosage over Ramadan, but assumed she had returned to the prescribed method after the month of fasting.

"Oh, no," Nadia answered. "She is no longer on the pills."

"But the doctor told her to stay with the pills for now," I said.

"Yes, he did, but she is no longer going to that doctor. We brought her to the *fqi*, to find out why she can't have children. And do you know what we learned? The problem is her aunt—her father's brother's wife."

"What about her aunt?"

"The *fqi* determined that she cannot have children because her aunt has put a spell on her. This woman is known to do magic, and she placed a spell on Jamila."

"Why would she do such a thing?"

"Because this woman's son wanted to marry Jamila. It would have been a perfect marriage, you know. They are the children of brothers. But Jamila went outside the family and married Yousef, and so now this woman has put a spell on Jamila. This is why Jamila's children are dying."

The *fqi*, I was told, divined this using numbers. "First, he asked Jamila her father's name, and then her mother's name, and then he put numbers to these words, looked the numbers up in a book, and divined that the person causing this trouble was the father's brother's wife." I was working hard to follow this, and Nadia was speaking quickly. For her this was almost obvious. "Then he asked Jamila if there was any trouble in the family, any fighting with this woman. 'Yes,' Jamila told him. 'Yes, there has been trouble with her.' 'So she is the problem, then,' the *fqi* said. 'She is the reason your children are dying. She is why you are unable to become pregnant again.'"

As soon as they had received this information from the *fqi*, they had organized the trip to the saint's shrine, to beg the saint for assistance.

But now Jamila was upstairs, sleeping. It was clear to me that she was not receiving the sympathy I thought might be due her as a result of this unsettling discovery. It was clear that, instead, Rashida and Nadia were angry at Jamila.

"She has been in bed for two days now, since we returned from the shrine. Now it is her toe that is hurt—she cannot walk." Nadia's voice was thick with sarcasm. "She is sickly, you know. She denies it. She claims that she was never sick before coming to this house, but that's a lie. Even her own sister says that she was always sickly, even before, in her own parents' house." And with this comment, Nadia's bitterness only seemed to increase and a torrent of venom spewed from her. She began with her opinion of Casablanca, the city of Jamila's birth, the city where her sister-in-law's family still remained.

"She is from Casablanca, you know, and Casablanca is a bad place. Once, when I was there, I had a watch stolen right off my wrist. Yes, it was taken from my wrist. That city is evil, and everyone in Casablanca does witchcraft. They are crazy for witchcraft in Casablanca. They do it constantly. Nothing like this exists in Fes. Compared to Casa, hardly anyone in Fes does witchcraft."

Nadia looked at me to be certain I had taken her point. I put a look of surprise and interest on my face. I had known that Jamila was from Casablanca and that Nadia's family had traveled there to be hosted by the bride's family at the time of the wedding. But such vitriol I had never heard. And then, when she was certain I was paying attention, Nadia went on. "This is how Jamila got Yousef. She got him using witchcraft, plain and simple." Rashida had been sitting with us, quietly, letting her daughter defame Casablanca, neither agreeing nor disagreeing. But as Nadia uttered this statement, the mother nodded slowly and definitively. This was certain. Nadia continued. "Yousef and Aisha's son—Si Muhammad—went to Khenifra once to visit the son of our father's third brother—the boy who was married to Jamila's sister. Together the three traveled to Casablanca, and that is when Jamila first saw Yousef. She saw him and immediately wanted him. She even told Yousef that she wanted him. To his face she told him this." A look of disbelief crossed my face, for I knew that such a thing was shameful, and I doubted, strongly, that Jamila, so meek and compliant in this household, would dare make such a move. Nadia responded, "This is shocking, but it is true." And Rashida continued to nod. I had heard another version of this story already: I had heard about the love letters that began with "*habibi, habibi.*" But I had not yet heard this.

"From that day on," Nadia continued, "from the moment Yousef saw Jamila, Yousef began to cry. He cried all the time, and he said that he would marry Jamila or he would die. And so we all went to Casablanca to visit her family." Nadia lifted a clay mug from the table to drink. This story was going to take a long time. "We saw her, and immediately we did not want her. We didn't want her because she did not know how to do housework well at all. She still can't do the housework well. My mother here has to do everything." And again Rashida nodded. "When I am out at work my mother has to get up and lift all the furniture out of the room to put it in the sun, because Jamila cannot do it. She doesn't know how to clean the room properly. I myself do the work on

Sundays, because I cannot bear to sit in a dirty room, to have people come over to a dirty room."

"We went to Casablanca, and we were not at all impressed. And so we came back to Fes, saying we would think about it. And then one week later, Jamila's father came to our house. We were terribly embarrassed. We had wanted time to think, and he had given us only one week—he came right away. And he said, 'If you want her, let's talk about the money.' Well, we did not want her, but we were so embarrassed. Plus, Yousef was still crying, still saying that he would marry her or die. What could we do? We talked to her father."

"They were married very quickly. That is how Casablanca girls do it: they marry when they can. As soon as Jamila came into our house, after the wedding ceremony in Casablanca, when we brought her back here, we noticed that there was a rock under the table. When her family left, leaving her with us, a rock was left behind. That is how we knew it was witchcraft. She had used witchcraft to get Yousef. That is why Yousef was crying so much after he met her, and that is why he took her so quickly. Now Yousef often says, 'Why did I marry?' He doesn't understand why he married at such a young age. He is only 26."

And as she spoke, it seemed that Nadia's bitterness increased. She said that Yousef had not passed his high school exam but that she had been prepared to work, to pay for him to complete his schooling at a private school. "Then," she said, "Jamila stepped in, and she put an end to that plan."

In my own calculations, it seemed to me that Jamila had appeared long after Yousef had left high school, but I did not argue.

"I myself would never want to do magic to get a man. This is never a good idea, because once you get the man, the magic begins to wear off, and he will soon start to hit you and dislike you." And Nadia began to repeat what she had said before—that Jamila was sickly and had always been sickly, that she was lazy and did not know how to do housework. "Yousef is so kind and gentle and nice to people that he tries to deal with her. He has patience for her."

And my mind flashed to the image of Jamila standing in the doorway of the house on that Ramadan night, saying that she never really liked to go outside, and the memory of Jamila sitting in the dark little room when Nadia and I had taken that stroll to Macro, saying that Yousef had already returned to the shop and it was too late for her to ask him if she could go. I wondered if Jamila was really asleep upstairs and whether she could hear us talking down here. And now I really felt sorry for Jamila.

•

We were eating *harsha*, flat cornbread that Rashida cooked on a gas burner that had been carried into the sitting room so she could cook as she sat with us. It was about 5 p.m. The phone rang in the narrow hallway, and Nadia jumped up to answer it. She spoke curtly for a few minutes and then returned to the sitting room. She did not sit back down. "Titia, do you want to go to Macro now?"

"Sure," I said. Nadia put on a new and colorful *djellaba* and wrapped a silken scarf around her neck. She stood in front of the small mirror hanging in the dark hallway and applied eye makeup and lipstick, which she urged me to share. I declined and she told me I should use more makeup and dress more fashionably, and then we left the house.

As soon as we stepped outside, Nadia told me the plan. "Titia, there is a teacher I met. He called me, and we are going to meet him at Macro." I was stunned. I had not expected Nadia to be secretly courting, given the rather conservative perspective she held on Jamila's life and the fact that it seemed to me that as far as I could tell, when she was not working, she was at home with her mother or sitting in Aisha's house. I was also worried. It would be considered shameful for an unmarried girl to be meeting a man, and the neighborhood was full of Nadia's relatives and family friends. We were sneaking out to meet a man for Nadia now, and if found out, I would be implicated in the scheme.

We moved quickly through the dirt roads of Ben Souda, toward the Meknes highway, and then headed out on the path along the side of the road to the supermarket. I was moving along, thinking I could not abandon Nadia now. She could not be seen walking alone. I was her cover. Within minutes a car driving past us pulled to the side of the road.

"I think that is him. That looks like his car," Nadia said.

"But it can't be him. Two men are in that car." And then the driver emerged from the car, and so did his companion, and we stood, all four of us, at the side of the Meknes highway, politely greeting each other in the long and drawn-out series of gestures and greetings Moroccans make when saying hello.

The young men suggested we all go to a café, and Nadia quickly agreed. I nodded my consent, but a creeping disquiet was coming over me. This girl, I thought, has three brothers, a father, and an uncle who own a business in the neighborhood. Everyone knows them. I do not want them to see me with their sister, riding around in a strange car with unfamiliar men. Word of such an event would spread quickly, and while there was surely no real risk here for me, I would find this situation embarrassing. Nadia's reputation would suffer and her family would be angry. Moreover, I was not interested in what seemed to be looking more and more like a double date. "Nadia," I said, grabbing at an excuse she could not refuse. "I am married. If someone told my husband I was in a café with these men, it would be very bad for me." Nadia agreed quickly— relieved, I thought—to avoid the café. She explained the situation to the men, who were graciously apologetic. They made a plan for us all to meet at the supermarket instead.

Nadia and I walked on and the men drove ahead of us. When we arrived at Macro, the men were standing right inside the electric doors, awaiting our arrival. Nadia and her date started off, strolling up and down the aisles of the giant store, a museum of imported goods rarely seen in Ben Souda. Nadia's date leaned in close to her as they walked, grasping her arm. The two immediately became engrossed in secretive conversation. I strolled behind them, accompanied by her date's friend. He informed me that he and his companion were both training to be high school math teachers. They were renting an apartment in Ben Souda until the end of July, when their training would end and when the government would assign them a teaching position somewhere in Morocco. They had no idea where in Morocco they would be posted.

After some time, Nadia and her friend separated, and she announced that it was time for us to leave. We set out back down the highway's side in the dark. "It is so obvious that this man is educated," Nadia began. "Titia, did you notice that he did not force me to go to a café with him? He never pushed me. He let me do what I wanted to do. This is because he is educated. An *arubi* [a person from the countryside, an uneducated person] would have forced me to go to the café. He would have been so crude, so uncivilized. I really cannot bear un-educated people. I can barely even speak to them." And thus Nadia praised her new friend, although Nadia herself had had little more than a year of formal schooling.

"I am surprised, Nadia, that you have a boyfriend," I told her, curious and still somewhat surprised by this incident. "I didn't think you had boyfriends. You never told me you had boyfriends."

"I don't. I have never met with a man before—and I told him that," she replied. "I told him that you were shocked because I never meet with men." I was certain Nadia had taken care to mention this to her date to ensure that he did not think of her as a loose sort of girl, a characterization she would avoid at all costs. "I'm ugly," she went on. "I know that. But still men follow me. They follow me on the streets, but I never speak to them. I do nothing when they follow me. I ignore them. But this man—I would like a man like this. He is a teacher, he has a car, and he is nice. He did not try to force me into anything."

And Nadia turned to musing about the opportunities for marriage that have never materialized. She reminded me of Aisha's brother, who had secretly promised that he would marry her, but then had died. She reminded me of her cousin in France who promised to marry her once he purchases a house. She said that, in fact, Jamila's brother wanted her. But there is no way she would accept an offer from him, she said, because he lived in Casablanca. Yes, he had a great job—he was the assistant to the manager of a factory somewhere in Casablanca. Yes, he was very nice—the nicest one in that whole family. Yes, he earned lots of money. But all these things were nothing to her, because she could not bear the way people speak in Casablanca. "For example," she said, "in Casablanca, when they want to say 'sit,' they say '*brki*' instead of '*gilsi.*' If I married him, before long I would be talking like him, and then my children would talk that way, and I could not bear it." I thought perhaps it was not entirely true that Jamila's brother wished to marry her. But I did not say this. Quickly Nadia returned to the object of her current marriage prospect.

"He told me that he could not wait to see me again. He said that Monday was too far away." It was Friday. The boyfriend was going to Meknes to spend the weekend with his family. He would call her when he returned to Fes on Monday. Nadia was speaking excitedly. This man drove a car, which he claimed was his own. He would soon have a teaching post. If she could marry this man, she could buy those things we had seen in Macro, and life, I think she thought, would be better.

As Nadia went on speaking about the teacher and the various hindrances she had thus far encountered on the road to marriage, I wondered what Rashida and Jamila thought when she received that phone call. Hadn't they been suspicious when Nadia returned to the sitting room but did not bother to sit down? When she got dressed in her finest *djellaba*, put on makeup, and raced me out the door? Perhaps Rashida simply turned her head, realizing that Nadia was out to meet a man, but choosing not to question this, hoping only that her daughter, long past the traditional marriage age and with no real prospects, would somehow manage to find her own mate. Another worker whom I had befriended, who at the age of 28 found herself free of nearly all family constraints, told me that her brothers no longer concerned themselves with her and her wandering because of her late age. At 28, she said, they believed she had her own mind. This girl, and Nadia, and many others are part of the first generation of Moroccan women entering their late 20s still single, a kind of disaster for them and their families. Perhaps it is simply that no one really knows what to do with them.[2]

•

After this initial meeting, Nadia met with her boyfriend several more times over a few weeks. They met in the streets, strolling and talking. She always brought along her friend, a neighborhood girl she had known a long time. Finally, one day the boyfriend telephoned and told her he needed to see her urgently. There was something he had to tell her. She hurried out of the house that day, stopped several streets away to pick up her friend, and went to the other side of Ben Souda, where she met up with him. And then the boyfriend told her that he was married and that he had a 2-year-old child. This was the family that lived in Meknes, and this was why he traveled there every weekend.

"After he told me this, he started to try to explain, and I just started laughing. I laughed out loud." And when Nadia said this to me, she mimicked the laugh, which was a sort of high pitched peal that did not sound at all like a response to something funny. "And he asked me, 'Why are you laughing?' and I told him, 'I am laughing at you.'" Nadia said she was shocked by this news; she had never suspected him. I knew her hopes had been dashed. She had liked this teacher. She had liked his job and his car and his lack of aggression. But that short shrill laugh, I think, was meant to show him she had not even cared that he tricked her.

"He told me he had to tell me the truth because he just could not lie to me anymore. He thought that once he told me the truth, I would be willing to continue seeing him." And here again Nadia laughed, again that strange, unfunny sound. Then she swore that she would not see him anymore. "Another girl would most likely continue to see him, but not me. He keeps calling me and asking me to meet him, but each time I tell him no. I am not like other girls." So although she would break the rules and stroll in secret with an unfamiliar man through the city streets, she would not dally with a married man. "I tell him no each time he calls, but I am always very polite," she said, "because I do not want to anger him."

I nodded my agreement, but I thought this strange—that she was afraid to anger him—because one of the qualities Nadia liked so much about this teacher was that he was not forceful. She continued, "He told me he no longer likes his wife, that they have a lot of trouble between them. They were students together, and she got pregnant, and that is why he married her. But he says that she spends all his money—she is always sick and wastes all his money on doctors. She constantly gives him problems and that is why he likes me. He even said he would marry me, now."

"You would be the second wife?" I asked, surprised at the idea for Nadia. And she laughed, bitterly.

"Of course not."

I felt sorry for Nadia and her terrible struggle, the hopelessness of her prospects for marriage. "Would it be possible," I asked her, "for you to let your family know that you have spoken with this man—that you have met with him outside the house? Could you tell them about what has happened?"

"Never. There is no in-between for us. Until there is an engagement, I cannot speak to a man. If a man wants to speak with me he must engage me first. Then my family will allow conversation. Girls like me can meet with men, but we cannot let our parents know. If they find out, they will say, 'We are not Christians. We do not behave in this way.'"

"But, Nadia, doesn't your mother know he has called?" I still wondered how Nadia's mysterious disappearances could have remained a secret.

"No," she insisted. "One time he called and my mother answered. And he said, 'Is Nadia there?' and my mother said, 'Who wants her?' He told my mother that his own sister, who he said was named Nadia, was coming to visit her daughter Nadia, and that he was looking for his sister."

"And your mother believed that?"

"She thought nothing of it."

The teacher continued to call Nadia for a few weeks, and she continued to speak about him. She said that the problems with his wife were terrible. But she always insisted these problems existed before she met him. She was not the cause of their marital strife. Her own father had left his wife—her mother— which meant he had also left her, and she would not be involved with such a crime. Even if this teacher were to leave his wife and child, she said, she would refuse to marry him, knowing what he had done to them.

But always, in discussing the teacher's marital difficulties, Nadia blamed his wife. Her pregnancy had led to the ill-fated marriage, and according to Nadia, "She is the one at fault. She knew what she was doing when she got pregnant."

Eventually the teacher stopped calling, and some time after that Nadia ran into his roommate in the street. The teacher's family, he said, had come to pick him up and return him permanently to Meknes. That was the last we heard of him.

•

Spring had set in, and the heat was becoming powerful. One afternoon when I arrived at Nadia's house, Rashida was sleeping on the banquette, her head thrown back and her mouth open, snoring loudly. Soon after I entered the sitting room, she woke with a start and righted herself on the banquette. She stood up, donned a scarf, and readied herself for the afternoon prayer. Nadia, too, put on a scarf to pray. Although I had seen Rashida pray, I had never before seen Nadia make a motion to pray. Although I knew Nadia saw herself as a moral and upright Muslim, she did not pursue the more formal Islamic practices. She did not (could not) read the Qur'an, she did not pray five times a day, she had not adopted the veil. Nadia and I had never discussed religion in the months I had known her.

As she was knotting the scarf under her chin, Nadia began to harangue Jamila. "You need to pray, you know. Why are you not praying?" she asked in a high-pitched tone that had an edge to it. And then mother and daughter left to make their supplications in the other room.

Left alone with me, Jamila defended herself in a low voice. "I cannot pray, you know. It's just too difficult for me to pray. When you are married and your husband touches you, you become dirty. I need to go to the *hammam* before I pray in order to get clean. It is just impossible for me to stay clean. So I cannot pray." I nodded emphatically so that Jamila would believe that I was on her side. Muslims, I knew, must go to prayer in a state of ritual purity. For women, this can be time-consuming. Jamila, like most young married women in traditional Morocco, felt unable to keep up with the purification requirements and thus did not pursue regular daily prayer. Nadia knew why her sister-in-law did not pray. But the tension was growing in the household, as if the family were heating up with the season.

Nadia and Rashida returned to the room only briefly and then left the house to visit an ailing neighbor, a woman who had developed a tumor on her shoulder from compulsive sweeping. (They had spoken before about this woman's proclivity to sweep, and they talked about it again now, laughing.) Quickly Jamila returned to her earlier conspiratorial tone, in a hurry to convey information to me that she would not be free to discuss in front of her in-laws. They had taken her to yet another shrine to resolve her problems. She had a painful sore on the heel of her foot, which had developed from her shoe rubbing there, on the walk to the shrine. She was planning her next visit to a *fqi* in Sefrou, well known for his ability to cure fertility problems.

"This is all because I don't have children," she said, and then corrected herself. "I do have children, actually—me and Yousef—we have children, but they die." She said this almost as a point of pride, as if at least she could claim to accomplish this. And she repeated part of the story, saying this time that the second child was taken from her in the seventh month. She said she had gone to the doctor several times once she realized she was pregnant, and she did not know the baby was dead until the seventh month. "I went in the seventh month, and only then did they tell me the baby was dead." I expressed my sorrow again. "And so now I have gone off the pill. I'm not going back to the doctor at all."

I had already heard this from the others. "But why not?" I asked.

"Because he has done nothing good for me. I have had those two surgeries. Two times they have taken the babies. And the doctor has already told me that if that happens again, it is likely my uterus will rip, and then I'll never have any children. So I'm not going back."

"Are you sure you won't try another doctor?" I asked, hoping she would stay with the advice of a medical professional. But Jamila only launched into a long story about the uselessness of doctors and their drugs. Hadn't I seen what had happened with Nadia? After spending 1,000 *dirham* on medications, she found a cure only from the *fqi*. And Nadia's most recent illness had been preceded by another illness, a skin ailment she had contracted in the months before I had arrived, that had cost her 1,000 *dirham* and that had gone uncured by the drugs prescribed.

"What does Yousef think of this?" I asked. "Does he want the children as much as you do?"

"Yes, of course he does, but he is worried about me, about my health. He says that he can wait awhile." This comforted me. "But I don't care. I need children now. It is better to have them when you are young. I am so bored in this house. I sit here all day. I sit here with no children." Jamila paused, and then voiced another thought. "It was better in the old days."

"What do you mean?"

"Look at my mother, for example. She got married when she was 11 years old. She lived in my father's house for three years, until she was old enough, and then they consummated the marriage. So she had her children young. She was young when she had my brother. This was better." I could not argue. At that moment, I could see that for Jamila, anyone's life seemed better than her own.

And then Nadia came back into the room. Nadia and Jamila took out a photo album and showed me a picture of them in Casablanca. Nadia, Jamila, and Jamila's sisters stood close together on a city street. Jamila's head was uncovered, her hair tied back loosely in a ponytail. She wore a skirt and shirt, unremarkable western attire that one might see on any street in Morocco, and yet this startled me. I had never seen Jamila wearing anything but the loose caftans and housedresses Moroccan women wear inside their homes. Her head was always covered tightly with a scarf.

"You are wearing western clothing," I said to her.

"Oh, yes, I always dressed like that. But now I only wear traditional clothes." Jamila laughed and pointed at the housedress she was wearing. "I used to get dressed up all the time before I was married. But that is usual. Young girls always get fancied up and wear makeup while they are living in their parents' house. They are concerned with nothing but themselves, that is why. But when you marry, all that stops. I never get dressed up or wear makeup anymore."

Wearing western clothing, I thought, means you are moving freely. Nadia, I knew, often wore skirts and sweaters when she left the house. The other factory workers I knew often wore western dress—not so much inside the factory, where they labored, but when they went outside to stroll, visit friends, shop in the *medina*. Jamila stopped wearing the western style of dress when she married because, with marriage, she was confined to her home. Wearing western dress in your own sitting room makes little sense. Unlike Nadia and the other factory workers, who must go out, Jamila could not go out. Jamila could barely step outside her door.

I asked her, "Did you go out when you lived at home with your parents?"

"No," she said. "Rarely."

"Why not?"

"My younger brother did not want me to go out. My mother and father never said anything. They never told me or my sisters not to go out. But my younger brother didn't want me to go out. He is the one who wanted me to stop working in the factory. So I didn't go out."

"In my culture this is just not possible," I said. "Perhaps a father or mother might be able to put limits on a daughter. But not her brother. Never her brother." I was unable to stop myself from implying that this was not acceptable to me.

"Listen, Titia," said Nadia, "here your brother, or your father's brother, or your mother's brother, or your father's brother's son, or a boy of the neighborhood—all of them have the right to control you." And she laughed, and Jamila laughed, and I laughed, too. "Everyone is in your business. Everyone feels they have the right to stick their nose in on you."

"But Yousef does not tell Nadia to stay home at all. She is allowed out," I said.

"Yousef tells Nadia to go out," Jamila agreed. But she seemed to have no explanation. She seemed not to question this.

I loved Morocco. I loved the dry smell of the heat. I loved the feeling that there was enough time to sit still. I loved the way people would speak with me as if they had always known me, even when we had met just moments earlier. The list of things I loved about Morocco was endless, but this I could not stand. The house was small and there weren't many windows, but at that moment it seemed to me that poverty was not the most troubling issue: it was the idea that Jamila could not go outside if she wanted to. Even though there was nothing out there but dusty roads and carts loaded with fruit for sale, the fact that Jamila could not, on a whim, step out there to look was something I could not accept. I asked Jamila the question I usually asked the factory workers that I interviewed. "Jamila, what do you think? Should a girl have freedom to move around?"

"Yes, of course. A girl should be given freedom. That is, parents should give a girl the opportunity to go out so she will know how to go out, how to get around on her own. If she is kept in too tightly, if she is too controlled, then she will not know at all how to behave when she does go out, and she will have a lot of problems. It's likely she'll do something stupid." Almost to the word, this was what the workers I interviewed always told me. "For example," Jamila continued, "if parents allow their daughter out, to go to the *hammam,* let's say, she should not be on the clock. They should not be watching the clock and after one hour say, 'Where has she gone?' A girl who is treated this way will never learn how to behave outside."

And to illustrate her point, Jamila told me a story. "Let me tell you about a girl who lived near us in Casablanca. She was kept in the house constantly. She was watched and kept at home, strictly controlled. And one day, she went into the kitchen and gave birth to a baby. No one in her family knew how this could have happened, since they watched her at all times. But then, when they asked her who the father of the baby was, she said she did not know. She had been with four men. Four men! This girl who was so carefully guarded."

"Where could she have met them?"

"Probably she found them in the street when she ran out for an errand. But this just shows you that it does no good to try to control a girl so tightly, like her parents did. There is no point to that."

"And what about a wife?" If Jamila thought girls should go out, at least a little, how did she reconcile her own position?

"A wife should not be given much freedom at all. She should have much less freedom."

"Why?"

"Because when a woman is married, she has no fear. A girl fears her parents and this keeps her on the straight path. But a woman does not have that kind of fear—she doesn't have the same kind of fear a girl has—the fear of her parents and brothers. A woman doesn't fear her husband in the same way. Therefore, a husband needs to keep her tightly under control."

Rashida had returned to the house sometime during this conversation. And now she nodded heavily, agreeing with this point.

"So do you ever go out?" I had not really seen Jamila leave the house. She had been to the clinic with Nadia, I knew, and she had recently been to the saints' shrines. She went out to the *hammam* once a week and twice a year she went to Casablanca to stay with her family.

"I do not go out. I never go out alone," she said, sounding certain and pleased. "If someone is sick, I might go out with them. I go to the *hammam* with Mama, but only if I tell Yousef I am planning to go." Rashida agreed with this point. Both of them seemed proud to hear Jamila say this.

"I went out when I was a girl," she continued, "because I went to school for a long time. I left in the second year of high school."

"Why did you leave?"

"My brother didn't think I should go to school anymore. That's when I started to work in the sewing factory, in the administration. Remember, I told you I worked there for six months. That was fun." And she laughed. Before, she had told me she hated work in the factory.

"What did you like about it?" I asked.

"You get up in the morning, and you leave the house. You don't have to do any housework."

"I told you she was lazy," Nadia interjected. Jamila looked at her and laughed. "I ate lunch at the factory every day. I bought my lunch there. I talked to the girls. At the end of the month, I had hardly any money left, since I spent it all buying lunch. And then my family said, 'Why should we let her work? She is working for nothing.' So they decided one day that I shouldn't go back," Jamila ended nonchalantly, as if none of it had really mattered.

Nadia and Rashida got up to put on tea, and Jamila remained sitting close to me. She returned to the conspiratorial tone. "I have been crying all morning," she whispered. "I have been crying my heart out."

"Why, what is the matter?"

"This is no good sitting in this house all day like this. There is nothing for me to do."

"You are bored," I said. And she started to mumble words that sounded like what she had said before, " . . . without having children, just sitting here with no children," and then Nadia came back into the room and Jamila stopped talking. And I realized that Jamila had no one at all to speak with. She had no ally. She was surrounded by in-laws—enemies. She needed her own children to counter them. It was worth risking her life for children.

We drank hot sweet tea, and they put on the television, and a photograph of the king and his sons appeared. "When the son comes to power, things will change," Nadia announced.

"How?" I asked.

"The son is much straighter than the father, and he will enact a law ordering all girls to stay in the house," Nadia said with satisfaction. "All the girls will be sent home. They will no longer be allowed to work, and the boys will take their jobs. Only the girls who are truly needy—who have no one to support them—will be allowed to remain in their jobs. The men will take the jobs the girls have now, and then the girls will be able to marry, because the men will have work."

"But," I said, "the garment factories will surely be empty. The men will refuse to work in those factories."

"It's true," said Nadia. "Men smoke, they demand money, they cause nothing but problems. They would never work like I do. They would go on strike."

"Anyway," I said, desperate to make a point about the seclusion of females, "it would be terribly difficult to live like that—to be told you can't keep your job, to not be allowed to go out."

"We are not like you, Titia," Nadia said.

I said nothing. What could I say? The choice here, clearly, was between marriage, being trapped inside the house hoping for children who could ensure your future, or a job, being trapped in a factory that paid little, hoping for marriage. Nadia was right. Those were never my choices. And then we just sat quietly for a while, breathing in the heat.[3]

•

Some weeks later, we were visiting Aisha. Nadia still had not returned to work. The new factory where she and Amina had been hired was ready to open, but there was a new glitch: in France, the workers who manufactured the cloth the Moroccan girls would sew had gone on strike. There would be no work until after the holiday of the Great Feast. After the feast they were to report to the factory. Until then, Nadia remained at home, spending more time sitting at Aisha's.

Nearly two months had passed since she had left Couture, and now she was becoming tired of her unemployment. She needed money, she said, to pay the phone bill and to buy sunglasses and new shoes for the summer months. "Who will give me money to buy things?" she asked me. Nadia did not worry about purchasing wheat or cooking oil, like other factory girls I knew. She lived in a house owned by her father and had two brothers working full-time. Although she liked to browse the aisles at Macro, it seemed to me that even if she had no job, Nadia and her family would eat.

More and more I had noticed she had lost all patience with her sister-in-law, Jamila. She nagged Jamila when we sat together in the sitting room at their home and gossiped about Jamila when we were out. As we sat in Aisha's sitting room late one afternoon, drinking tea, Nadia turned to the topic of Jamila, whom we had left behind. Nadia recounted for me the story of Jamila's early days. "Do you know, Titia," she began, "that shortly after Jamila and Yousef married, I came here, to live in Aisha's house for three months?"

"Why?" I asked.

"Because Jamila is full of poison. She is so full of poison that out of nowhere, she began to fight with me, to criticize me constantly. Suddenly she started to say that she wanted to leave our household. That she would go with Yousef to live in a rented place, those two alone—without us. For no reason, she stopped speaking to me. She would not even come down the steps. She just stayed upstairs, alone. She refused to be with us."

"But what did Yousef do? What did he want to do—about living alone?" I really wanted to know if Yousef had considered the possibility of leaving the household. He had a job, I knew. There were so many people in that small house, and clearly they did not always get along. But Nadia would not address this question.

"I did not want to tell Yousef what Jamila was saying. I didn't want to tell him how nasty she was being." Nadia tended to portray herself as a saint. But even if she bore her suffering quietly, wouldn't Yousef have noticed that she had moved out? I couldn't pursue these thoughts because Aisha cut in.

"It was during this time that Jamila was *tuwahem*ing. This all occurred at the beginning of the first pregnancy."

"It is certain that Jamila's actions could be attributed to this," I said. I felt sorry for Jamila. I liked her, and I felt like she was trapped. But Nadia said no.

"She took the opportunity to act badly when she could blame it on the *tuwahem*, that is all."

"This is true," Aisha agreed. "Titia, you will never really know how evil Jamila is, because you are always a guest. She really is a bad person." And then, as further evidence, they launched into the story of the betrothal of Jamila and Yousef. "Jamila," Aisha said, "is the one who told Yousef she loved him. This is shameful."

"But how do you know this for sure?" I asked.

"Jamila and Yousef exchanged letters during this time, and Jamila wrote this in a letter." I had already heard about the "*habibi*" letters.

"But how did you find the letters?"

"A letter was left just here, on a table, in their sitting room," and Aisha gestured to show me how a piece of paper was left lying about, on a table, and how she picked it up and read it. It was written in Arabic and Aisha can read Arabic, although Nadia cannot. And so this was the source, I realized, of the story I had heard from the beginning, the story of how Jamila had written of love to Yousef.

And in a mocking tone Aisha added, "She has had all those miscarriages, but she does not even want to tell people what is wrong with her."

I said nothing. I could not speak. What had Jamila done to them? Nadia and I had left her that afternoon, sitting alone in the sitting room, the television on. When we walked out, she kept asking us, "When will you be back?" But Nadia would not be tied down. "Should I make tea?" she had asked. "What time should I start the tea?" But Nadia wanted to go out and sit somewhere else. Jamila, we all knew, was not allowed to come along. There was nothing I could do for her.

And my mind wandered to the other factory girls I knew and their desperate desire for marriage as a solution to their dull work life and their economic woes. It is crucial, I thought, that they take caution. A girl must marry into a family she knows and trusts. At this economic level, she may well be forced to live with them, in a small set of rooms from which she will likely not be permitted to venture out. It is not so much the man and his whims that she will have to tolerate—it is his family. One factory girl, telling me she had so far refused three offers of marriage, because she did not think she would like the men's mothers, pointed out: "I will have to eat that woman's food—for a long time." For the teachers, the professors, engineers, and doctors, the young couple quickly moves to a separate space. This is not the case for the people in Ben Souda and the other factory districts. Jamila is stuck—not so much with Yousef—but with his sister and his mother.

And then, as I let my mind wander, in part because I could no longer bear this conversation which I thought was borne, at least in part, out of frustration and boredom, I began to think that perhaps part of the problem is that Jamila wanted Yousef. Nadia had no say in choosing her sister-in-law, nor did her mother. "We did not want her," she had told me. "She cannot cook well." Traditionally mothers in Morocco were able to influence the choice of a wife for their sons, and among the factory workers, I had noticed that the girls play a role: factory girls often choose friends and set about arranging the marriage of their brothers. But neither Nadia nor Rashida had a hand in selecting Jamila. And this, I thought, is making them mad.

And so I rejoined the conversation. "Jamila is beautiful," I said, "and I think she is very nice."

"It's true," Aisha agreed, but only, perhaps, because people in Morocco do not like to disagree with a guest. "She is a beauty."

.

It was the middle of April. Nadia had not found a new job and we spent more and more time sitting in Aisha's sitting room. Aisha was happy to have the diversion. She liked me, the foreigner. She liked me because my presence sparked conversations that people might not otherwise have bothered with. With me there, people were forced to articulate the rules of the culture. People spoke comparatively, contrasting Morocco with what they knew—or thought they knew—of other places. Aisha had a sharp mind and she was curious. I was someone she could teach, and so she instructed me. Lecturing me was interesting—for me, of course, but also, I felt, for her. In the end, of everyone I met from Nadia's family, I felt that I knew Aisha the best. Perhaps it was because she was so open and articulate. Aisha felt she had nothing to hide.

Aisha was a big woman, not just fat but tall and imposing. Rashida said that she weighed 90 kilos. She ate with gusto. Her features were even and her skin smooth. It is certain that she was beautiful as a girl. At this time she was 38 years old and had six children, one boy followed by five girls. Aisha always said she liked having children. One day, in the sitting room, her daughter announced that she herself would have only two children. "When I have one baby, I'll wait five years before having the next," the girl announced.[4]

Aisha looked at the girl and said, "Five years with no baby? That is terrible."

Aisha was one of ten children, "somewhere in the middle of four boys and six girls," she had told me. When she was a girl, her father sent her to school until she reached the fifth grade and earned the primary school certificate. That is why she could read Arabic, a skill she used handily to read Jamila's love letters to Yousef. Although he allowed her to go to school, her father was otherwise extremely strict. He let her out of the house for school only. He did not allow her to go visit friends or to attend weddings. She went "from school to the house from the house to school. Nowhere else."

Aisha married at the age of 16. She knew her husband before the marriage because he came from her family—he was not a blood relative, but the in-law of a blood relative. When Aisha was a child, the man who would become her husband frequently visited her family's home with his first wife. Ultimately, he divorced this wife because she was barren. And then one day, with his wife gone, the man came to ask for Aisha. Her father agreed, and the wedding was held one month later. Once I asked Aisha if she had spoken to her husband before the ceremony. "Never. I was a girl. He would be visiting with his wife. Was I going to speak to him?" After the wedding, she had five babies in quick succession, her sixth baby coming after a few years' reprieve.

When Aisha was young, few girls were working. There were none of the factory districts that surround Fes today. Very rarely did girls work. She herself never worked outside her home.

"So what do you think?" I asked Aisha one long afternoon as we sat in the heat. "Do you think the girls should be working, like they are these days?"

"It's okay for girls to work if they need to. Girls can work outside the house; they can go to school. But they must not dally in the streets, stroll around, and speak with boys. They should not even be in the streets. They should go directly from house to school—school to house, or from house to work—work to house." House and school, house and work, for Aisha these were binary pairs—opposing concepts. "Men are for the street, women for the house. This is the division."

I knew that Aisha's own daughters had attended school, with varying success. The two eldest, ages 19 and 20, had dropped out long before fifth grade. The eldest was now attending a sewing school, and the second eldest, an obese young woman who the others mocked, remained at home. The three younger girls were still in school, although no one knew how far they would go.

"So you let your own daughters go out?" I asked.

"Yes, they go out 'with the law'—with limits. They must tell me where they are going and why, and they must return on time. I watch them."

"And Si Muhammad?" I asked.

"Well, of course, he comes and goes as he pleases. He does not need to tell me where he is or when he will be coming back. Of course, you know why this is so?" And with this Aisha gestured toward her stomach, reaching her hand around in a gesture to demonstrate an enlarged belly, a pregnancy. I nodded.

"And you—do you go out?"

"Well, for myself, I too go out only 'with the law' as well. My husband must tell me if I can go out or not." And Aisha explained that she does not go out without asking him first. She does not go out until she tells him where she is going and when she will return. If he is not home, she cannot ask for permission, so then she does not go out at all. "Unless it is something small—something really close by," then she might go without asking him.

"Where could you go?"

"When I go out, I go to the *hammam* or to my mother's house, maybe."

"Can you think of anywhere else you might go?" But she could think of nowhere else.

"Let me tell you, when I was first married, I never went out. I didn't even know the road back from here to my mother's house. I had never been to Ben Souda when he brought me here." And Aisha continued, now in her storytelling mode. "At first I lived with him in his parents' house, with his parents and his older brother, his older brother's wife, and their two children. Once, when I was first married, there was a wedding in the house, and everyone was in one room, men and women mixed, and he would not allow me to come into the room. I was young and very beautiful then, and he did not want anyone to see me. I stayed alone that night, in a room on the side of the house. And I cried. I cried all night. Even though I was accustomed to not being allowed out—since my father had been so strict and I had never been allowed to go to weddings or friends' houses as a girl—still I cried that night."

"That's so sad," I said, and Aisha just shrugged. "At the beginning, when I was first married, I wore a face veil whenever I did leave the house. But after I had had many children, he let me take it off."

"Why?"

"He saw that the customs were changing, and women were no longer wearing face veils. But also he could see that when I went out, I came straight back to the house, and so he began to trust me, and he let me take off the face veil."

"And so now that he trusts you, you can go out more?" Aisha did not really answer this.

"One day, just a few weeks ago, I went to visit my friend, and when I returned, he hit me."

"Why?"

"I had left some bit of housework undone that he wanted done. So he hit me. Mostly he does not like to go out and not find me here when he gets in at night. From time to time he lets me go to my mother's and sleep there, but when I do he tells me, 'Tomorrow, when I get home from work, I want to find you here.'" Aisha waved her hand at this, brushing it off. "I have to be here anyway. There is too much work in the house, the children are here, they're fighting. How can I go out with all this?"

And then Aisha said how much she would like to come to my house—to see the apartment I lived in. She dearly liked seeing where and how people lived, and she had never been to the home of a foreigner. I urged her to come and tried to arrange for a day when Nadia could lead her there. But she would not set a date and kept repeating, "*Enshallah, enshallah*" (God willing, God willing). So I stopped urging her.

Later, as the dark was falling, I got up to leave and again I reminded Aisha that she would be most welcome at my house, and softly, almost under her breath but so that I could just barely hear her, she said, "He doesn't let me out."

And then I remembered that at the start of the afternoon we had left Jamila alone in Nadia's sitting room. When we walked out, nobody but Jamila was left there. Jamila had not wanted us to leave. When we got up to go, she had asked, "You're coming back, aren't you? You're coming back here after Aisha's?"

"I think so," I had told her. I was officially Nadia's guest.

She had asked Nadia, "What time will you be back? Should I get the tea started?"

"Not yet, wait a while," Nadia had said. And we had walked out, leaving Jamila there, in the dim light.

•

Of Aisha's six children, the three eldest have completed what they will of their education, and the three youngest are still in school. Si Muhammad was being brought into the family business, although, it appeared to me, he had plenty of free time on his hands. The eldest daughter was sent to a sewing school and the family purchased a knitting machine for the second eldest, so that she could remain at home and practice this craft. There would be no reason for these girls to pursue factory work—the only work for which they might be qualified, given their low level of education—since they had a father who could support them. Even if they had wished to work in a factory, their parents would not permit it.

"Aisha," I asked one afternoon, "are you planning to have your daughters marry soon?"

"No, I won't marry my daughters until they are a little older—24, maybe, or 25."

"But you married so much younger than that," I said, curious.

"Yes," she said. "But it's not good to marry so young. You are not wise then; you're not awake yet. You don't know anything; you cannot do the housework, even." And so Aisha is now working to teach her daughters the proper way to cook and to do the housework, so they will be prepared for marriage. She has put the second eldest in charge of all the cooking for the household. This is the hugely fat girl, who it is said cried one day when she weighed herself on a scale Si Muhammad brought home.

"How will they marry, since you protect them so and don't let them out? Your second-born girl stays home all day. How will someone even know to marry her?"

"A man will hear of her and come to the house to find out about her. And my husband and I will talk with him."

"Will the girls be able to talk to the man, too?"

"Not until we sign the marriage act," Aisha said with certainty. "The man can look at her, and she can look at him. That is all. What do they need to discuss? There is nothing for them to talk about. My husband and I will discuss things with him. That is all. It is the parents' job to do the talking."

And this idea set Aisha into a long diatribe about the many problems with marriage and children these days. "The problem with marriage today is that there are no good girls left. For example, if I marry Si Muhammad to a girl, after a while she will be fighting with my daughters. This is what is happening today—the new wife will fight with her husband's sisters. She will not necessarily fight with me. although she may do that, too. But she will surely fight with his sisters. And then, very soon, she will tell Si Muhammad, 'We need to go away from this house. We need to rent our own place.' This is extremely common today. All the girls are doing this." Now Aisha was leaning forward. She was impassioned. These problems were real.

"This really is the problem with marriage today. Now, for example, when I was married, I moved right into the house with my husband's parents, his brother, his brother's wife, and their two children—a boy and a girl. My husband's brother and his wife traveled all the time. They were never home, and I was left to care for these children. I never said a word to my husband about wanting to leave that house, to move out alone with him. Did I tell him I didn't want to care for his brother's children? No, I did not. I raised those children, took care of them until they were both married. I never said a word. I never asked to move out. But there are no girls left like this anymore." Aisha was shouting now. These thoughts made her angry.[5] But Aisha's opinions were widely held among people of Fes, as Abdul-Haq had once assured me.

Why aren't men marrying today in Morocco? The biggest problem is that of the feminist. The feminist woman wants to take the place of the man. In the house there used to be only the woman. The woman alone stayed in the house, cared for the house. The woman alone decided what she would cook, what the family would eat. A man would work and give all his money to the woman who would, by herself, work out the family budget, shop for the food, and decide what the family would eat. Perhaps the man would make tea. This is the only household duty that he would perform.

Actually the budgeting and purchasing really did not appear until the time of the French—because before the French, the woman did not go out. . . . Today, though, you will see women everywhere. Women are the ones who are in the souks making purchases. Men sell, and women buy. And on the buses, a greater number of passengers are women. And in jobs, even, women are holding the majority of jobs today. Every time you walk into an office you will see a woman who is sitting at a desk. She is sitting there, although she is never ever working; she is just sitting and knitting or talking on the telephone. She knits or talks. That is all she does, although she holds a job.

So why don't men want to marry? Because women want to take men's place.

"What would you do," I asked, "if Si Muhammad married a girl who wanted to leave this house, who wanted to live on her own with him?"

"What could I do?" she said, sounding tired. "The son chooses between the mother and the wife. The wife tries to pull the son away from the mother, and the son has to choose." For Aisha, the correct choice was clear: the mother should be chosen over the wife.

"Yousef always chooses his mother. He has told our mother that he will not leave," Nadia said.

Aisha nodded. She had heard this. "Yousef is a good man. This is the correct thing to do. But there is another problem that we have here today. You should know about this, Titia. Listen. I might take someone's daughter and give my daughter to them. Then, if there is any problem—for example, if I divorce their daughter, they will turn around and divorce my daughter. Whatever I do to their daughter, they will do to my daughter. This is very bad. If I divorce their daughter, does that mean they should divorce my daughter?" She looked at me for an answer, but I could not think of what to say. She did not wait long, though. "No, of course not. This is not how it should be with these kinds of exchanges. But this is what people are doing nowadays. This is a big problem with marriage."

Now Aisha had gotten herself going, and she needed to cover other, tangentially related problems with marriage. "Men are bad. Some men are so bad that they will say to their wife, 'If this is not a girl baby, I will divorce you'—that is, if the wife has had many boys. Or they will say, 'If this baby is not a boy, I will divorce you.' This is a terrible thing that men do. Is such a thing in the hands of the woman?"

"No," I answered, shaking my head emphatically.

"No," she said. "This is in the hands of God, but men will threaten women like that." And I remembered what Nadia had told me, how each time after the birth of Si Muhammad, Aisha had been certain the next baby would be a boy, and how each time, five times in all, the next baby had been a girl.

•

Nadia's prospects for work in the factory that was soon to open were looking increasingly dim. Her relationship with the teacher was definitively over, but she still mentioned him from time to time, now claiming that she had always suspected he was a liar. Nadia believed that she was wasting away and complained of how thin and weak she had become from just sitting around, inside the house, unemployed. Rashida believed, too, that her daughter was becoming weaker from the loss of her work. I could see that Nadia was becoming more and more frustrated, bored, and angry. But I myself had not noticed a physical change.

The Great Feast was soon to arrive, when people would celebrate Abraham's reprieve from the slaughter of his son and his covenant with the one God. Work would stop for days, and people would eat and visit. When I arrived at Nadia's one afternoon, the family put a film in the VCR for me to enjoy—a home movie of their celebration of the Great Feast two years earlier, before the arrival of Jamila.

"This was just before Jamila came," Nadia told me. "Before Yousef went away and saw her and wanted her." And so I sat and watched, thinking it was surreal—me, sitting on a banquette in the heat, watching them on the television, in this very house, slaughter the ram and slice up the carcass, Rashida squatting in the courtyard in front of the open fire in the *mishmar*, piercing the meat onto skewers, roasting it, the sons sitting on the very banquettes where I sat now, stuffing their mouths with meat—all of this playing out on the television screen. In the video the women were talking to the men, calling in from the courtyard to the sons seated in the sitting room, being feasted with meat. And then suddenly Rashida's face figured large on the screen, Rashida pressing the cheeks of a young man close to her own, hugging him, and telling the camera that he was her son. But he was not blood. He was just a young man who was a dear friend of the boys, whom they had known since childhood—like blood.

We watched the video until it ran blank, and then Nadia turned to me and asked, "Titia, why is it that you can get a visa to come here—to Morocco—but we can't get a visa to go to America?"

I sat, thinking. I was to depart in August and now it was May. Nadia had been asking me more and more frequently about visa requirements. Her questions were becoming pointed, and I was beginning to see where they were headed: Nadia was thinking that I could take her with me to America. She would no longer need to struggle for a job or a husband. Instead, she would go to America. The Promised Land. With me.

Over the year I had explained many times, to many people, that I could not secure visas to take them home with me. I told people that the United States had made it nearly impossible for Moroccans to secure visas unless they were already employed by an American factory or firm. And I explained that I did not own a factory or firm, and I could not hire them. I was not as rich as the Americans they saw on television. I could not find anyone a husband (or a wife), because Americans did not like to marry people they did not know. At every turn Moroccans had offered me countless kindnesses, and throughout the year I had tried to repay these with small gifts or with whatever inconsequential favor I might be able to provide at the moment. But a visa was something I could not provide.

From Nadia's point of view, I owed her something. Nadia had not just been a friend—she had helped me with my research. She had introduced me to other factory girls to interview. She had allowed me to sit with her family and listen to them speak of their lives. She had talked to me, giving me information, patiently, openly. I did owe her something.

But I could not take her with me to America. I was certain that Nadia would not be able to secure a visa. She spoke no language other than Moroccan Arabic. She had been to school for a little over two years. She could not even read numbers, from what I could tell. Nadia had never been away from her family. She had rarely left Ben Souda. She had no money at all. Even if she could have secured a visa, as remote as that possibility might be, I knew I was not able to financially support her through what it would have required for her to live independently, and alone, in the United States.

"Nadia, it is impossible nowadays for people to get visas to America. They will not give them. There are just too many people trying to get in. But even if I could get you one—and I don't think I can—I don't know what you could do in America. I cannot get you a job there." These excuses, for her, were weak. And again she began to argue, saying she could sew, she could clean houses. I gave in. "Okay, listen. I'll go to Casablanca. I'll go ask about a visa for you. I'll go next month. Or maybe the month after that." I knew I would be traveling to the coast within the next few months, before my own departure. And I decided then that I would, in fact, research the visa requirements. And then, perhaps, I would have some official reason why I could not take her with me. As I settled this idea in my mind, my thoughts wandered back to my first few encounters with Nadia, when she had so warmly insisted that I visit her family. Abdul-Haq had been eager to explain Nadia's hospitality:

> There are three reasons why Nadia might want you to come to her home, to visit her and to do interviews. [Here Abdul-Haq began his counting, pinky first.] The three possibilities are that:
> 1. Nadia likes you.
> 2. Nadia is a police agent.
> 3. Nadia wants something from you.
> [Abdul-Haq went straight to point number two, which is one of many reasons why I suspected he himself never liked me.]
> Nadia could be a police agent. Agents are everywhere in Morocco. It is very likely that when you leave, the police will come after the people you have spoken with and harass them, continually interrogate them, and possibly put them in jail. . . . Even people who simply buy a newspaper every day have been taken by the police. [This thought terrified me. I had Moroccan government permission to conduct research and had no evidence that what Abdul-Haq said was true. And yet his words haunted me all year.]
> Point three: Nadia wants something from you. Moroccans believe that foreigners can help. They believe this because when the French were here, many fantastic things happened to people, fantastic things that people can-

not forget. For example [and here Abdul-Haq switched into a storytelling mode]:

It rains a lot in the winter in Morocco, and in the past it used to rain much, much more. In the past, the winters were full of rain. And one winter there was a Frenchman walking through Fes El Djedid, and it was raining and dark, and his clothing was soaked through, completely soaked through to his skin. And a boy, who worked in the public oven, the boy who lifts the bread in and out of the fire, saw this Frenchman soaked through to the skin. This boy did not know any French; he could speak no French at all. But somehow the boy was able to speak with the man, and he invited him back to his home. And he took him inside his own house and gave the French-man the clothes of his elder brother, which were clean and dry, to put on. And he lit a fire in the small brazier, so the Frenchman could stand over it and warm himself.

And the Frenchman stayed in the boy's house. He slept there for a few days, perhaps two or three days. And when he left, he went back to France, and not long after, he sent back to Fes El Djedid, he sent for the oven boy's older brother. He sent for him to come to France. And the boy went to France and worked with the Frenchman, and eventually he sent for the entire family. The entire family slowly moved to France, and they bought land, and now they all live in France, owning land.

My mind was on this story of Abdul-Haq's and the deliverance of the poor boy, and then Nadia interrupted my thoughts. She started talking about the king again, about his son, and how in the future things would be so much better because the new king would force all the girls and women to stay in the house. This, she said, was the only solution to the problem.

"This will be difficult, too, though," I said, because I could not keep listening to this talk without saying something.

"We are not like you." Nadia said.

"Oh," I said, because Nadia had already said this to me before, and what could I say? Nadia was angry. I sensed that now she felt she had wasted all these months sitting with me, a foreigner with a bad accent. And for what?

"There is no solution to our problems," Nadia said. I was quiet and then I got up to leave, and as I was leaving she said, "Titia, come back. Come back and celebrate the Great Feast with us." And I told her I would.

•

I returned for the Great Feast and spent the day in the sitting room with the brothers, being encouraged to eat pieces of roasted ram while Nadia, Jamila, and Rashida dashed in and out of the courtyard where they were grilling the meat Yousef had slaughtered. Nadia told me she had gone back to work two days earlier and then quit that very same day. She had taken a job in Sidi Brahim, worked one full day, and left the factory, intending never to return. The factory was near the train station and she had found it with her friend Amina. They needed workers, so she got up in the morning and arrived early. She sat at her machine and sewed all day long and at 7:00 p.m., she just got up from her seat and told the owner she would work no longer. The girls in that factory work until 8:30 every night, she had discovered, and the factory provides no transportation home. Sidi Brahim is far from Ben Souda, and she will not make that trek every night, so late in the evening. The pay was good at that factory, but it was so hot in there, and she wants to work in a factory where they start work at 8:00 a.m. and shut down by 5:30 or 6:00 p.m. She does not want to work all night. In any case, she has a friend who knows the floor manager there, and the friend says he is bad, very bad. So after a day's work, she walked out. She got no pay for the day. I knew she would never be able to retrieve her pay for those hours worked.

•

The next time I stopped in, late one afternoon, Nadia was not at home. She was visiting a friend, Rashida said, in the *medina*. "She has become weak, very weak," Rashida told me. "She is getting tired of not working. She is bored."

Jamila and Yousef were still in Casablanca, where they had gone to stay for almost two weeks, visiting Jamila's family for the holiday. The two oldest brothers, Brahim and Hassan, were in the sitting room. Brahim was showing his mother pictures of a weeklong vacation he had taken with Aisha's son, Si Muhammad, in Si Muhammad's car, over the holiday. The two had driven throughout Morocco, visiting the cities of Casablanca, Marrakech, and Agadir. Brahim had taken hundreds of pictures—or perhaps Si Muhammad had taken them—for there were pictures of Brahim posing all across Morocco. "Fes is nothing, Mother," Brahim was telling Rashida. "Compared to Marrakech, Fes has nothing. There is nothing here. Marrakech is far better." Rashida listened and studied each picture with great care, perhaps because he was her son, or perhaps because she herself had never been to these places. And I thought that this was certainly a trip that Nadia would never take; even if she could put together the money, Nadia would never be allowed to drive around the country, in a car, with just one friend, stopping where she pleased, posing for photographs.

And while we sat, Yousef called from Casablanca. He called to tell his mother he would be home the following day, and his brothers in turn took the phone to speak with him. Rashida began to weep, saying how she missed her son and how she wanted him to return. And then Rashida got up to make tea, and Nadia returned, and we drank the tea and then walked together, Rashida, Nadia and I, to Aisha's house, because Aisha had sent for us.

As soon as we arrived, Aisha blurted out a piece of information. "Did you know, Titia," Aisha said quickly and loudly, "Hassan is planning to marry?" Nadia and Rashida stopped short and looked blankly at Aisha. I could see that this bit of information was not supposed to have been revealed, at least not to me. I was embarrassed and sat, silently. Immediately my mind went to images of Hassan, Rashida's second son, washing dishes in soapy water, helping Rashida with laundry, jumping up to answer the door while we females sat still. Hassan, from what I could see, did not work. How would he marry? But I could not ask this question.

"The woman Hassan has found to marry has a daughter already—a child older than my youngest girl," Aisha continued. Still I didn't say anything. Nadia and Rashida just stared at Aisha. Was Aisha laughing at them? Was she taunting them? "She comes with a guarantee, that is what Hassan says," Aisha went on. "At least we know she can have children, better than the one who sleeps upstairs in Rashida's house." Nadia and Rashida remained silent. I knew that Aisha should not be speaking, that she was touching a sore spot that was supposed to go unmentioned.

And then Aisha started imitating Jamila, announcing, "I am going to the clinic," mocking Jamila's barren state. Rashida remained silent. I was uncomfortable with the cruelty of laughing at Jamila's tragedy, and I sensed that Aisha was not supposed to be mocking Jamila in front of Rashida. Jamila's barren state was a real problem for Rashida's beloved son. And then, with none of these conversation starters very fruitful, Aisha started to mock the wedding festivities hosted by Jamila's family in Casablanca. "The family served plain rice. They placed tiny bowls in front of us, filled with nothing but plain rice. No sugar, no milk on it. We refused to eat this."

And finally Rashida joined in. "This was truly shameful. Shameful to give us plain rice at the wedding when they should serve chicken or meat."

But I could not let the discussion of Hassan's impending marriage go. It was too curious. I had never understood Hassan's role in the household. He was so often in the house—the other brothers did not dally in the sitting room where the women sat—and he carried out chores appropriate only for females. "Will Hassan move his new wife into the house with you?" I asked Rashida, unable to think of where this new pair could possibly fit.

"Of course, where else would they live?" she responded. She sounded angry, but I knew she was not angry with me. There was something else going on, but I would not be told what.

As we walked home from Aisha's house, we passed an old woman heavily carrying her girth down the dirt road, her hand wrapped in cloth. Rashida grabbed my arm and pulled me to a stop so I could look at the woman. "Do you see her—her arm? Her daughter-in-law hit her and broke her hand." My face showed disbelief. "It's true," she said. "If my daughter-in-law did that to me, I would strangle her." I looked at Rashida. She was dead serious. I had never heard her speak so viciously. She was always so measured and reassuring and kind. She was so often leaning over a Bunsen burner, cooking flat breads or heating water for tea. And now this.

"Imagine," she continued, "that woman's own son feeds the wife. He clothes her and he shelters her. Her own son buys everything for that wife, and that is what the wife does to his mother. If my daughter-in-law did that to me, I would kill her." Nadia knew of the story and agreed with her mother.

"And now," Rashida muttered, "Hassan will bring in another one, another one who will do that to me."

•

Nadia had despised her job at Couture when she left it, and now she had come to despise her own inactivity. One afternoon she told me about the job she held before she worked for Couture, a job in a factory in the *medina*. "Things were good when I worked in the *medina*. Every day I got up at five in the morning, I drank my tea, and I went to meet my friend at the bus station. We took a bus to the *medina,* and as soon as we arrived, we'd buy some yogurt and cornbread at a small shop near the bus depot. We'd start work and then at ten, the bell would sound for the break, and we'd share a long loaf of bread and some cheese. We'd split the cost. And then, at one o'clock, the lunch bell would ring and we'd eat lunch together, and then we'd eat again at four—we'd stop working for a snack. And then when we left the factory, we'd stop and buy a treat for the way home. And when I arrived here, I'd eat dinner. I was fat then. The work made me fat, and this was good. And now I am weak and thin—from not working at all."

Shortly after she told me this, Nadia did find a job. For a few days she worked for the wife of Couture's owner. There are a few families in Fes who are said to own everything, and one family in particular, the Benhay family, is known to own and operate many of the garment factories in town. The owner of Couture is a Benhay. He is married to a woman who is also a Benhay. She and her friend (yet another Benhay) had decided to open a fashion boutique in the Ville Nouvelle. The women, Nadia told me, had placed two sewing machines on the ground floor of a villa in which one of them lived, a lovely villa with a swimming pool, surrounded by a fabulous garden. And they had hired Nadia and another former Couture worker to sew for them. The girls would sew clothing using the fabrics and patterns from Benhay factories, and this clothing would be sold in the rich women's boutique.

Everything was good about this position, although Nadia's manner showed little enthusiasm. "We can be late for work, and the women do not scream at us. We can take as long as we like for lunch. In fact, they told us not to bring our lunch, because they will have lunch served to us. And we will get paid by the week instead of at the end of the month. This is good, because if I decide to quit, I can wait and get my pay first. And the pay is good. But what's most important is that these women do not scream at us." And here Nadia demonstrated to me how these women spoke with her and her friend. "They ask us things. They want our opinion because they know nothing at all about sewing. We have to advise them on how to sew the things." This Nadia repeated several times, and several times again she mentioned that these women do not scream and yell.

"Why are these women starting their own factory?" I asked.

"These people are rich. They have everything they need. But still these women cannot sit alone all day doing nothing. And they work separately from their husbands so that they do not fight with them, and the husbands then cannot enter into their affairs and boss them around." Nadia said this with a kind of admiration. "All of these rich women are opening boutiques. It's what they're doing now. Have you seen Abdou's wife? She has short hair and smokes cigarettes. She is a foreigner."

"She is?"

"No, she's not really foreign. She's Moroccan. But she owns so much, she has everything, she lives the good life—like a foreigner." Nadia continued, "They're not like us. Look at us. We can't do anything. I'd like to start something, but we can't start anything. It's all about money. They have the money to get things started."

Nadia, I knew, was acutely sensitive to the class status of the Benhay women. I, too, knew exactly where these women stood, as Abdul-Haq had clearly outlined the class system for me:

There are three classes of people in Morocco:

1. The first class is the popular class, also called the poor people. These are the people who live with other people: if you go to their house, they will have you eat with them, they help each other on the street, they know each other and speak with each other. . . . At this level people earn about one thousand dirham a month. You will find these people in the popular districts, the industrial districts.

2. Then there are the people in the middle. . . . They are the kind of people who live in apartment buildings like the one you live in, in the Ville Nouvelle. These are the teachers, the bureaucrats.

3. Then there are the "heads of money," the rich. These are what we call the bourgeoisie. They are alone in their own class. . . . They have no tradition, no respect. A girl from the bourgeoisie is likely to sit in front of her father and smoke a cigarette, wearing a short skirt. This is very bad. The bourgeoisie do terrible things. For example, they do not eat the middle of the bread. They pull out the inside part of bread and eat only the crusts. They then use the insides of the bread to wash or dry off their hands after dinner. This is extremely upsetting to the popular people. For the Moroccan people, bread is thought of as something holy. If they see a piece of bread on the ground, they will pick it up and kiss it and then put it high up, put it off the ground, perhaps on the branch of a tree. . . . But not the Bourgeoisie.

•

It was early June. From noon until four or five in the afternoon, the streets were quiet. People left their houses to do what business they had in the cool of the early morning and returned home for the noon meal. Then, if they could, they stayed inside until the sun began to set. The heat was a dry heat like the heat that shoots out of a hair dryer. Except this heat surrounded your body, and there was no escape from it.

Late one afternoon I arrived at Nadia's house. The family had removed the furniture from the sitting room and piled it in the courtyard, where it would remain until September. The furniture, they said, holds the heat, and without it the room would be cooler. But still the room was stifling. We sat on a rug on the bare floor, trying to feel the cool of the cement walls and floor. Nadia and

I sat alone. Rashida and Jamila had been to the *hammam* and, depleted from the heat, were sleeping upstairs.

Nadia and I went to see Aisha, who we had heard was sitting alone, too. Aisha's closest companions, her eldest daughters, had traveled for the day to Sefrou. Si Muhammad, accompanied by Nadia's eldest brother, Brahim, had driven them there. This trip had been arranged because Aisha's second eldest daughter had been crying bitterly the day before. She was complaining, Nadia said, that she was never allowed to leave the house. "She gets up in the morning, and she makes the bread. She prepares breakfast for everyone and then she cleans and organizes the house. Then she prepares the lunch. After lunch she washes the clothing and prepares dinner. The little girls go to school, the eldest girl goes to sewing school, Si Muhammad goes out all day in his car, and her father, of course, leaves for the shop. And she cannot go out," Nadia reported.

As we walked, Nadia told me that she thought them all ridiculous. "Si Muhammad," she says, "actually yells at his sisters for peeking out the window. He tells them not to peer from the windows because he is afraid that people will see them. They beg him to take them out in his car, but he claims always to be busy and never takes them anywhere. He just does not want them to go out."

"This is a bit unpleasant," I said, feeling disgust but not wanting to express the extent of my own distaste.

"It isn't a bit unpleasant. It is very unpleasant," Nadia replied forcefully. "If a girl is kept so strictly controlled, she will go wild if she goes out just once. She will lose control. She won't know how to behave in the street."

"It would be far better for them to work in a factory," I suggested.

"But why would they? They do not need the money. I know plenty of girls who don't work, who are allowed to go out to the *medina* once a week. Aisha's girls cannot even do that. Si Muhammad won't let them. Their father won't let them."

"But why doesn't Aisha intercede for them?" I asked. "Why doesn't she ask her husband to let them out?"

"'They are on their own with their father,' that's what Aisha says," Nadia said. "Aisha refuses to intercede for them."

"I think she is afraid of her husband."

"No, that's not it."

"Well, is she just so traditional herself?"

"Aisha thinks that if a girl goes outside, she will simply talk to boys and get into trouble. Remember I told you Aisha does nothing? She does no housework at all. The girls do it all. So why should she let them go out? Then she'll have to do the housework herself."

"Well, you're lucky you at least can go out."

"Oh yes, I go out," Nadia said proudly. "But it's not because I am lucky. I'm straight, and my brothers know it. I am so straight, and so honest, they know they can trust me. I never do stupid things. I don't do anything crooked. I don't do the *zigzag*." I did not want to remind her of her secret boyfriend.

We sat with Aisha and waited for the girls. They returned from the festival at 7 p.m., dashing up the cement steps. The day was a hot one, and the daughter who had so desperately wanted to be taken out appeared in a black velvet *djellaba* that encased her obese body. I could see how the curly hair near her ears was wet with sweat. Her skinny sister, dressed in dark blue jeans covered by a baggy long-sleeve shirt, was sweating, too.

We did not visit long with these girls, though. The moment they entered the room, Nadia raced down the cement steps to speak with Si Muhammad before he drove away in his car. Aisha's husband, it seemed, had arranged for Si Muhammad to take Nadia to the home of a man who was heavily indebted to him. This man's wife was the floor manager of a large sewing factory in Sidi Brahim, and she would be obligated to offer Nadia a job. The position with the Benhay women was not as lucrative as it had first appeared, and Nadia felt that this opportunity might be an improvement. Nadia came running back up the steps: Si Muhammad and Brahim would be willing to take us. Aisha grabbed her head scarf. She had been given permission to go. And we three jumped into the back seat of Si Muhammad's four-door sedan and went out into the night. It was very exciting.

Si Muhammad drove, and Brahim sat in front next to him. We traveled to a new section of the city, a section not more than ten years old. As we drove, everyone talked about how recently the buildings had been planted there, how they remembered when this part of the city was nothing but empty space. We arrived in front of one of the countless cement block apartment buildings that lined the road. Si Muhammad parked the car in the dust. We all got out, and Si Muhammad knocked loudly on a metal door.

We were welcomed into a small apartment and brought through a hallway into a sitting room. This apartment had all the elements of the houses I had visited in the factory districts of Fes, and yet it was different. The apartment was tiny but immaculate and purposefully decorated. But what was so different was that this building—this apartment—was completely finished. None of the walls were uncovered cinder blocks. There was no cement left to pour. Portions of the interior walls were covered with tile—not the hand-painted ceramic tile found in the *Medina* but shiny new, factory-produced tiles printed in bright blue geometric patterns. The fabric on the banquettes in the sitting room was shiny and new. The low serving table in this room was covered with a carefully embroidered tablecloth and stacked with embroidered napkins. Knickknack shelves hung on the walls, lined with tiny decorative ceramic figurines—the kind that could be purchased in Macro. This was the apartment of a family who had nearly reached the middle class, a family that could purchase novelties and baubles that had no real use. This was the apartment Nadia wanted.

It was the indebted man who greeted us, the floor manager's husband. He assured us his wife would return shortly and graciously treated us as guests. As he moved back and forth between the sitting room and kitchen, preparing coffee, Aisha mimicked and mocked him, saying his hospitality was due only to the fact that he owed her husband millions, and she laughed at the figurines on display.

We sat and drank the coffee we were offered until finally the floor manager returned home, trailed by her two finely dressed young sons and a tiny girl whose filthy clothing signaled her position as the family's child maid. Unpleasantly surprised to find us awaiting her, the floor manager went immediately into a back room to change and emerged after some time in a shiny polyester Chinese gown tied around her large stomach with a wide belt. Harshly she began to interrogate Nadia, asking her where she had worked before and what she had previously earned. Nadia became shy and incoherent. She mumbled her answers and looked at the ground. Finally, though, it was agreed that Nadia would report to the woman's factory the next morning. The woman would instruct the guard to admit her.

So it was decided and the deal was closed. Then there was a hitch: Nadia mentioned, almost as we were leaving, that she would be unable to start so quickly. She wanted to be certain to collect her earnings from the Benhay women before beginning this new job. She would need to finish the week with them. "This is not a problem," the floor manager said. "Just go and tell those women that you are ill and that you need to go away, to stay with your sister—in Casablanca perhaps. They'll have to pay you. They won't be able to compel you to continue working with them—not under this situation." We were, at this point, standing together in a group near the door, and everyone agreed that this was the best way to go about things. So the plans were set for Nadia to take the new job. Nadia would be at the factory gate at 8:00 a.m.

We left and climbed back in the car. And as soon as the doors were shut,

Nadia said, "I have worked with that woman before. She does nothing but scream. She is full of screaming. I worked with that woman for one full day once, and she would come right up to my machine and scream, 'Hurry, hurry!' Why do people scream like this? What is the point of that screaming? I'm not going to that factory. I have no wish to work with her." And then Nadia started to talk about the intermittent work she had found with the Benhay women. "This is better work. And if I stay with them, and these women ever manage to open a factory, I would probably become a manager, since I was the first one there."

"It's true, there's no reason you should leave what you have now," Brahim advised his sister from the front seat. And it was agreed that Nadia, in fact, would not be appearing at that woman's factory the next morning.

Si Muhammad headed the car into the Ville Nouvelle, where he would drop me off. He stopped in front of my building, and I got out. Before I could shut the car door, Aisha had dashed out of the back seat and was on the sidewalk behind me. She was coming in to see my apartment. There was no stopping her now; she was out of the car. The men in the front seat said nothing, and Nadia followed along. I unlocked the door to the building and led them up the cement steps and into the apartment.

The apartment was dark and empty. Aisha walked directly into my bedroom and opened the doors of my closet. She started looking through the clothing hanging there, commenting on what I owned. She pulled out a sleeveless dress I never wore, because I knew that no respectable woman flaunted her arms on the streets of Fes.

"This is beautiful. Why don't you wear it?"

"I don't like to wear it here. I'm embarrassed."

"Really, you shouldn't be embarrassed. It is good. You should wear this to make yourself look more beautiful."

Once, when she had become impassioned discussing the behavior of Moroccan girls, Aisha had said that the girls who stroll around Fes in miniskirts, baring their legs for all to see, were shameless. "Girls like that," Aisha had said, "should have their legs cut off." But now she was exempting me from this indictment. It was as if she were saying, "I wouldn't criticize you if you wore this dress with no sleeves. I recognize that you are different, and I accept your foreign ways."

And then she moved into my sitting room, where there was a large window that looked out onto the street. The room was still dark because we had not switched on the lights. We sat down on the banquette in front of the window.

The glow from a street light illuminated the pattern on the cushion where we sat.

"Titia, this is good," said Aisha. "You have the light from the street coming in here. You can make use of this light at night, and then you won't be forced to pay so much for electricity." Then Si Muhammad started to honk the horn, and Aisha and Nadia left my apartment.

•

The next time we arrived at Aisha's house, we found Aisha had visitors: Nadia's aunt and her newly married daughter were in the sitting room. I had previously seen the wedding pictures of this young woman. Her skin is black and she is hugely obese. Sitting next to her was her mother, who was light-skinned and very thin and frail. I was struck immediately by the contrast between the two. I had met many of Nadia's "aunts" before and had long ago accepted that I would never fully comprehend the genealogical connections between these people. But this young woman's skin was dark—as dark as a glass of Coca-Cola—a phrase Nadia herself had once used. How could she be this fair-skinned woman's daughter? But skin color was not the most noticeable trait for Nadia.

"This one is fat, isn't she, Titia?" Nadia joked after we had all carried out our greetings. I smiled, not wishing to agree too readily.

The girl smiled with little sign of dismay. "My mother, as thin as she is now, was fat when she was young. She weakened and grew thin from bearing children. This is what will happen to me, I think."

The fat girl told me that she, like me, had married last year. She was 28 and had married at the end of Ramadan. "I married an old man," she said bluntly, "a very old man. He is so old that his children are my age, and they are all married."

"And how do you like it then—this marriage?" I asked.

"It is good," she said. "We live alone in the house, and the house is quiet. I can leave every afternoon to go and visit my mother." She seemed pleased with the arrangement. At the age of 28, I thought, she was too old to have found a younger, more desirable man. And she was far too fat, even in Morocco, where women do not strive for skeletal figures. He was too old, and she was too fat. But in Morocco, "marriage—like death—is necessary." That is what people say.

Her problem, as I might have expected, was that although she had been married for a year, she had not yet become pregnant. She wanted children, and the conversation very quickly turned to her medical history and her most recent doctor visits. And as we talked, Nadia unrolled a plastic bag that she had brought along with her to the house. I had noticed the bag, but had not asked what she was carrying. On the table in front of us, Nadia carefully pulled from the bag a huge pair of white pantaloons, the baggy cotton pants that women wear underneath their robes. The pantaloons were giant and stained with a reddish brown mark—the stain of dried blood. These were the wedding pants of the fat black girl. Nadia, it seemed, had been walking around with these pants on for the last three days.

As it turned out, the family was quite certain that a spell had been placed on Nadia. Nadia was getting old—she was 26—and she had had many opportunities for offers of marriage, but no offers had been made. This clearly was an ongoing problem. But recent events had convinced the family that there was some sort of foul play. In the space of several days Nadia had thrown up repeatedly, even though she was not ill. The vomiting always followed upon her drinking buttermilk. There was a large jar of buttermilk in the house and each time Nadia drank from it, she threw up. The women decided that they should start to take some action on Nadia's behalf, and so they began with the pantaloons of this recent bride. The hope was that by wearing these pantaloons, Nadia might remove the spell and improve her chances of finding a mate. But this was just the first step. The women were making plans to go and visit a *shuwafa*, a fortune-teller who might provide them more insight.

•

Nobody mentioned the pants again, and I could learn nothing of a visit to a *shuwafa*. Nadia never appeared at the factory of the screaming floor manager, and the wealthy factory wives seemed to have halted in their efforts to stock their boutique. Nadia was angry. As we walked to Aisha's house, she told me of the troubles of her good friend Amina, who was also still unemployed. But for Amina, things were far worse. Amina was married. "Her husband is forcing her to find a job," Nadia told me with outrage. "She tries to act like he is not forcing her, but I can see that he is. Whenever I am there, he says, 'Why don't you two go out together now, to look for work?'" Amina's husband, I knew, was employed at a factory as well.

"Why is he so desperate for her to work?" I asked. "Doesn't he have a pretty good job?"

"He has a job," Nadia said, "but he gets about 1,500 *dirham* a month, which is just not enough. Their rent is 800, and after paying for electricity and water what good will 1,500 do? And the baby is sick. Amina needs to bring her to

Rabat, to the hospital, but they don't have the money. And so he keeps telling her to get a job."

But the point of this conversation was not Amina. It was Nadia and her own life. "I cannot stand these conditions," she said, gesturing around her. "This house, this way of living, I can't stand it. I don't want to have to work. Okay, I'd work to help my husband. We could help each other. But I don't want to work by force. He can't force me to work. I don't want him to be depending on me for money. He shouldn't need money. He shouldn't have to ask me for my wages.

"You know Amina sold her gold. She sold all her gold because her husband needed the money. This is not what I want. I don't want to be selling my gold for my husband. You sell your gold if you need to, but then you should be able to get it back later. In marriage you should be able to increase the amount of gold you have, not lose gold. This is what you should be able to do in marriage."

We arrived at Aisha's house only to hear more bad news, news that Nadia had already known. Aisha was pregnant and in a state of despair. She had been suffering health problems ever since the birth of her last daughter. Her doctor had told her this pregnancy would be difficult. Aisha did not want any more pregnancies.

Nadia, already in a rage with her own life, had no patience for Aisha's dilemma. She knew with certainty what Aisha must do. "Listen to me, Aisha," she began loudly, with little of the tenderness I would have expected in this situation. "You have had too many children already. Si Muhammad and Fatima [Aisha's firstborn] are the only ones who should be alive anyway—the rest of them should not even exist. I admit it. I should not even exist. I am the fifth born, and there are just too many people. Think about it. Every child should be clean and well dressed. This takes money. People should not be having all these children. We all know that. Get rid of it, Aisha. Take it out. That's what you should do."

Abortion is legal in Morocco, although a woman would need the signature of her husband in order for the doctor to perform the procedure. Still, I was surprised by Nadia's behavior. She had no patience for Aisha's low mood and her indecision.

"What did the doctor tell you, Aisha?" I asked. Aisha was usually the loud and brusque one, the joker. But today she was sitting quietly, chewing her bottom lip.

"He just said it will cause me problems," Aisha said.

But Nadia had no time for anyone's reaction to this pregnancy but her own.

"You people might say I am crazy, that my opinion is no good, but you are the stupid ones. One or two children are enough. Look at the woman who lives next door to us. She and her husband live on the bottom floor of the house, in two rooms only, two rooms that her mother gave her to live in. First she had two children, a boy and a girl. Perfect. And her husband was working at a company, and it was good. But then he lost his job and had to get a cart and started selling bananas and apples. Then she had twins and then twins again. Two times she had twins. Even her father came and told her to stop having children. It is ridiculous."

"Why does she keep having children?" I had to ask.

"I have no idea why. She is stupid. There are no jobs. Everyone is living with terrible difficulties, in terrible conditions, and she keeps having twins." Nadia stopped to take a breath. Her point was made.

•

Nadia's feelings were not lifting. The unemployment was making her hopeless, I felt. She worked a day here and there for the wealthy wives, and then finally they sent her home, saying they wouldn't need her for a while. They had stocked the boutique. At Aisha's one afternoon Nadia was telling us how bored she was with her life, how she felt she couldn't bear her situation.

"Look, my friend," Aisha said, leaning forward to get closer to Nadia, who sat on the banquette opposite her. "Life is like that. The moments of happiness are short; they pass quickly. But the moments of sadness and boredom pass quickly, too. Look at me. A few weeks ago, I was strangled. I felt I was being strangled," and she made the gesture of being choked, wrapping her fingers around her neck. "And now I feel better. I was going crazy because I was so bored. I was insane. And look at me now. I'm okay."

"When was this, Aisha? When were you feeling this way?" I asked, not remembering Aisha expressing these thoughts.

"When I knew I was pregnant. Before I had the abortion. That was how I felt." I was taken aback by Aisha's announcement. No one had mentioned the abortion again, and I had assumed that Aisha had not pursued this option, that she was, in fact, still pregnant. Then I felt a deep admiration for Aisha, for what she was telling Nadia. Aisha was trapped in that sitting room. I wondered how she—or any of them—could bear that. And now I knew that she did in fact sometimes feel like she was suffocating, but still she kept on joking, holding court on her banquette.

•

Late one afternoon, I invited Nadia to come with me to "stroll the *medina*," to help relieve the boredom. When I arrived at the bus station where we had planned to meet, I found Aisha with her. Both were dressed in their finest clothing. Nadia was wearing a new black pantsuit with a long white polyester shirt whose front was lined with yellow gold buttons. On her feet were the high-heeled plastic sandals that all the factory girls had purchased this spring and that, I imagined, would surely produce painful blisters. Aisha was wearing the black velvet *djellaba* which I had seen on her daughter. It made her look glamorous, but in the heat of early June, it was surely the cause of the thin stream of sweat running down her face. Aisha's black hair was pulled back tightly and today it was uncovered. I sensed that her hair had just moments earlier been hidden by a head scarf, which Nadia had instructed her to remove. Both wore matching lipstick—which was Nadia's. They were dressed for an afternoon out of the house.

We went through our greetings and looked carefully at each other in this new setting. And then Nadia suggested that instead of touring the *medina* we take a bus to visit Aisha's mother, who was, of course, also Nadia's aunt.

Aisha was tempted. She liked this idea. "But he'll be mad," she said. "My husband will be very angry. He has let me out to go to the *medina*, and he thinks that is where I'm going. He'll be mad if he hears I went to my mother's." Aisha was nervous, unable to decide. She bit her lower lip.

"How could he be mad at you for visiting your mother? Going to your mother's can't be a bad thing, can it?" This seemed to push her into a decision.

"I'll go," she said. "But I'll lie to him. I'll lie." I could sense a fear in Aisha. She kept chewing her lip as if she were thinking hard, contemplating this decision and its consequences, and I regretted having said anything. I tried to backtrack and suggest we stay with our original plan, but now Aisha was determined to go see her mother. We boarded a bus to take us south of Fes, down the road toward Sefrou. And I watched Aisha's face as we traveled.

Aisha's mother lives out on Route Immouzer where it intersects with Route Sefrou. As we moved further from Fes, the concentration of houses thinned. Large, ornately decorated villas began to appear, new structures where the wealthy were settling far from the noise of the town. Occasional blocks of two-story apartments dotted the landscape. As these signs of the city began to disappear and the dry hills, looking untouched, rose up before us, we arrived at a small settlement of dirt treks and squat, cement houses. We prepared to get off the bus, and Aisha announced that she had decided what she would tell her husband.

"I'll tell him that the American needed to go down Route Sefrou, to get something for her husband from a teacher's house. I'll say that Nadia decided to go with the American and that I was afraid to go to the *medina* by myself, that I did not want to separate from Nadia. I'll tell him that is why I went with you two on the bus to Route Sefrou."

"Will you tell him you visited your mother at all?" I asked.

"No, I won't tell him that."

"Well, what if your mother mistakenly mentions that you were at her house?"

"That will never happen," she said quite confidently. She asked Nadia for a handkerchief and began to wipe the lipstick from her lips, saying she would be ashamed to appear like that in front of her father. Nadia removed her lipstick as well.

We started off down a dusty trail of dirt. The air was noticeably quiet, absent of the constant sounds of the city. Aisha pointed here and there. "We used to play in the irrigation canal right here," she said. "And there, where those houses are, it was nothing but olive trees. We'd play in the trees. It was beautiful here." Aisha's elderly parents lived in a house that her brother had financed with the earnings from his thirty years of labor in France—despite his greedy wife's desperate attempts to keep the money for herself. "She wants all his money for her own family."

When we arrived at Aisha's parents' house, we were warmly welcomed and immediately—upon seeing her daughter—Aisha's mother began to cry. There had been an assassination attempt on the Egyptian president, and his near-death reminded her of the death of her youngest son, the son whose funeral I had heard about. We settled in a small room on old banquettes, and the women began to speak, quickly turning to the discussion of Jamila and the recent dis-coveries about her inability to become pregnant. Nadia eagerly delivered the news of the witchcraft that had been uncovered. "Someone," she told Aisha's mother, "is killing the children before they are born, in the womb. It is most certainly witchcraft." Aisha's mother was very visibly horrified. Her daughter, however, showed less interest in this side of the story. Aisha was focused on her most recent criticism of Jamila: Jamila was wasting all her time and too much money on doctors.

Finally, the subject of my own childbearing, or lack thereof, was introduced. I had married just before coming to Morocco, they knew, and as time passed, more and more they spoke about my lack of children. "She has been married almost a year now," said Nadia. "And nothing." Aisha's mother looked at me.

She said she was unconcerned, that in fact some people do not have children until three, even five years after marriage.

"But," Aisha tuned in, "she is 30 already." And with this, the old woman looked at me again, this time with alarm in her eyes. But it was growing late, and we had to get back to the city before dark, so the conversation was cut short. We nearly had to run from the house to be certain to get the next bus home. After racing through the still hot and dusty road, Aisha sat down heavily on the seat of the bus. She was tired, she said, tired from running. Tired from being out. The bus ride from the Ville Nouvelle to Aisha's mother's house had taken us over an hour, although I suspected the distance was not more than fifteen miles. The bus ride from Ben Souda to the *Ville Nouvelle* would take at least another forty-five minutes. The buses were hot and crowded. For them it would take almost two hours to get home.

"That is because you do not go out enough," Nadia told her. "You never get out, so you are tired when you go anywhere." Aisha said nothing.

CHAPTER 7

Taking Leave

It is now the end of July, and my departure is near. Fes is enclosed by mountains, and these mountains trap the heat inside the city. I feel like I am baking, and I want to go home.

For months I have been visiting Nadia and her family. I have been engrossed with Jamila's and Aisha's sagas and Nadia's quest to establish herself as a worker and as a wife. The preoccupations of their lives, however, are not nuanced. Marriage. Pregnancy. Sickness. These topics seem always to be at the center of our conversations. It can be stifling, like the heat.

I know there is more to talk about in Morocco. My friends at the university discuss feminism and interpretations of American novels in careful English. A group of professors I know argue over the impact of French colonialism on the structure of the Moroccan university. I continue to visit with other workers, especially with Hayat and her family, who tell of life on the move, raising sheep in the hinterlands. All of these conversations are intriguing and diverting and remind me of life beyond the cinder block sitting room walls.

But then I catch myself. Nadia and the women of her family have not had the privilege of a sustained education and the hope it offers for an expanded horizon. Among this group, only Nadia has stepped over the threshold and out the front door of the family house into the public world of work. And even this foray has now stalled. Television offers very little; they have no real entertainment or distraction. They rarely travel beyond the limits of Fes, and even a car ride is an exceptional event. Their worlds are largely confined to the rooms in which they sit. Within these walls, though, they fight Herculean battles to protect what is important to them and secure their own futures. I know that this talk of marriage, pregnancy, and sickness is, in fact, the talk of life and death. I know this is true, and yet I am weary of this talk and wish to leave it behind. Soon I will. That is the difference between me and them.

•

I waited until almost evening to go to Nadia's. I planned to invite Nadia to go with me to Macro, where I might purchase gifts for friends before my departure. I carried with me two large potted plants, plants that looked like small palm trees that I had purchased soon after my arrival in a vain effort to make my apartment cozy, and Nadia had admired them. These plants I had dragged through the dirt roads from the taxi stand to the house, and I arrived sweating and dumbstruck, so hot that I felt I could not speak. When I entered the sitting room, I found Nadia, Rashida, and Jamila's teenage sister, who would be staying with the family through the summer months, all lying in the room, suffering from the heat. "It's so hot, it's so hot," Rashida was moaning.

Nadia sat up to greet me. "It is hot in America, too, Titia," she assured me. "People are dying from the heat. In California two people have died—from heat alone." I have heard this already. There is a heat wave in the United States, and the deaths of Americans are being broadcast daily. "Why is it," Nadia asked, "that you people die from the heat? We are always hearing that Americans die when it is hot."

I shrugged. I had been asked this before. I had no idea why Americans die in heat waves while there seem to be no media accounts here of Moroccan heat-related deaths. I had made up an answer that sounded plausible. "It's sick people," I said. "It's the sick—and the very old. They become exhausted and die. This probably happens here, too."

"Look at us. Look at this heat. We're not dying from it," Nadia said. I nodded. It was true.

And then Rashida, acknowledging the plants, began to talk about my departure. "We will cry," she assured me. "We Moroccans get used to people. You have come into our hearts, and we will not find it easy to separate from you." And with this big tears began to drip from her eyes, and Rashida spoke of how much she would miss me. And then she talked of the German they had once known and how painful the separation from him had been. Perhaps it was the heat or my overwhelming exhaustion with my work, but I felt that Rashida's tears were not real. Rashida, I felt, was crying out of hospitality. I was a guest. I had been a guest. I would leave and not come back, and it would not matter that much. But Rashida was a fine hostess, a kind and generous woman. She would work to make me feel I had been cherished here. "You are one of us now, Titia," she continued. "You can come here any time. You are always welcome here. Bring your mother with you. Bring your sister. Don't stay in a hotel. Stay with us." I sensed Rashida was using her best hospitality, and I liked her even more for her efforts.

Nadia had walked to Sidi Brahim that morning looking for work. "My God," I said, "the heat. How could you walk so far in this heat? Can't you just wait until September now?" Rashida agreed that since so much of the summer had passed, Nadia should wait until the heat subsided to look for work.

"Probably now I will," said Nadia. "I'll probably not be working until September now. Anyway, Couture is going to send for me in September. They told me they would be reopening then, after the August vacation. I'll go back there."

"You'll go back there?" I asked. "Even though you really hated it?"

"What am I going to do? I have to work. I can't just sit here."

"It's so close," said Rashida. "It's a good job because it's so close. She can get there easily." And I felt like Nadia had come full circle, the same circle other workers had described to me. She had worked at a factory until she was completely fed up with the conditions. She had not staged a strike, but she had fought with the floor manager and complained to the owner. She had tried for many months to find another job, saying she would never accept a job as bad as that one again, and she had sat at home, at first glad for the reprieve and then made desperate by her boredom and her need for money. And now she would return to the same bad job and the same bad conditions—if, indeed, Couture called her back in September.

But there was still one hope for Nadia: me. And so she again asked about a visa, this time in the third person. "Titia, how could someone get a visa?"

This time I was well prepared for this conversation and I had the answer. I had gone to Rabat and to Casablanca and had visited the U.S. government offices where I could find out about the visa process. "I went to Casablanca," I said, "and they told me there was no such thing as a 'guest visa.' There is no such thing as this in America."

"But there *are* 'guest visas.' I know so many people who have taken them to get to France."

"But France is not America. There is no such thing as a 'guest visa' from Morocco to America. And anyway, they told me there is nothing that I can do. If a person wants a visa to America, they must come themselves to fill out the papers, pay the money, and then just wait." Nadia was listening, and I had determined to make her understand why I could not take her back with me.

So I continued. "There are two cases where you could easily get a visa: one, if you are a student"—and here I started to count on my fingers, pinky first, to make my point—"and two, if you have a special skill. For example, if I owned a company and needed a person with your particular skill, I could get you a visa. That is all."

And now I would put an end to this discussion, I hoped. "Nadia, I am just a student. I don't own anything. I don't own a factory or a company. I can't hire you for anything. I cannot guarantee you the work you would need to get a visa out of Morocco."

Nadia was quiet. And then she recalled someone she knew who had taken a visa, gone to France, and had been saved. "But France is different from the United States," I told her. "They have a different relationship with Morocco there. That's why they have this sort of visa. That is France. I'm from the United States." I was sure that Nadia must understand the difference, but still she continued with her stories.

"What about the neighbor's son, for example? He was poor, unemployed. He lived right next door. He married his cousin—his mother's sister's daughter. She was old and ugly. Much older than he, and ugly. He was young and handsome, but unemployed. She was living in Holland, so he married her and went to Holland. That was it. Next time we saw him, he was driving a car. And he was fat. They came back here from Holland in a car. The woman had had children—two little girls. But really, this is no surprise. They are Riffis, and Riffis always take care of themselves. They always marry inside the family, so everybody can share the wealth.[1] That's what's wrong with us. We don't do this. Look at Aisha's brother. He's been in France for years. But he never brings anyone from their family to France. His wife does, but he doesn't. And when he comes home for the August vacation, what does he bring Aisha? A scarf." Nadia took a breath and then continued. The stories of Moroccans redeemed by the visa, I knew, were legion.

"Then the neighbor on the other side of us, how about their son? He spent all his money. The whole family spent their money on him, and he got a visa— for fifteen days only. Fifteen days is nothing, but he got to France and right away he married a foreigner. That is how they do it. They get the fifteen-day visa and marry right away, so they can stay longer. Then he came back with the foreigner and a car."

Eventually the conversation sputtered. Rashida was watching her daughter speak, agreeing, but adding nothing. She had no desire, I sensed, to see her children leave for France or for America, car or no car. And then Jamila came down the stairs just as Nadia had left the room to get ready for our walk to Macro and Rashida ascended to the roof.

I had seen Jamila only rarely since she had returned from Casablanca after the vacation of the Great Feast. She had nearly stopped appearing for my visits, often just coming down the stairs as I was preparing to leave. She was said to be upstairs sleeping. Now she stepped into the sitting room looking groggy and tired. She said that she was sick again. She had a cold and was suffering terribly from the heat.

I spoke politely with Jamila, asking if she was enjoying her sister's visit, if the two had been able to go out together. They had not. I asked if perhaps they would come along with us to Macro, thinking that perhaps with her sister in tow, Jamila would be permitted to escape. "No, I cannot go out," she answered me, her voice flat. "Every day, I cannot go out. Yousef does not let me. He does not want me to go into the street. The street is bad."

I already knew that Jamila was not permitted to go out, and Jamila knew that I knew this. So why did she repeat this to me? Was she complaining? If she was complaining, why did she then remind me that the street is a bad place? Something, I felt, was wrong with Jamila. But I did not know what. And I could not help her.

Jamila is an obedient wife. Several days earlier when I was visiting, Jamila had come downstairs, and suddenly Yousef called from upstairs. He called her name, and she jumped and ran to him. When he called, Jamila jumped; her whole body reacted. And as she moved from the sitting room, I understood that her position here was precarious. Jamila is married, and she cannot produce children. She has trouble with the women in this family, for reasons I will never fully understand. She cannot make trouble with Yousef. If he divorces her, she will be forced to return home to another poor household struggling to make ends meet. Jamila has no options—except to become ill.

Nadia returned, dressed in a fashionable white sleeveless shirt and a wide, puffy navy blue skirt with big white polka dots on it. She wore the black suede sandals she had recently bought for the summer and carried a matching black purse. She was glad, she said, very glad to get out of the house, despite the heat.

Aisha's house was on the way to Macro, so, of course, we stopped for a visit. The house was full of people as so often it was. Women lined the banquettes. This time they were gathered around a neighbor who had lost her ability to speak. The speechless woman sat squeezed between the others on a banquette, gesturing wildly with her hands whenever someone spoke to her.

"This woman," Nadia explained to me, "is filled with *jnun*."

The jnun are demons. If a person has jnun in them, they are truly crazy.
This is much more severe than a person who just has spirits in them. Spirits
are relatively benign.

    Jnun are often found in frogs, cats, and dogs. Jnun transform themselves
and lodge themselves in frogs, cats, or dogs. So at night a person might see
one of these animals and not realize that the jnun are really hiding under-
neath the animal mask. If a person kicks a cat in the street at night and
hurts the cat or deforms it or kills it, the person will then be transformed
and bear that deformity. So it is dangerous to go out at night, and it is dan-
gerous to kick cats or dogs, etc. Jnun particularly hang out near the water.
They inhabit water, so it is especially dangerous near water. Or near an
empty place, because jnun fill up empty places.

"The *jnun*," Nadia continued, "are telling her they will only let go of her if
she becomes a *shuwafa* (fortune-teller). But the woman refuses. She does not
wish to become a *shuwafa*."

"Why not?" I asked.

"Because then, if she becomes a *shuwafa*, she will have to travel constantly
to Sefrou to visit the saints' tombs there, and she will be forced to go to visit
the tombs of all the saints, and spend days there, sometimes as many as three
days, sleeping over."

"Why would she have to do that?"

"She would need to be there to help the sick people who go to visit the saints.
That is what the *shuwafa* do. But her husband would never tolerate this. He is
young, and he will marry again. She has two little girls. The real fear is that he
will marry again and then she will really be in trouble."

"Well, if she can no longer speak, how do you know all this? How do you
know the *jnun* are telling her to become a *shuwafa*?"

"She told us."

"But she can't speak."

"Although she cannot speak, she mumbles in such a way that we understand her." And with this Nadia demonstrated to me someone mumbling
words with jaws clenched tight, for this is how the woman was communicating now. "The other day she was downstairs, and her son was upstairs, and
the *jnun* came over her. They told her that her son would be mute, too. They
would render her son mute if she did not acquiesce and become a *shuwafa*.

This, of course, terrified her, and she ran upstairs, and there were hands on the throat of her son."

"Whose hands were these?" But Nadia disregarded my question.

"The *jnun* are threatening her that she must become a *shuwafa*. She must. But she is resisting. Her stomach has become distended and completely hard from the *jnun*. They are making her sick."

"This is very sad." This woman, I thought, must surely have had a stroke.

"So we brought her to a *fqi*. It is a Berber *fqi*. But before we went, the *fqi* warned us not to tell her we were going to visit him. So we tricked her. We told her we were going on a trip to get a wife for Si Muhammad—that we were going to propose for him. We all went together—Si Muhammad, Brahim, Aisha, and me."

"Si Muhammad drove?"

"Yes, he drove. The *fqi* was outside of town. He read the Qur'an to her over and over to try to get the *jnun* to leave."

"But they haven't left." I could see the woman sitting there in Aisha's sitting room, speechless. There was nothing we could do. We got up to continue on to Macro.

We walked the aisles of Macro. I bought nothing and Nadia bought several small containers of yogurt. We stood in line behind a family whose cart was full, almost spilling over, with plastic containers, cans of sardines, cartons of Coca-Cola. An older woman dressed in a *djellaba* held the handle of the cart, gold bracelets jangling ostentatiously on her wrist. Standing next to her was a man in a new polyester shirt. We watched as their items were rung up by the cashier and as they paid with cash. They spent 700 *dirham*.

"Uneducated country folk," Nadia muttered scornfully behind them. "They could buy that Coca-Cola at the corner store. Obviously, he's just returned from France. Now she's going to spend all the money. *Facances*—that's all they are."

Facances are what people in Ben Souda call the Moroccans who hold jobs abroad, often in France. These migrant laborers return during the vacation months each summer (*les vacances*, in French, from where the term *facances* is derived). They often return loaded down with consumer goods from Europe, with extra money to spend on luxuries for their families. As the season warms up, everyone in Ben Souda becomes aware of the presence of the *facances*, who, it is believed, could be easily recognized because they drive cars while others walk and they wear fancy clothing that others could never afford.

And as we walked home down the dark path from Macro, Nadia spoke about the *facances* and their showiness and how they were everywhere, all over

Ben Souda now that it was late July. So when I left her house and made my way back to the taxi stand, I looked earnestly around the dark dusty streets of Ben Souda for evidence of the *facances*—for snappy-looking people driving comfortably in handsome cars. I did not notice any.

•

I was going to make my last visit to Nadia. I would be leaving Fes later in the week. I wrapped the gifts I had purchased for the family in fancy paper I had bought in the Ville Nouvelle. A feeling of dread sat in my stomach. I was tired of Fes, tired of Morocco, tired of the heat and the strange and sad stories people told me. I was bored with sitting in Nadia's small sitting room in the dark, watching television, feeling trapped with dust everywhere and nowhere to go but Macro. But this good-bye was final. I would not be back.

Nadia's people had been kind to me. I thought of Rashida, her fat cheeks, the big smile that made her wide nose spread across her face, her short legs and swollen feet. All year she had reassured me. "*Behal, behal,*" she would say. "You are the same as us, Titia. *Benadem*—we human beings—we're all alike." Each time I left her house she would call out in her loud voice, the voice of a country woman, strong and unrefined, "Come back, don't stay away, come back to see us. We like people here."

I took the taxi to Ben Souda and arrived for lunch. Nadia and I sat and talked about my departure. Nadia kept repeating that she could not relax—she could not even eat—knowing that I was going. We drank warm Coke and watched a television program about market women in West Africa. The African women dominated the market; they sold their products freely, shouting prices and joking with customers, which women in Morocco are not expected to do. "That is great. It is really nice those women can do that," Nadia remarked. I knew that Nadia fiercely defended her own tradition but that she was curious and interested and tolerant, and I remembered that this was why we had become friends in the first place.

We got up and went into the small courtyard. The furniture was no longer stacked there. Nadia had returned it all to the sitting room because, she said, she was ashamed to have her family sitting on the floor all day like country folk. Someday, she said, she would build a roof over the courtyard to make it into a separate room, perhaps even a bathroom with a shower. And then as we stood there, to cool the house down, Nadia began to throw water on the floors, swishing the water around with a large cloth and pushing it down the front hallway and out the front door. The water streamed around my feet as I stood in the courtyard.

I looked at the plants I had brought some days ago, pushed against the courtyard wall, and when Rashida saw me staring at the plants, she said, "It is good you did not give those plants to Aisha. Aisha's plants always die on her. That's because Aisha's heart is no good. Her heart is black. That's why plants die on her." I had heard mutterings earlier about Aisha and knew that a dispute was in the air. Rashida, I knew, would not tell me directly what was happening, but she continued to hint. "You give Aisha a plant one day, and the next day, that plant is dead. That shows you the condition of her heart." I only smiled, and I understood that I would never know why Rashida was talking this way. I was leaving now.

And then we moved into the hallway where the water had just passed through and sat on the pitted cement floor there with the front door open. The cold water had cooled the ground and a breeze blew past us on its way to the courtyard. Then Rashida went over the instructions on how to make cornbread so that I would know how to prepare it when I returned to my home. Jamila came down the stairs, groggy from sleeping, a long flat braid hanging down her back. We moved into the small sitting room to eat the cornbread Rashida had prepared.

We sat and ate, and then very suddenly I stood up. "I need to go now," I said. Nadia ran from the room to get me a belt, a wide gold colored sash that belonged to an ornate robe they had given me as a good-bye present at the time of my last visit. I lifted the gifts I had for them from my bag. I handed a gift to Jamila, and she wept and told me I would leave an empty space behind me. I handed my gifts to the others. Rashida hugged me and held her fat smooth cheek against mine for a long time. I began to cry, the tears streaming silently, the salt in my mouth. I knew I was glad to leave this place. I could not bear to pass any more afternoons in the dark little room. But I cried for how they had welcomed me and told me I was one of them—even though they knew I was not. I cried because I liked them and because I felt sorry for them—for their sicknesses, for their joblessness, for their lack of children, for the smallness of that room. I cried because I had not been able to help them at all. We wept for a while, and finally Nadia and I walked out the door and down the dirt road to see Aisha, both of us weeping still.

We arrived at Aisha's. My tears had dried. Aisha was in her usual place on the banquette, her eldest daughter next to her. Aisha's hair was tied back in a black hair net, and she was wearing a tent-like polyester dress with short sleeves that showed off the plump smoothness of her arms. The terribly fat daughter was mixing a special bread in a clay bowl, and the mute woman sat near her, watching. Nadia explained that I was leaving, that I would not be back. My departure was sooner than had originally been expected, and Aisha began to weep. I felt as if I could cry no more. I wanted to be gone. Nadia told the story of my departure, and she reviewed and repeated the things I had said earlier. "She will remember us always, she told us," Nadia reported to Aisha. Aisha began to imitate the things I had said to them, the phrases I most often used, perfectly mimicking my faulty Arabic.

"Remember, she would come in and say, 'Excuse me, please, I would just like to speak with you,'" Aisha said, and I recognized myself in her clever imitation.

"She told us," said Nadia, "that she was unable to sleep last night, knowing she would not be back after today. She said that she is terribly upset to be leaving now."

Rashida entered the room then, still crying, and we sat looking at each other, wiping tears. "When the German left, it wasn't this bad," Rashida said. "This one is worse than the German. The boys never liked that German, but they liked her. They would sit with her, talk to her."

"That's because she speaks Arabic," Aisha said. And everyone agreed that I was good. Everyone liked me.

I began to feel that I had died. I was no longer there. I had already become a rich and interesting story that could be told and retold for years to come.

Finally I stood up to go. Aisha insisted I stay. She would send her youngest daughter for Coca-Cola, and we would drink together. I said I had to leave and gave Aisha the gift I had brought her. She began to weep anew and acted angry, insisting I should have brought her nothing. "Why? Why did you get me a gift? You should not have gotten me anything."

"Because you were my friend," I said without thinking, knowing this was the truth.

Aisha began again to weep, and she repeated this line, over and over. "I was her friend," she said. And I knew that sentence had become part of the story that I had passed into.

And so I hugged them all, the women in the room, and to stop the crying, Rashida said loudly, "Enough, enough. That is enough," which is what Moroccan women say when there is too much sorrow. As I headed to the door, Rashida called out, "God help you."

"God help you," I called back, and I walked to the taxi stand and got into a taxi headed for the Ville Nouvelle.

Epilogue

For a time, after I left Morocco, my friends and I passed letters back and forth across the ocean. As with many of the workers I had befriended, Nadia could not read or write, but Aisha's daughters could write for her. We sent best wishes to one another. They asked about my health and the health of my husband, mother, sisters, and brother. I reported details about my work and life. They wrote that Jamila had given birth to a son at last. They assured me that they thought of me often. I told them they were not forgotten and promised I would always remember the time we had spent together. Nadia wrote that she wished to send me a package, a collection of gifts that would remind me of Morocco, but troubles with the post kept preventing her from getting the bundle off. Eventually our correspondence petered out, as if the bridge between us had collapsed, the weight of our differences overcoming us at last.

Conclusion

All over the world, local communities experience the impact of globalization. Neo-liberal economic reforms in 1980s Morocco opened the economy to new investments and fueled the development of the garment manufacturing industry. Young Moroccan women flooded into sewing factories, providing the cheap labor needed to power this wave of industrialization. Industrial districts rose up on the edge of Fes in fields where once onions were planted. Girls from lower-class families, whose mothers had married at puberty and given their lives to bearing children, began to leave their homes to work in the new factories. How did these girls and their families experience this change?

A faithful adherence to their identity as Moroccan females guided the factory girls in Fes. Factory labor and earning a wage did not persuade workers to refashion their understanding of the feminine or to adopt western feminist notions of female autonomy. Instead, workers integrated their factory labor and the wages they earned into existing notions of what it means to be a good Muslim daughter. They interpreted their labor in industry as another form of service that dutiful daughters provided—they earned money to support their families just as they might cook, or clean, or wash clothing at home. They labored in factories to serve their families, and thus they worked for a wage without significantly altering their idea of what it was to be female. The working girls held tight to traditional markers of female identity, they took pride in their housekeeping skills, they worried about and guarded their reputations, and they talked incessantly about marriage, husbands, and sexual purity.

Even if the working women had been in search of an alternate concept of the feminine self—and they were not—factory work provided a limited scope to reshape the traditional female identity. Garment factory jobs were uncertain and precarious, temporary at best, and no worker could count on working in the future. Salaries were meager and did not provide sufficient support for an individual, much less a family. Moreover, the conditions of factory work were completely incompatible with the role of wife and mother. The factory shift lasted longer than an eight-hour day, and workers could be kept overtime—even into the night—without warning. A factory worker's hours would not allow her to rear children or maintain a household, which were required components of a married woman's position in Morocco. Moreover, the low status accorded garment factory workers was particularly troublesome for a married woman; her employment in a factory would bespeak her husband's inability to support the family. Taken together, these circumstances led the girls to think of their factory work as a transitory phase in their young lives.

The work itself was tedious and tiring, and conditions in the factory were difficult, but workers had little opportunity to organize against the power of the owners. Workers were widely aware that resistance would be met with termination of employment. Given their families' low economic status and reliance on their salaries, most workers were reluctant to organize for improved conditions. If the possibility of being fired for labor activism was not sufficient to dampen worker resistance, the owners were able to capitalize on the workers' intrinsic sense of duty and to cultivate in workers a powerful loyalty toward the factory. Altogether, the impossibility of taking action to improve factory conditions, combined with a sense of the precariousness of their jobs, led workers to understand factory work as something they would endure until a husband could be found. Thus in many ways, factory employment induced the workers to reaffirm and reemphasize traditional notions of self in the face of the difficulties and the contradictions the work imposed.

What the working girls longed for was to marry, bear children, and manage their own households. Marriage was the way out of the factory. It also marked the traditional entrance into adulthood for Moroccan girls—only through marriage could a girl authenticate herself as a mature adult, a valuable woman in the community. For lower-class females with so little earning power, marriage was the only way to secure an economic future. No factory worker could support herself with her own wages, and no girl had any hope of economic survival without the support of a husband. But because of the high levels of male unemployment, the young workers found themselves waiting for marriage long into their 20s.

It is important to note that in the opinions of the factory girls, wage-earning and employment in the public domain was as laudable for females as it was for men. It was not the idea of women's employment itself that was difficult to integrate into the Moroccan ideal of proper female comportment. Factory workers heartily endorsed female wage labor that could accommodate women in their roles as wives and mothers. Workers maintained that had they been educated—had they attained positions as teachers, engineers, or secretaries—they would be eager to remain in the workforce, long after marriage and even after childbearing. It was specifically factory labor that was problematic. This work could not accommodate the schedules of a wife or mother. Moreover, factory labor was widely considered low-status work. The Fes community demeaned factory girls as uneducated and unskilled and accorded them low regard. This denigration was particularly bothersome to the workers.

Thus workers labored in the factories while endeavoring to hold on to a notion of themselves as traditional females unaltered by their exposure to the public realm of the factory. Fes factories were staffed almost entirely by females, and workers claimed that this single-sex space helped them feel secure; they likened what was a public space to a private space, metaphorically transforming the factory into a home. They spoke of the factory as a family. They often praised the factory owner, comparing him to a protective patron or sometimes even to a father. They behaved with deference inside the factory, controlling their emotions and rarely voicing opposition. Yet, despite their efforts to adhere to cherished notions of traditional female ideals, the factory space and all that factory work entailed were vastly different from the realm of home and family. Despite their verbal allegiance to traditional norms, young females were in fact transformed by the factory.

Inside the factory, girls mastered and used skills unfamiliar to their mothers. Moroccans place great value in learning and in mastering a skill, and the workers took pride in their own competence. They were eager to speak of how they could tag garments, sew rapidly enough to keep up with extreme production demands, and assemble their own clothing. Some young women took on positions of authority, supervising large numbers of their peers, negotiating with other skilled workers, managing conflicts. They honed their manual and interpersonal skills in a much broader sphere and with a far wider array of activities than would be available to them at home.

Even for the less skilled workers in the factory, those who would likely never advance into managerial positions, the factory afforded new kinds of social opportunities. On average, the workers had attained no more than a fifth-grade education. As was the norm among members of their class, the factory girls had remained at home after leaving school early in childhood. Some had worked in neighborhood carpet workshops or attended artisanal training centers, but most had little opportunity to venture much beyond the house. Their social worlds were composed of kin. Work in the garment factories afforded these young women a whole new social sphere. Inside the factories, the girls would meet with hundreds of other young women from different districts of the city, each with different histories, families, and life experiences. Inside the factory, they expanded their social worlds, learned from peers, exchanged information, all beyond the purview of supervising kin—mothers, fathers, brothers. Inside the factory, girls heard things they would not otherwise have heard—"the talk of this one and that one," as they would say. The workers were aware that their level of social exposure went beyond the norm, and they understood it was often deemed inappropriate for young girls to be so worldly and aware. And yet it was this socialization—the opportunity to meet and talk with other girls—that the workers most valued in their factory experience.

Moreover, employment in the garment factories opened up a new space in which young women of the lower class could freely maneuver: the street. Typically, Moroccan girls of the lower class are carefully guarded, and their movements outside the home are closely monitored by kin. Working in a factory, however, demanded that the young girls have more mobility. Most factories were located on the margins of the city; although many Fes factory owners provided company buses to transport workers (in an effort to assure factory parents that their daughters remained protected), the demands of the commute left many workers to negotiate the city streets independently. Alone or in small groups, factory girls walked or took city buses to and from the factories. They wandered the streets unchaperoned after work, independently deciding where they would go and when they would return home; the factory regime (or sometimes the demands of the job hunt) provided a ready justification for their absence. Young girls who otherwise would have had no reason to escape household demands now had an excuse to explore the city unmonitored. Although workers generally gave the bulk of their salaries to their mothers, they often held onto a small amount of money—perhaps only pocket change—to support their wanderings. This freedom from parental control, a sense of autonomy, and the ability to physically move through new spaces were available to them because they had taken on factory work. Thus engagement with the factory altered workers' behaviors and attitudes, despite their public attestations of support for traditional values.

Inside the home, factory labor and a factory salary did not necessarily alter the status of the working daughter, nor did it lessen the labor demands placed on workers as daughters. For the most part, workers continued to defer to parents and brothers, respecting traditional kinship hierarchies in the home.

Working daughters, who were contributing a substantial portion to the household budget, were expected to exhibit obedience even to unemployed fathers and brothers, and they did. They were expected to perform household tasks conventionally assigned to daughters, and when at home, they were shown no lenience due to the strenuous factory routines. Factory girls spent all their free time at home doing housework, performing tasks that reinforced their status as daughters: cleaning, washing clothing, serving family members.

This being said, workers' activities in the streets—their wanderings, open discussions with unrelated men, independent purchases of small commodities—belied their obedience to parental regulations. What's more, families, often informally, accorded a new kind of status to working girls who had been contributing to the household over a long period of time. These workers, frequently in their mid-20s, reported that their families awarded them a high degree of trust and respect for their abilities. Although these families often did not directly acknowledge the girls' financial contributions, they implicitly recognized these daughters as important breadwinners. These daughters were often free to leave the house with relatively few questions asked and to make purchasing decisions independently, and it was not uncommon for them to speak their minds at home.

While there were differences in the level of physical freedom from mother to daughter, the mind-set of factory workers was not significantly different from that of their mothers: workers, like other women of their class, recognized and respected the traditional Islamic ideals about gendered behavior for females. They spoke about maintaining the proper social boundaries and respecting God-given limits. They sought to display modesty and worried about their own reputations and how others regarded them. In practice, though, the working girls of Fes extended and expanded their own boundaries through factory work.

Factory work, however, did not lead to real economic improvement. Women toiled long hours under strenuous conditions. They did not feel that they were respected inside the factory walls and in the city streets. They endured a relentless cycle of seeking jobs, holding jobs, losing jobs. The work they secured paid poorly and provided little relief to a worker's economic woes over the long term. Factory work would never pay enough for a woman to provide for herself or her family. It offered little hope for personal or professional advancement. Workers expected that eventually they would marry and leave the factory forever. Ultimately, they endured factory work and waited patiently for marriage.

·

What has happened in Morocco, and in the Moroccan garment industry, since the end of the millennium?

The Moroccan economy has grown steadily in the first decade of the millennium, although unemployment rates in the country remain high—estimated at 25 percent in the cities, similar to rates in the 1990s and still most severe among young job seekers. Agriculture continues to employ some 50 percent of the labor force, a figure unchanged since the time of research. This dependence on agriculture renders the Moroccan economy highly susceptible to weather patterns, and the economy's erratic performance over recent decades has been linked to cyclical drought. Despite the rise of a middle class, significant disparities between the rich and the poor persist in Morocco.[1]

In 1999, King Mohammed VI assumed the throne upon the death of his father, Hassan II. Mohammed's government has intensified the former king's inexorable march toward the globalization of the Moroccan economy by liberalizing the economy and encouraging free trade. The government has retained an export-oriented model of economic development, continually opening Morocco's doors to international investors. Under Mohammed, the Moroccan government has strongly supported the manufacture and export of textiles and clothing, and the textile industry continues to develop, albeit unevenly.

Today the textile sector (a category that includes the manufacture of cloth and thread, as well as garments) accounts for over 40 percent of industrial employment in Morocco. Three out of four workers in this sector are women, most working in sewing factories. Textile exports make up 25 percent of Morocco's total exports, and the majority of these are clothing exports. Many features of the industry remain similar to conditions at the time of research. The sector is still dependent on export and is focused on trade with the European Union—today France, England, and Spain together purchase more than 70 percent of Moroccan textile and clothing production.[2] Forming trade unions continues to be extremely difficult.[3] Most of the industry's workers are still girls and women. The industry is still highly volatile, and factories frequently close, downsize, and reopen in an unpredictable manner—vacillations that workers typically experience as job loss.[4] This volatility, similar to the volatility at the time of research, is linked to the manufacturing structure of Moroccan clothing production; the industry remains based on subcontracting. Today, as in 1995, Morocco provides the labor to assemble materials imported from abroad and then exports the finished garments.

As noted in the introduction, subcontracting the world over is associated with a "flexible" workforce—temporary, itinerant employment, often with degraded work conditions. In recent years, women's associations in Morocco have denounced the exploitation of women in Moroccan industries, the garment industry included, and have argued against the rampant wage discrimination against women in Moroccan industry, the majority of them in garment manufacturing. Export firms in Morocco continue to increase profits by employing young and unskilled female labor.[5] The current working conditions still reflect those witnessed at the time of research.

Throughout the first decade of this millennium, Moroccan garment manufacturers have struggled fiercely to compete with new exporting countries whose competitive advantage lies, at least in part, in the low wages they pay their workers. Morocco's struggle to secure a position among international garment exporters has been reflected in the high level of job insecurity that the workers face. For instance, in 2005 the Multi Fibre Arrangement expired. This trade agreement, in place since 1974, had placed quotas on the amount of textiles that developing countries could export to developed countries. When it finally expired, clothing exports from China and other Asian nations (such as Bangladesh and India) surged into Europe, competing with Moroccan products. This competition badly damaged the Moroccan garment industry, and in early 2005 many factories closed, putting at least 30,000 workers out of work.

In the years since the dissolution of the Multi Fibre Arrangement, Morocco's government has renewed its efforts to help its garment manufacturers resume trade with the European Union. The government has crafted a series of trade agreements with a variety of countries, progressively eliminating trade barriers and expanding international cooperation. For instance, Moroccan textile manufacturers have joined forces with Jordan, Egypt, and Tunisia in their efforts to fend off the competition from China. The government has negotiated a bilateral free trade accord with the United States and a similar bilateral accord with Turkey. It has drawn up a new partnership with the European Union and is currently negotiating for the creation of a Euro-Mediterranean Free Trade Area, to be completed by 2010. These trade agreements have helped Morocco ward off the threat posed by Asian producers, improve trade with foreign clients, and bolster the Moroccan garment industry.[6] It is not certain, however, how these particular accords have affected conditions for women working in the sewing factories.

In addition to trade agreements, the Moroccan government has stepped up its liberalization of the economy. The government has continued to increase tax incentives to garment companies operating in Morocco, enticing large foreign operatives to open their shops in the country. The state has reduced tariffs and has opened a large export processing center in Tangiers. It has worked to improve communications and transport to and throughout the country, building a major industrial port in Tangiers and improving access to all industrial centers. It has streamlined customs procedures and actively marketed Morocco as the crossroad between Europe and the Middle East. Altogether, these strategies have helped to offset the effects of the loss of the Fibre Trade Arrangement and have increased international market share in the garment sector.

Governmental efforts to increase the flow of international capital into Morocco have had an impact on the size and the ownership of garment factories. Today 60 percent of Moroccan garment production is handled by large companies: 872 garment factories are operational today, and these factories employ 153,010 persons. At the time of research, some 786 garment factories employed 95,000 persons. Thus the overall number of garment workers has grown, and so has the size of individual factories. At the time of research, the majority of Morocco's factories were relatively small, and many were Moroccan-owned, particularly those in Fes. Today 60 percent of Moroccan garment production is handled by large companies. One-third of the garment factories have foreign ownership or involvement. This fact reflects government efforts to open Morocco's borders to international capital and encourage foreign investment in Morocco. Whether women and girls working in larger, foreign-owned factories hold more secure positions and work under better conditions remains to be documented.

Since the completion of my research, the Moroccan garment industry has expanded and the number of jobs in the industry has increased. Foreign investment in the sector has grown significantly. The industry remains based in subcontracting and is highly dependent on economic forces far beyond Moroccan shores,[7] with all the attendant implications for women working in the global factory.

Appendix 1: Inside the Factory

Sewing Factory Personnel

Abderrahim:	One of the few men on the factory floor, he manages one sewing line.
Absellem:	A sewing line manager, he is one of two male line managers and one of the few men on the factory floor.
Amal, owner's sister:	A young woman who, having regretfully left the university, works in the factory office as an administrator.
Factory owner:	Actually, he is the owner's son, who runs the factory.
Fadela:	Zaynab's 20-year-old sister, who works as a factory maid. Fadela has a hidden source of income.
Fatiha Alami:	As manager of quality control, Alami works downstairs in the packing department. At 29, she is one of the oldest workers I met. Alami is unique in that she is well educated, having completed high school and a technical training course as well. She believes she could secure a career position in the agriculture department if she could save enough of her earnings for a bribe.
Fatima Zahara:	A new worker, young and difficult. She often refuses to cooperate with her bosses.
Fatima:	Manager of a line of sewing workers. She has spent seven years laboring in factories. Her family relies on her wages as well as the wages from her mother's job as a cleaning lady and her brother's part-time work in a coffee shop.
Fouzia:	Salima Bendoun's friend
Hajja:	The owner's aunt.

Hannen:	The manager of the packing department. A stylishly dressed young woman whose family, although lower class, is relatively well off economically.
Hayat:	A young worker who lives in a rented room with six of her relatives.
Ilham:	A young worker who gets sick at work one day.
Kenza:	A girl at the lunch table whose marriage contract has been signed but who has not yet begun to live with her husband.
Latifa:	A 19-year-old worker who works, along with two of her sisters, to support their parents. She believes her father is "crazy."
Mariam:	Fatima's best friend.
Mina:	Another girl in the packing department
Naima:	A 15-year-old worker, new to the factory. She has never attended school and is on the verge of marriage.
Najia:	A fairly educated worker who completed high school and works in inventory, an enviable position. Najia is veiled in the style of a Muslim sister, and her clothing is always beautiful.
Salima Bendoun:	A worker who considers herself to be a lost girl, having lost her reputation in a previous love affair that is never explained. Salima's father served in the Moroccan military and now draws a pension, which provides the family with a steady, if small, source of income.
Saudi:	A married worker who disappears from the factory scene early in my own tenure. She is forced out of the factory following excessive absences caused by her daughter's illness.
Si Wardi:	Factory floor manager, an older man who seems to have little involvement in running the factory.
Sylvie:	French manager of the factory, responsible for production on the factory floor.
Sylvie's husband:	Helps with factory inventory.
Zaynab:	A 21-year-old worker who has recently joined work in the factory with her younger sister, Fadela. Several brothers, who have remained in the family home with their own wives and families, contribute to the household income.

Appendix 2: Inside the House

Nadia's Household

Nadia: A factory girl, age 26
Rashida: Nadia's mother
Brahim, Hassan, Yousef: Nadia's three elder brothers
Jamila: Yousef's wife

Aisha's Household

Aisha: Nadia's cousin through her mother
Aisha's husband: Nadia's uncle (her father's brother)
Si Muhammad: Their only son
Fatima: Their eldest daughter
Saida: Their third daughter
The second eldest and the two youngest daughters in the household go unnamed

Aisha's husband is Nadia's paternal uncle, her father's brother. But Nadia is also Aisha's cousin. Aisha is the daughter of Nadia's mother's sister. The relationship between Nadia and Aisha most likely has other overlap as well: Nadia's mother and father are said to be relatives.

Aisha and her family are a source of constant companionship for Nadia, her mother, and her brothers, and their households are inextricably linked.

Nadia's father remains legally married to her mother. However, he married a second wife, and they settled in a house nearby with their small child.

Nadia has an elder sister who lives somewhere in Fes.

Acknowledgments

I would like to thank the working girls of Fes, who spoke to me so freely of their lives. I owe a debt of gratitude to their families as well, for their hospitality, open-mindedness, and tolerance. I thank the Fes factory owners who endured my questions and the one owner in particular who allowed my daily observation in his factory.

I thank the editors at the University Press of Florida for seeing the book through publication and Cynthia Nelson for her invaluable editing. I am grateful to the Wenner-Gren Foundation, the Social Science Research Council, and Fulbright for the financial support for the research on which this book is based.

Finally, I thank my husband, Jerry Kurlandski, for his persistent encouragement, sharp editorial eye, and equanimity.

Notes

Introduction

1. In the Middle East, beginning in the 1980s, economic restructuring led to an influx of females into garment manufacturing, in Morocco and Tunisia specifically. See Drori on Arab Muslim females in garment factories in Israel. On Bangladeshi girls who are Muslim but not Arab, see Feldman and Kabeer. Also see Ong 1987 on Malaysian females, who also are Muslim but not Arab.

2. Anthropologists such as Powdermaker, Bowen (Laura Bohannan writing under a pen name), Shostak, Behar 1993, Brown, and Dettwyler have recorded ethnographic experience in varying narrative forms. A number of anthropologists working in the Middle East and in Morocco specifically have made use of alternative ethnography, including Fernea 1989, 1975, 1970, Friedl 1989, Abu-Lughod 1993, Crapanzano, Rabinow, and Dwyer 1982. *Anthropology and Humanism* 32, no. 2, investigates, as its central theme, "The Art of Ethnography: Narrative Style as a Research Method." See here especially Behar 2007 and Narayan.

3. *Anthropology and Humanism* takes the question of "what it means to be human" and the search for narrative forms of expression as its guiding inquiry. It is essential to note the contributions of feminist researchers to the development of narrative in ethnography. See, for example, Behar 1997, Behar and Gordon, Stacey, Tedlock, and Visweswaran.

4. Frobel et al., Fuentes and Ehrenreich, and Nash and Fernández-Kelly are the earliest widely recognized volumes. Since then, a plethora of research has been published. This literature has been reviewed from the anthropological perspective first in Ong 1991 and then in Mills 2003.

5. Tilly and Scott and Dublin.

6. The gendered impact of economic restructuring has been well researched in Latin America and particularly in the Caribbean. See Benería and Feldman, 1992.

7. Mills's 2003 review of the literature guides the discussion of major issues here.

8. Early researchers in Asia coined the term "dutiful daughters" to describe the young girls whose families removed them from school and placed them in factories, often using their wages to support the education of brothers. See Salaff, for example. Later Wolf, Mills 1999, and Lynch studied daughters as workers. In contrast, the labor of women who are wives and mothers invokes a different set of issues. For example, Lamphere details the complexity of child care arrangements among working women.

9. Braverman's work stimulated thought on capitalism's "deskilling" of workers. Prentice describes Trinidadian women who develop and use dressmaking expertise outside the factory; I did not see Moroccan workers make great use of their skill at home.

10. There is an abundant literature on the lives of workers in Mexico's global factories that points to the sexualization of female bodies. For one example, see Tiano.

11. Freeman, Lynch, Mills, and Ong 1987 all see females becoming new consumers; Root notes that the Malaysian government linked factories with HIV/AIDS, with no reasonable epidemiological data supporting the link; Lynch takes note of news accounts of physical assault of girls in Sri Lanka's export processing zones; many writers have suggested that the overt sexualization of Mexican females is a factor behind the mass murders of women in Juarez. See Livingston, for example.

12. Pun reports on nightmares and menstrual problems in China, Ong 1987 describes spirit possession in Malaysia, and Kim documents female militancy. Bourqia has mentioned hysteria in Morocco, specifically in Casablanca, although I never witnessed such a phenomenon.

13. The European search for the cheapest form of labor put females in factories where, a decade earlier, males would have been hired. Before the 1980s, the workers in Moroccan sewing factories (like nearly all Moroccan factory hands) were predominantly male (Joekes 1982, 1985). By 1995 nearly all sewing factory workers were female. Belghazi and Baden and Bourqia have documented the process in Morocco as well.

14. In my time spent in Fes I met only a handful of workers who claimed to hold a work registration card, although I never actually saw such a card. Standing describes the increasing flexibility of the labor force, and this is an example of that phenomenon. See also Horton.

15. In 1995 the exchange rate was approximately 10 *dirham* to 1 dollar.

16. The concept of Taylorism refers to the principles of scientific management first systematically introduced by Frederick Winslow Taylor, in which management develops a highly standardized method for performing individual tasks; workers are trained to perform with minimal decision-making input and maximum efficiency. Taylorism risks deskilling the worker and dehumanizing the workplace.

17. It is difficult to accurately assess these claims because no official record of the strike exists.

18. While the country's gross national product did increase during the decade, the per capita gross national product actually declined significantly during this decade. The gains may have been offset by population increases: the population nearly tripled between 1950 and 1990. The Moroccan economy was not growing fast enough to keep up with the population growth.

19. During this period, the typical poor worker earned one-third the average wage or half the legislated minimum wage. See Moghadam 2001.

20. These statistics and others on the nature of the female factory workforce in Fes are based on the results of two formal surveys I took in two Fes factories. The survey results are compiled in two articles (Cairoli 1998, 1999). According to my surveys, 76 percent of workers were single, 16 percent were married, and 8 percent were divorced. All of these workers were young: 92 percent were between the ages of 13 and 25.

21. See, for example, Pun, Wolf, and Mills 1999, who discuss issues of rural to urban migration. The workers described in these contexts also work in large factories (with 300 or more workers) in export processing zones that include electronics assembly plants as well as garments and textiles. Such zones do not exist in Fes. Fes industry is limited (for the most part)

to textiles, garments, and vegetable processing plants. It is smaller in scale and often locally owned.

22. Moghadam 2001 notes that throughout the 1990s Morocco did not have universal primary and secondary school enrollments, and the gender gaps in school enrollments were wide. Given the high fertility rates in the previous decades, families of seven or eight children were not uncommon among the workers. The workers had already left school before they entered the factory; most reported they had been unsuccessful and could not pass end-of-year testing. See Wagner on schooling in Morocco. Mothers did not require the assistance of multiple unmarried daughters to manage the housework in this urban setting; the wages of daughters were needed instead.

23. There is an almost unlimited collection of research on the topic of women, gender, and kinship in the Arab and Muslim context. Eickelman and Bates and Rassam provide an overview of the material in their texts on the Middle East. See Fernea and Bezirgan and Beck and Keddi for early collections. Other comprehensive surveys and collections include Fernea 1985, Ahmed, Barakat, Nashat and Tucker, and Keddie. In Morocco specifically there are a number of ethnographies describing the lives of women. For example, see Dwyer 1978, Davis 1983, Davis and Davis 1989, Mernissi 1975, 1989, Fernea 1975, Kapchan, and Newcomb. Here I touch on some of the cultural ideals that influence the workers I knew.

24. Mohammed VI, who took the throne in 1999 after his father's death, instituted a new family code in 2004 that improved women's legal status.

25. The cultural explanation which argues that Islam—or perhaps "Arab" family values— keeps women out of the wage labor force has been refuted repeatedly. Hijab noted that Jordanian women stepped in and out of the paid labor force in response to economic growth and decline, not cultural values. Assaad notes that structural adjustment policies in Morocco pushed females into factories, while similar economic policies in Egypt caused a decline in female wage labor participation. Given that Morocco and Egypt have similar cultural notions of gender, he argues that cultural values alone cannot be used to explain the presence or absence of women in factories in these two countries. Ross describes how, in the Persian Gulf countries, the economic policies of the oil industry have prevented women from joining the labor force en masse. In this region, oil—not Islam—keeps women from wage labor.

Chapter 1. Finding the Workers

1. Questions about the ethics and impact of anthropological research, including questions about informed consent, are discussed in Fluehr-Lobban.

2. In Morocco, women have long practiced weaving, embroidery, and sewing in the home. They also produce goods for the artisanal markets. Most often it is little girls who are put to work in carpet factories. Older girls and women take pieces home from tailors in the market and sew at home for a wage. These activities bring minimal income. Clancy-Smith provides a history of women's artisanal work in Tunisia and Algeria. See White for a detailed ethnography of women's sewing in Turkey.

3. The idea of *tuwahem*, a kind of craving during pregnancy that can affect the fetus, is common among lower-class women in Morocco, particularly those who have had little access to formal schooling. It is discussed again here in chapter 5.

Chapter 2. Gaining Entrée

1. Pun notes that gender is invoked when the control of the laborers is at stake. In China's factories, she has quoted male bosses as saying, "You're a girl. How can you speak to me like this?" "Don't you know that you are a girl? You should treat the work more tenderly" (p. 143).

2. In this particular situation, ethnic divisions (French vs. Moroccan), informed by a history of colonialism, affected the relationship between management and workers. In general, however, ethnic division does not play a pervasive role inside Fes factories. Most frequently in Fes, the factories are managed by Moroccans. Differences in ethnic identity do not play a role among workers either. In Fes, all the working girls identify as Moroccan, and all the workers I encountered spoke Arabic as a primary language. Although some girls did claim Berber roots when questioned, this identity appears to be inconsequential for workers and their families.

3. Familism is the way in which workers themselves explain and interpret their relationships inside the factory. Although the workers imagine the factory as a family, owners do not attempt to hire sisters. I found that although several sisters from a single family may work in the factories, they often work in separate factories. Workers do attempt to help their own kin, neighbors, and friends by recommending them to factory managers. But factory jobs are scarce, and recruitment is not strictly based on ties of family or friendship. Familism as an ideology is common in factory settings; see Dublin. Also see an earlier article on Fes specifically (Cairoli 1999).

4. Writers in the Caribbean describe factory workers using the factory as a place to develop personal entrepreneurial enterprises. This was not common in Morocco, although occasionally workers seemed to have something to sell. See Freeman and Prentice.

5. Other writers have seen female workers' discourses about femininity and their glorification of motherhood and marriage as a form of resistance to the factory regime. In India, lace workers work full-time at lace making, but they perceive themselves not as workers but as mothers and wives. See Mies in India. In Turkey, White describes how women produce handicrafts at home for the capital market while continuing to view their work not as labor but as an aspect of their roles as mothers and wives. In China, Pun believes that the women's talk she hears in the factories helps to "suture their female identities" and also helps young girls to develop themselves in their own processes of sexualization.

6. Susan Schaefer Davis describes the Moroccan woman's ability to be patient, to withstand, to endure, as central to her power. She describes the frequency with which Moroccan women use the phrase, meaning "be patient, endure."

7. Moroccans often legalize a marriage and sign the official papers months (even years) before a couple begins to cohabit. This process has the advantage of legitimizing all social interaction between the couple, securing the girl's reputation, and ensuring that a spouse has been found for both boy and girl. Families might delay the festivities that signal the practical start of the marriage for financial reasons: the wedding ceremony requires a significant financial input, and the young husband must be fully capable of supporting his new wife and future children of the union. It is widely assumed that the salary of a factory girl belongs to the family of origin until she cohabits with her husband, so this might be a financial incentive for a family to delay the practical marriage of their daughters. I met only one worker who had delayed marriage for this reason. Otherwise, this issue was not mentioned by factory girls. Marriage prospects for all the females in the popular classes were scarce due to the shortages in the labor market that

made it impossible for young men to secure employment that would allow them to support a wife.

8. By the mid-1990s, immigration laws in Europe (and specifically in France, where many Moroccans traveled for work) had tightened, slowing Moroccan emigration. Men—and not women—had been the ones to migrate out of the country for wages. Given the tightening of immigration laws generally, it was unlikely that girls would begin to leave the country to work. However, the fact that so many young women so fervently spoke to me about their hopes or plans to emigrate signals a new kind of mobility for Moroccan girls.

9. In her memoir, Fatima Mernissi (1994) describes her mother and aunts' desire for chewing gum and cigarettes, items not allowed to them in their home in Fes in the 1940s. According to Mernissi's mother, "A woman who chews gum is in fact making a revolutionary gesture. Not because she chews gum per se, but because gum chewing is not prescribed by the code" (p. 187). However, the girls' choice of commodities that highlight a western ideal of female beauty, while allowing them to resist the authority of local males, also makes them susceptible to new forms of domination, as Abu-Lughod 1990 notes among Egyptian Bedouin women.

10. Sending little girls out to serve as maids in the homes of wealthy families was common in Morocco during the period of study. It was under attack, however, by enlightened Moroccans and social service organizations that understood this practice to be exploitative. See Belarbi, Davies, and Human Rights Watch.

11. In speaking and working with factory workers, I noticed an inordinate amount of sickness among workers, who suffered from hair loss, skin disorders, head scars, unexplained pain, etc. I noted many obvious illnesses among workers' families as well, and among women illness was an issue of concern. I did not carefully track the claims of illness or research them. I assume they are related to the overall poverty of factory households and the families' lack of reliable access to medical resources. Pun describes pervasive menstrual problems and pain among factory workers. She cites the work of Arthur Kleinman, who sees pain as an expression of bodily refusal.

Chapter 3. The Girls in the Packing Department

1. There is a well developed system of what are called *nadie*, sewing schools, in Fes, many of them run by the state, some of them private.

2. Here Latifa expresses her salary in *riyals*. There are 20 *riyals* to a *dirham*, so workers expressing their salary in *riyals* would quote numbers in the thousands. I leave this here in *riyal* form because workers with great frequency quoted their earnings in terms of *riyals*. The *riyal* is useful when describing currency values less than one *dirham*, and might be used in purchases at souks, vegetable markets, and in the *medina*. Quoting a number in *riyals* signals a class status to some extent—only those who are relatively poor calculate in terms of the *riyal*.

3. Wolf notes that in Indonesia it is also believed that the workers don't really need to earn money. There, the notion is that because workers' families operate farms, they are in fact supported by agriculture. Of course, this is not true, and workers' families often end up funding the workers who need help with living expenses in the city.

4. It is important to note that in 1995, the Islamic veil had been adopted mainly by girls in the university; still at that time, only a fraction of university girls had begun to veil. Today use of the Islamic hijab is far more widespread in Morocco, due in part to King Mohammed's

liberal approach to the rise of a local Islamic political movement. The veil is commonly used at all class levels, and there are indications that workers now widely wear the Islamic hijab inside factories.

5. In other factory contexts, workers form close connections to an adolescent peer group through continual contact in factory dorms or shared apartments. See, for example, Pun, Wolf, and Mills 1999. In Fes I found that workers never transferred their allegiance from kin to peers. Factory friendships, in most cases, were fragmented and fragile due to the unsteadiness of the employment itself. What's more, workers had little free time to devote to peer activities—workers all lived at home, and weekends and evenings were spent performing household labor.

6. Wolf found workers in Java earning about $24.00 per month in 1988 and noted that wages in Indonesian manufacturing were among the lowest in the world. A woman in Java would need to work three hours to buy a bar of soap. During this period in the factory, Hayat earned 250 *dirham*—$25.00. A kilogram of dates, food typically eaten during the Ramadan breakfast meal, cost approximately 10 *dirham*. Since she had worked approximately 20 days that month, she would have worked one day for a kilogram of dates.

7. I analyze this fully in Cairoli 1999.

8. Factory workers around the globe break traditional spatial boundaries and thus are accused of immorality. However, the spatial options available to young females in Fes are more limited than those available elsewhere. The karaoke clubs, dance halls, bars, and movie theaters that female workers frequent in Indonesia, China, and Mexico, for example, are either unavailable or closed to women in the provincial town of Fes (and in Morocco generally). There is no nightlife for girls in Fes as there is in other contexts where the global factory has opened spaces to women. The space that becomes available to these girls is, quite literally, the street. Girls stroll the avenues, ride the public buses, and shop in souks during the day—except for during Ramadan, when people exit their homes at night. Factory girls still do not enter the cafes or movie theaters of Fes.

9. Freeman notes that Caribbean women working at global processing firms see motherhood and work as going "hand in hand." What is crucial to note here is that men in Fes preferred nonworking wives at the time of this study.

10. Wealthy families in old Fes might have hired a male guardian—long ago he would have been a slave and maybe a eunuch—to guard the door, so that no stranger could get in and no woman could get out without her husband's permission. See Mernissi 1994.

11. Ultimately I collected survey data on the majority of workers steadily employed in the factory during the period I was there. The data included workers' ages, marital status, educational attainment, and years of factory service, as well as factory parents' place of origins, presence or absence of fathers in factory households, number of siblings, number of employed persons in family, etc. No such data had ever been collected on the workers. Much of this is presented in Cairoli 1998. Workers were usually questioned in groups and in pairs; there was little opportunity for me to work individually with workers, given their time constraints. Moreover, the highly social ethos of the factory rendered all conversations public.

12. There is a high rate of blindness in the industrial quarter named Ben Souda. This phenomenon is documented in many unpublished theses housed at the University of Fes, which link the blindness to cousin marriage.

13. Females in Fes, and Fes residents generally, frequently use this particular phrasing, placing in opposition the idea of "controlling a girl" or "giving her freedom" when discussing the

proper comportment for females—daughters, sisters, wives. "Controlling a girl" means closely watching and limiting her movements and interactions outside the home. "Giving her freedom" means allowing her to move and to interact with others at will outside the home. I often posed this question in these terms in an attempt to delineate the limits and to see whether anyone would argue against them. My questioning often produced the sort of response Latifa gives here. In answering this question, people often invoked the Islamic idea of the "boundaries," God-given limits that humans must respect. For females, in practical terms, these boundaries are spatial limits that must not be crossed.

14. Again see Cairoli 1998. The familism that reigns in Fes factories might, in practical terms, protect girls from the sexual exploitation seen in other factory settings. In Mexico, managers sexually harass workers; in China, Pun notes that factories are called "peach orchards," a kind of sexual reference where the workers are peaches available to be picked by men. In Fes, I did not see an overt sexualization of workers inside factories. Rather, the factory workers and factory community strove to conceptualize factories as safe places, inhabited only by females, who are protected by men. With the exception of Latifa's comments about a previous owner, and another comment by a worker who claimed that the owners of the small artisanal factories in the *medina* prey on the workers, workers did not complain or comment about sexual harassment. I do not know if such harassment is in fact as rare as it appeared, or if the shame attached to harassment (females would be blamed) prevented workers from discussing it. However, the pervasive representation of the factory as family—with the owner as father and workers as sisters—and the fact that owners strove to keep the factories as single-sex operations (all female), helped mitigate some of the sexualization of workers that has occurred elsewhere, I believe.

15. Adolescence is not a traditionally acknowledged period in Morocco. Historically girls were married shortly after puberty. The factory girls are the first generation of Moroccan females to step into a long period of adolescence, an extended series of years in their teens and early 20s when they remain unmarried. See Davis and Davis 1989 on adolescence in Morocco and Friedl 2002 on the prolonged adolescence of females in Iran.

16. The problem with factory work has to do not just with gender but with class: factory work connotes a low class status.

17. Wolf (p. 147) quotes Ut, an Indonesian factory worker, as saying, "We are not like our mothers."

Chapter 4. Final Days

1. At the time of my research, workers in the hijab were said to be turned away from factory doors. This was not universally true, as some (though few) workers did wear the hijab. This worker's claim that the owners wished to see the girls "wear makeup and dress nicely" does not conform to what I saw. I saw no pressure, implicit or explicit, on the part of management pressing the women to adopt a particular form of dress or to sexualize themselves. The vast majority of workers traveled to the factory dressed in the *djellaba*. The *djellaba* covers the form of the body and expresses modesty in the streets. A minority wore scarves on their heads, but those whose heads were bare wore their hair tied back. Once inside the factory, with their *djellaba*s removed, workers often wore the same sort of clothing they wore inside the house: housedresses with pants or pantaloons underneath and layers of sweaters during the cooler months. Many workers wore *tablies* over their clothing inside the factory—light blue overcoats

often worn by schoolgirls to protect their clothing from dust. These also are baggy and cover the female form. In other regions around the globe, management has in fact encouraged females to adopt sexualized forms of dress (e.g., miniskirts and high heels), and in some places factory beauty contests are commonplace (see Tiano, Pun, Mills 2003). The industrialization reframes female bodies as highly sexualized. This is not the case in Morocco.

2. In Thailand and Indonesia (Mills 1999, Wolf), girls often choose factory work against their parents' wishes. Girls spend a significant sum of their own money, often on self-support. In Indonesia, Wolf notes, families cannot control a girl's wages. She attributes this to greater economic autonomy of females in the bilateral kinship system, as opposed to female positions in a patrilineal system.

Chapter 5. Introductions

1. White describes piecework sewing as ubiquitous throughout the lower-class urban neighborhoods of Istanbul. Although women do piecework in Fes, it did not appear to me as ubiquitous as White described in Turkey.

Chapter 6. The Women in the Sitting Room

1. Nearly every account written on female workers in the global factory notes that the new factory girls become participants in the market for new kinds of commodities, whose purchase defines these girls as modern and urban.

2. In many regions, participation in industry has allowed girls greater control over their own life decisions—choice of a spouse, control of sexuality, control over fertility. The factory girls of Fes carry out courtship rituals that generally involve strolling in the streets and souks with a chosen man. Although families never officially cede authority to an unmarried daughter, I noticed that families seemed to significantly loosen control over daughters who remained unmarried well into their 20s and whose economic contributions to the household had been crucial. These workers seemed to come and go as they pleased, in an almost unspoken arrangement.

3. In other regions of the world, factory girls enter industry amid national debates about modernity and questions of how industrialization—and the girls participating in it—can affect the nation's progress. See Pun, Mills 1999, Lynch. In Morocco, the issue of factory work gets steeped in questions about whether employment in the factory fits into Islamic tradition. This question would not come to the fore, perhaps, in a better economic context. Few in Morocco question whether the work of female engineers, or college professors, or primary school teachers fits into the Muslim tradition. Educated people—men and women alike—are respected in Morocco. These discussions may also have reflected growing interest in conservative forms of Islam around the globe for this period.

4. I found that young women in the age category of factory girls (13–25 years old) consistently reported that they would bear only one or two children, with the goal of educating these children well. Demographic studies reveal that between the 1970s and the 1990s, fertility declined by 44 percent in Morocco. By 1995, the total fertility rate in Morocco was 3.3 children

per woman, low when compared with the past. By 2007, the total fertility rate in Morocco had declined even further, to 2.4 children per woman. See Althaus, Eltigani, and UNICEF.

5. Aisha, and the workers who so often complained about the difficulties of finding husbands, were in fact reflecting a significant shift in marriage trends in Morocco. In 1995 the female age of first marriage in Morocco was 26.3 years, a significant drop from 1980, when the age at first marriage was 21.3 years, itself at variance with traditional notions that girls are best married at puberty. Rates of marriage had declined as well. In 1995, 52 percent of Moroccan women of reproductive age were married, and 42 percent were single. As indicated before, the convention is that all females must marry, and traditionally all persons have married young. See Althaus, Eltigani, and UNICEF.

Chapter 7. Taking Leave

1. "Riffi" refers to Berber groups native to the Rif mountain range of northern Morocco.

Conclusion

1. Central Intelligence Agency.

2. Moroccan Association of Textile and Clothing Industries.

3. As yet, Morocco has not ratified ILO Convention 87 on freedom of association and protection of the right to organize. The government interest in supporting the textile and garment export trade, a key to their efforts to reduce high levels of unemployment, reduces state interest in workers' rights.

4. World Bank.

5. Naciri.

6. Despite efforts to increase trade with the United States, this source of trade remains relatively small; distance is a problem.

7. Moroccan Association of Textile and Clothing Industries.

Works Cited

Abu-Lughod, Lila. 1990. "The Romance of Resistance: Tracing Transformations of Power through Bedouin Women." *American Ethnologist* 17: 41–55.

———. 1993. *Writing Women's Worlds: Bedouin Stories.* Berkeley: University of California Press.

Ahmed, Leila. 1992. *Women and Gender in Islam: Historical Roots of a Modern Debate.* New Haven: Yale University Press.

Althaus, F. 1997. "Rising Contraceptive Use and Age at Marriage Lower Fertility Levels in Morocco." *International Family Planning Perspectives* 23 (1): 46–49.

Assaad, Ragui. 2005. "Why Did Economic Liberalization Lead to Feminization of the Labor Force in Morocco and De-feminization in Egypt?" Paper prepared for the Center of Arab Woman Training and Research (CAWTAR) Mediterranean Development Forum. Cairo: Population Council.

Barakat, Halim. 1993. *The Arab World: Society, Culture, and State.* Berkeley: University of California Press.

Bates, Daniel G., and Amal Rassam. 2001. *Peoples and Cultures of the Middle East.* 2nd ed. Upper Saddle River, N.J.: Prentice Hall.

Beck, Lois, and Nikki Keddi, eds. 1978. *Women in the Muslim World.* Cambridge: Harvard University Press.

Behar, Ruth. 1993. *Translated Woman: Crossing the Border with Esperanza's Story.* Boston: Beacon Press.

———. 1997. *The Vulnerable Observer: Anthropology That Breaks Your Heart.* Boston: Beacon Press.

———. 2007. "Ethnography in a Time of Blurred Genres." *Anthropology and Humanism* 32 (2): 145–55.

Behar, Ruth, and Deborah A. Gordon, eds. 1995. *Women Writing Culture.* Berkeley: University of California Press.

Belarbi, A. 1991. *Situation de la Petite Fille au Maroc* (The conditions of the young girl in Morocco). Casablanca: Imprimerie Najah el Jadida.

Belghazi, S., and S. Baden. 2002. "Wage Discrimination by Gender in Morocco's Urban Labor Force: Evidence and Implications for Industrial and Labour Policy." In *Women's*

Employment in the Textile Manufacturing Sectors of Bangladesh and Morocco, ed. Carol Miller and Jessica Vivian, 35–60. New York: UNRISD Publications.

Benería, Lourdes, and Shelley Feldman, eds. 1992. *Unequal Burden: Economic Crises, Persistent Poverty, and Women's Work*. Boulder: Westview Press.

Bourqia, Rahma. 2002. "Gender and Employment in Moroccan Textiles Industries." In *Women's Employment in the Textile Manufacturing Sectors of Bangladesh and Morocco*, ed. Carol Miller and Jessica Vivian, 61–102. New York: UNRISD Publications.

Bowen, Elenore Smith. 1954. *Return to Laughter*. New York: Harper.

Braverman, Harry. 1998. *Labor and Monopoly Capital: The Degradation of Work in the Twentieth Century*. New York: Monthly Review Press. (Originally published in 1975.)

Brown, Karen McCarthy. 2001. *Mama Lola: A Vodou Priestess in Brooklyn*. Berkeley: University of California Press.

Cairoli, M. Laetitia. 1998. "Factory as Home and Family: Female Workers in the Moroccan Garment Industry." *Human Organization* 57 (2): 181–89.

———. 1999. "Garment Factory Workers in the City of Fez." *Middle East Journal* 53 (1)9): 28–43.

———. 2007. "Girl but Not Woman: Garment Factory Workers in Fez, Morocco." In *From Patriarchy to Empowerment: Women's Participation, Movements, and Rights in the Middle East, North Africa, and South Asia*, ed. Valentine M. Moghadam, 160–80. Syracuse: Syracuse University Press.

Central Intelligence Agency. "The World Factbook: Morocco," http://www.cia.gov/library/publications/the-world-factbook/geos/mo.html.

Clancy-Smith, Julia. 1999. "A Woman without Her Distaff: Gender, Work, and Handicraft Production in Colonial North Africa." In *Social History of Women and Gender in the Modern Middle East*, ed. Margaret L. Meriwether and Judith E. Tucker, 25–62. Boulder: Westview Press.

Crapanzano, Vincent. 1980. *Tuhami, Portrait of a Moroccan*. Chicago: University of Chicago Press.

Davies, Deborah, Daoud Kuttab, and Ilan Ziv, producers. 2000. *Home, or Maids in My Family*. New York: Icarus Films.

Davis, Susan Schaefer. 1983. *Patience and Power: Women's Lives in a Moroccan Village*. Cambridge, Mass.: Schenkman.

Davis, Susan Schaefer, and Douglas A. Davis. 1989. *Adolescence in a Moroccan Town: Making Social Sense*. New Brunswick, N.J.: Rutgers University Press.

Dettwyler, Katherine A. 1994. *Dancing Skeletons: Life and Death in West Africa*. Long Grove, Ill.: Waveland Press.

Drori, Israel. 2000. *The Seam Line: Arab Workers and Jewish Managers in the Israeli Textile Industry*. Stanford: Stanford University Press.

Dublin, Thomas. 1979. *Women at Work: The Transformation of Work and Community in Lowell, Massachusetts, 1826–1860*. New York: Columbia University Press.

Dwyer, Daisy Hilse. 1978. *Images and Self-Images: Male and Female in Morocco*. New York: Columbia University Press.

Dwyer, Kevin. 1982. *Anthropology in Question*. Baltimore: Johns Hopkins University Press.

Eickelman, Dale F. 2001. *The Middle East and Central Asia: An Anthropological Approach*. 4th ed. Upper Saddle River, N.J.: Prentice Hall.

Elson, D., and R. Pearson. 1981. "The Subordination of Women and the Internationalization of Factory Production." In *Of Marriage and the Market: Women's Subordination in International Perspective*, ed. K. Young, 144–66. London: CSE Books.

Eltigani, E. 2000. "Changes in Family-Building Patterns in Egypt and Morocco: A Comparative Analysis." *International Family Planning Perspectives* 26 (2): 73–78.

Feldman, Shelley. 1992. "Crisis, Islam, and Gender in Bangladesh: The Social Construction of a Female Labor Force." In *Unequal Burden: Economic Crises, Persistent Poverty, and Women's Work,* ed. Lourdes Benería and Shelley Feldman, 105–31. Boulder, Colo.: Westview Press.

Fernea, Elizabeth Warnock. 1970. *A View of the Nile*. Garden City, N.Y.: Doubleday.

———. 1975. *A Street in Marrakech*. Garden City, N.Y.: Doubleday.

———. 1989. *Guests of the Sheik: An Ethnography of an Iraqi Village*. New York: Random House, 1969; reprint, New York: Anchor Books.

———, ed. 1985. *Women and Family in the Middle East: New Voices of Change*. Austin: University of Texas Press.

Fernea, Elizabeth Warnock, and Basima Qattam Bezirgan, eds. 1978. *Middle Eastern Muslim Women Speak*. Austin: University of Texas Press.

Fluehr-Lobban, Carolyn. 2003. *Ethics and the Profession of Anthropology: A Dialogue for Ethically Conscious Practice*. 2nd ed. Philadelphia: University of Pennsylvania Press.

Freeman, Carla. 2000. *High Tech and High Heels in the Global Economy: Women, Work, and Pink-Collar Industries in the Caribbean*. Durham, N.C.: Duke University Press.

Friedl, Erika. 1989. *Women of Deh Koh: Lives in an Iranian Village*. Washington: Smithsonian Institution Press.

———. 2002. "A Thorny Side of Marriage in Iran." In *Everyday Life in the Muslim Middle East,* 2nd ed., ed. Donna Lee Bowen and Evelyn Early, 111–20. Bloomington: Indiana University Press.

Frobel, Folker, J. Heinrich, and O. Kreye. 1980. *The New International Division of Labour*. Cambridge: Cambridge University Press.

Fuentes, Annette, and Barbara Ehrenreich. 1983. *Women in the Global Factory*. Boston: South End Press.

Hijab, Nadia. 1988. *Womanpower: The Arab Debate on Woman at Work*. Cambridge: Cambridge University Press.

Harrell, Richard S., ed. 1966. *A Dictionary of Moroccan Arabic: Moroccan-English*. Comp. Thomas Fox and Mohammed Abu-Talib, with the assistance of Ahmed Ben Thami et al. Washington, D.C.: Georgetown University Press, 2004.

Horton, S. 1999. "Marginalization Revisited: Women's Market Work and Pay, and Economic Development." *World Development* 27 (3): 571–82.

Human Rights Watch. 2005. "Inside the Home, outside the Law: Abuse of Child Domestic Workers in Morocco." *Human Rights Watch* 17, no. 12E, http://hrw.org/reports/2005/morocco1205/.

Joekes, Susan. 1982. "Female-Led Industrialization and Women's Jobs in Third World Export Manufacturing: The Case of the Moroccan Clothing Industry." Research Report no. 15. Brighton: Institute of Development Studies.

———. 1985. "Working for Lipstick? Male and Female Labour in the Clothing Industry in Morocco." In *Women, Work, and Ideology in the Third World*, ed. Haleh Afshar, 183–214. London: Tavistock.

Kabeer, Naila. 2000. *The Power to Choose: Bangladeshi Women and Labour Market Decisions in London and Dhaka*. London: VERSO.

Kapchan, Deborah A. 1996. *Gender on the Market: Moroccan Women and the Revoicing of Tradition*. Philadelphia: University of Pennsylvania Press.

Keddie, Nikki R. 2007. *Women in the Middle East, Past and Present*. Princeton: Princeton University Press.

Kim, Seung-Kyung. 1997. *Class Struggle or Family Struggle? The Lives of Women Factory Workers in South Korea*. Cambridge: Cambridge University Press.

Lamphere, Louise. 1993. *Sunbelt Working Mothers: Reconciling Family and Factory*. Ithaca, N.Y.: Cornell University Press.

Livingston, Jessica. 2004. "Murder in Juárez." *Frontiers: A Journal of Women Studies* 25 (1): 59–76.

Lynch, C. 2007. *Juki Girls, Good Girls: Gender and Cultural Politics in Sri Lanka's Global Garment Industry*. Ithaca, N.Y.: ILR Press.

Mernissi, Fatima. 1975. *Beyond the Veil: Male-Female Dynamics in a Modern Muslim Society*. Cambridge: Schenkman.

———. 1989. *Doing Daily Battle: Interviews with Moroccan Women*. New Brunswick, N.J.: Rutgers University Press.

———. 1994. *Dreams of Trespass: Tales of a Harem Girlhood*. Reading, Mass.: Addison-Wesley.

Mies, Maria. 1982. *The Lace Makers of Narsapur: Indian Housewives Produce for the World Market*. London: Zed Press.

Mills, Marybeth. 1999. *Thai Women in the Global Labor Force: Consuming Desires, Contested Selves*. New Brunswick, N.J.: Rutgers University Press.

———. 2003. "Gender and Inequality in the Global Labor Force." *Annual Review of Anthropology* 32: 41–61.

Moghadam, Valentine M. 1997. "Morocco and Tunisia: Export-Led Growth and Working Women." In *Women, Work, and Economic Reform in the Middle East and North Africa*. Boulder: Lynne Rienner.

———. 2001. "Women, Work, and Economic Restructuring: A Regional Overview." In *The Economics of Women and Work in the Middle East and North Africa*, ed. E. Mine Cinar, 93–116. Amsterdam: JAI Press.

Moroccan Association of Textile and Clothing Industries. "Data of the Sector," http://www.textile.ma/amith.

Naciri, Rabea. 1996. "Essential Matter: Policy Dialogue on Women's Industrial Employment in Morocco." *Viewpoint: United Nations Research Institute for Social Development*, December 1, http://www.unrisd.org/unrisd/website/newsview.nsf/(httpNews)/.

Narayan, K. 2007. "Tools to Shape Texts: What Creative Nonfiction Can Offer Ethnography." *Anthropology and Humanism* 32 (2): 130–44.

Nash, June, and Maria Patricia Fernández-Kelly, eds. 1983. *Women, Men, and the International Division of Labor*. Albany, N.Y.: SUNY Press.

Nashat, Guity, and Judith E. Tucker. 1999. *Women in the Middle East and North Africa: Restoring Women to History*. Bloomington: Indiana University Press.

Newcomb, Rachel. 2008. *Women of Fes: Ambiguities of Urban Life in Morocco*. Philadelphia: University of Pennsylvania Press.

Ong, Aihwa. 1987. *Spirits of Resistance and Capitalist Discipline: Factory Women in Malaysia*. Albany: State University of New York Press.

———. 1991. "The Gender and Labor Politics of Postmodernity." *Annual Review of Anthropology* 20: 279–309.

Powdermaker, Hortense. 1966. *Stranger and Friend: The Way of an Anthropologist*. New York: W. W. Norton.

Prentice, Rebecca. 2008. "Knowledge, Skill, and the Inculcation of the Anthropologist: Reflections on Learning to Sew in the Field." *Anthropology of Work Review* (Special Issue on Embodiment and Work) 29 (3): 54–61.

Pun, Ngai. 2005. *Made in China: Women Factory Workers in a Global Workplace*. Durham, N.C.: Duke University Press.

Rabinow, Paul. 1977. *Reflections on Fieldwork in Morocco*. Berkeley: University of California Press.

Root, Robin. 2006. "Mixing" as an Ethnoetiology of HIV/AIDS in Malaysia's Multinational Factories." *Medical Anthropology Quarterly* 20 (3): 321–44.

Ross, Michael. 2008. "Oil, Islam and Women." *American Political Science Review* 102: 107–23.

Salaff, Janet. 1981. *Working Daughters of Hong Kong: Filial Piety or Power in the Family?* New York: Cambridge University Press.

Shostak, Marjorie. 1983. *Nisa, the Life and Words of a !Kung Woman*. New York: Vintage.

Stacey, Judith. 1988. "Can There Be a Feminist Ethnography?" *Women's Studies International Forum* 11 (1): 21–27.

Standing, G. 1991. "Global Feminization through Flexible Labor: A Theme Revisited." *World Development* 27 (3): 583–602.

Tedlock, Barbara. 1991. "From Participant Observation to the Observation of Participation: The Emergence of Narrative Ethnography." *Journal of Anthropological Research* 47 (1): 69–94.

Tiano, Susan. 1994. *Patriarchy on the Line: Labor, Gender, and Ideology in the Mexican Maquila Industry*. Philadelphia: Temple University Press.

Tilly, Louise A., and Joan W. Scott. 1978. *Women, Work, and Family*. New York: Holt, Rinehart and Winston.

UNICEF. 2009. "At a Glance Morocco." *The State of the World's Children 2009*, http://www.unicef.org/infobycountry/morocco_statistics.html.

Visweswaran, Kamala. 1994. *Fictions of Feminist Ethnography*. Minneapolis: University of Minnesota Press.

Wagner, Daniel A. 1993. *Literacy, Culture, and Development: Becoming Literate in Morocco*. Cambridge: Cambridge University Press.

White, Jenny B. 1994. *Money Makes Us Relatives: Women's Labor in Urban Turkey*. Austin: University of Texas Press.

Wolf, Diane L. 1992. *Factory Daughters: Gender, Household Dynamics, and Rural Industrialization in Java*. Berkeley: University of California Press.

World Bank. 2006. "Morocco, Tunisia, Egypt, and Jordan after the End of the Multi-Fiber Agreement: Impact, Challenges, and Prospects?" Report no. 35376 MNA, December, http://go.worldbank.org/3LK9LK3PU0.

Index

M. Laetitia Cairoli is professor of anthropology at several universities in New Jersey. Her research on the workers of Fes has been published in *Human Organization* and the *Middle East Journal*.

CPSIA information can be obtained at www.ICGtesting.com
Printed in the USA
BVOW08s1653080916

461480BV00003B/35/P